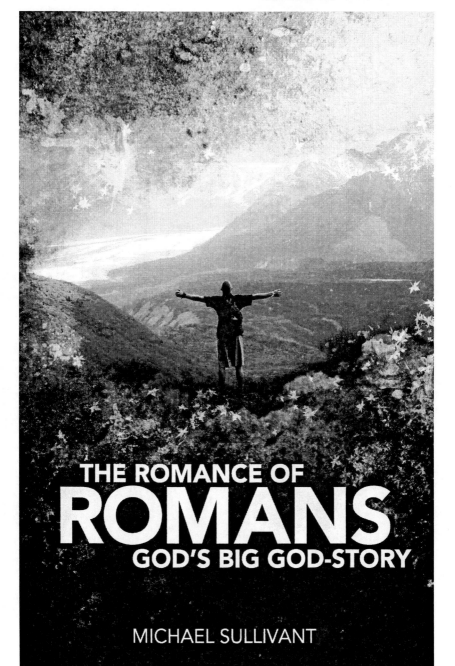

THE ROMANCE OF
ROMANS
GOD'S BIG GOD-STORY

MICHAEL SULLIVANT

The Romance of Romans: God's Big God-Story
An Interpretative Paraphrase of Paul's Letter to the
Romans

Copyright © 2011 by Michael Sullivant

Cover design by Dave Gilbertson.

Printed in the United States of America

ISBN-13: 978-0615481920 (Radius Books)

ISBN-10: 0615481922

TABLE OF CONTENTS

PREFACE

Some years ago, as a part of my devotional times, I attempted to put the book of Romans into a more modern idiom that I believe express what Paul meant. I've called it an interpretative paraphrase. I'm sure that many of the ways in which I rephrase our English translations are not perfect ... they certainly are not literal. The exercise is akin to what preachers do when they take a passage and attempt to teach the meaning of God's Word to their listeners. No preachers do this without some inaccuracies along the way—sometimes rather major inaccuracies. Still, there is great value in taking in biblical teaching from others who have studied and meditated on Scripture. Believers still need to do their own study, search the Scriptures for themselves and sift through what teachers teach. Additionally, this is not just a personal matter. I believe that one of the most important spiritual disciplines of the community of God's people has always been to "wrestle together" with the Scriptures and their meaning in a spirit of love for God and for one another. I am still searching out what the book of Romans really teaches.

A few years ago, I started making my paraphrase

into a series of devotionals for my "Blog": www.michael-radius.blogspot.com. This book is the compilation of those devotionals, with some necessary minor tweaking. I offer it to my readers with my sincere prayers that God will use this book in ways that will never be calculable on earth. Please consider reading this devotional in tandem with a more literal translation of Romans and comparing the paraphrase to the literal text.

I dedicate this book to my amazing (and growing!) family. My wife, Terri, is an exquisite person and follower of Jesus Christ. She has taught me so much since we met at college during a move of God and then married in 1977. Terri, thanks for being my personal life coach through so many years! To Luke (and Beka/Jonah), Lisa (and James), Samuel (and Caitlin), Mike (and Jeri), Steve (and someone wonderful, I'm sure!) and to all the grandchildren that God will surely give to us in the coming days— each of you has touched my life on a profound level, and you continue to do so as each year passes. Your mother and I will be with you all the way as life happens. Thank you for living from your renewed hearts so consistently. I am well pleased with who you are. Our Father in heaven has blessed us to be a family.

INTRODUCTION:

THE FELLOWSHIP OF THE MYSTERY

... How that by revelation he made known to me the mystery ... which in other ages was not made known to the sons of men, as it has now been revealed by the Spirit to his holy apostles and prophets ... and to make all see what is the fellowship of the mystery, which from the beginning of the ages has been hidden in God who created all things through Jesus Christ; to the intent that now the manifold wisdom of God might be made known by the church to the principalities and powers in the heavenly places, according to the eternal purpose which he accomplished in Christ Jesus our Lord. (Ephesians 3:3, 5, 9–11)

Jesus the Messiah (his Person and Work) is the integrating reality that brings God's Big-God Story of divine/human history together into the grandest adventure, mystery and love story that has ever been conceived. I use this language to refer to the meta-narrative of Scripture in which all the many smaller stories and the theology they teach us find their larger context. The smaller stories are ingeniously "nested" in the grand divine drama. The Bible tells one greater story that presents Jesus the Christ as the main character. It has been widely understood by many believers that the narratives, poetry and prophecies of the Old Testament scriptures, at times obviously and sometimes cryptically, pointed forward to the Messiah (which is a transliteration of the Hebrew word that correlates to the Greek word "Christos," or "anointed one"), in addition to simultaneously addressing real people and matters in their historical context.

However, the importance and impact of this unified story on our macro-view of God's eternal purposes has not translated into creating sufficiently wondrous hearts in many Christ-followers. This is because the Bible has too often been taught in bits and parts. Yet we, who have been born since the first coming of Christ, have a tremendous advantage in decoding the Old Testament scriptures. Not because we are so wise (this is for sure), but because we have much personal, clear and divinely-inspired commentary of both Jesus and his first apostles in the New Testament on the specific ways that a vast amount of Old Testament prophecy was fulfilled through the Messiah's first coming. For us, it's like being able to take an open book test. It's even more like obtaining the answer key to the big test ahead of time. (God knows that we need some special help in order to get a passing grade, given our track record!)

Still, too many preachers and believers throughout history have not taken the time to deeply study and comprehend the "answer key"—the New Testament writings—which become for us an interpretive template that can be laid over the Old Testament writings. (An old adage captures this concept: "The New Testament is in the Old, concealed. The Old Testament is in the New, revealed.") We would be wise to strive to understand how Jesus and his first apostles understood the Old Testament storyline, its characters and prophecies, the implications of him "showing up" on earth the way he did, and the historical/theological implications of his message. This message was not, in any way, disconnected from all that went before. But none of the biblical scholars or religious sects of his day could have fully anticipated who he would be, what he would do, and how he would re-frame and illuminate biblical theology and eschatology (the doctrine of the end of this age). Saint Peter said that even the prophets who wrote these kinds of words didn't understand the fullness of what they were referring to. (1 Pet 1:10-12) More tragically, this fullness has not been well understood by many Bible teachers, preachers and religious movements since he came. We desperately need this fact to change!

The point I have been referring to is illustrated beautifully in the mysterious encounter the two disciples on the road to Emmaus had with the risen Jesus.

> *Then he said to them, "O foolish ones, and slow of heart to believe in all that the prophets have spoken! Ought not the Christ to have suffered these things and to enter into his glory?" And beginning at Moses and all the Prophets, he expounded to them in all the Scriptures the things concerning himself ... Now it came to pass, as he sat at the table with them, that he took bread, blessed and broke it, and gave it to them. Then their eyes were opened and they knew him; and he vanished from their sight. And they said to one another, "Did not our heart burn within us while he talked with us on the*

road, and while he opened the Scriptures to us?"
(Luke 24:25–27, 30–32)

Jesus and his apostles established their world-
wide message around this dynamic of "opening the
[Old Testament] Scriptures" to clueless people and
causing their hearts to burn within them through
the fire of the Spirit's revelation. Wouldn't you have
loved to have heard the risen Messiah expound on
the meta-narrative of the scriptures—God's Big
God-Story? What on earth do you imagine he said
to them exactly? Do you think that maybe some
of his insights were captured by his apostles and
later recorded in the gospels and apostolic epistles?
And, if they were, how important and authoritative
do you imagine Christ's insights into the Old Testament actually are?

We actually can comprehend Jesus and his apostles' very personal insight into the Old Testament.
We can simply study Old Testament cross-referenc-
es in the New Testament, and then allow the implications of those passages to shape and, if necessary, re-shape, our theological presuppositions and
paradigms. This long and fascinating journey will
not only blow our minds, it will cause our hearts
to burn within us. We will discover that we, like
the first disciples, are living in circles of friends in
Christ that are bonded together in the fire of divine
zeal.

> *Then he said to them, "These are my words that
> I spoke to you while I was still with you, that
> everything written about me in the Law of Moses
> and the Prophets and the Psalms must be fulfilled."
> Then he opened their minds to understand the
> Scriptures, and said to them, "Thus it is written,*

that the Christ should suffer and on the third day rise from the dead, and that repentance and forgiveness of sins should be proclaimed in his name to all nations, beginning from Jerusalem. You are witnesses of these things. And behold, I am sending the promise of my Father upon you. But stay in the city until you are clothed with power from on high." (Luke 24:44–49)

ROMANS CHAPTER ONE

1. The Gospel Is Grounded in Old Testament Prophecy (1:1–7)

This is a letter from Paul, a servant of Jesus Christ, called to be a divine ambassador. I was apprehended for the express purpose of spreading the good news of God that was spoken of in times past by the prophets in the holy Scriptures. This message centers on his Son, Jesus Christ our Lord, who, in his humanity, was the Son of David. He was also proven to be the Son of God when he was raised from the dead through the power of the Holy Spirit. Through the same Spirit, I have received this ambassadorial commission to introduce many people from many nations, for the honor of Christ, into the passionate pursuit of God that flows from genuine faith. You are a part of this great company that has been chosen by Jesus himself. Yes, I write this to all the believers in Rome who are loved by God and called to be his holy ones: Grace and peace be yours from God our Father and the Lord Jesus Christ.

Comments —————————————————————

Many believers in our day long to tap the power that comes through prophecy. In my view, this

9

has resulted in both healthy and unhealthy spiritual dynamics. One way that we can properly inform our eagerness for the prophetic is to embrace a clear, foundational priority that properly shapes any other forms of genuine prophecy. This priority is the passionate understanding that communicating the gospel of Jesus itself is the most prophetic message that Christ-followers could ever speak. This Great News revolves around the availability of a new quality of righteousness to all the peoples of the earth. Through Christ, God's own righteousness is offered as a free gift to all who would open their hearts to him as they humbly and gratefully receive it. This righteousness also involves the reality and promise that he has and will, in his time and manner, heal his good creation. Evil has dramatically and tragically invaded his creation, but he will turn everything right side up through who Jesus is and what Jesus has done.

The gospel is rooted deeply in the prophetic Scriptures and promises of the Old Testament, although it was significantly shrouded until the events actually came to pass in human history and the Holy Spirit provided 20/20 hindsight.

This divinely prophetic message is what fueled both Paul's and the whole Church's apostleship ("being sent forth") into the cultures of this world by the power of the Spirit for the honor of Jesus Christ.

2.   A Mutual Exchange of Faith (1:8–15)

I want to first thank God through Jesus for all of you, because your faith in Christ has become known throughout the whole world. Before God, whom I serve

*with all my heart in spreading this good news, I'm not
exaggerating when I say that I pray for you constantly.
My hope and prayer are that God may finally allow me
the joy of coming to visit you. I long to meet you and
impart to you the spiritual gift that God has given me to
firmly establish believers in Christ. Beyond this, I want
us to experience the encouragement that comes through
a mutual exchange of faith—we both have something to
give each other.*

*I want you to know that I have many times planned
to visit you, that I might have the privilege of winning
some Romans to Jesus, as I have had in other places.
However, it wasn't God's time. I feel obligated to win
all kinds of people to Christ, both the educated and the
uneducated. So, I am very excited to preach the good
news in the "melting pot" of Rome, if God wills.*

Comments ————————————————————

What stands out to me in this section of Romans
1 is Paul's reference to the mutual exchange of God's
grace that he anticipated would take place when he
met the believers in Rome. I have had the honor of
meeting believers from many nations and cultures
through the years. An amazing phenomenon has
always accompanied these opportunities—you immediately feel the "family connection" with these
people whom you have never met before. It is a powerful experience that lends a lot of credibility to the
reality of the gospel of Jesus. You see the love of God
in their eyes and in their smiles, and feel it through
their hugs and prayers of thanksgiving. You immediately feel at home when the music plays. Your eyes
become wet with tears as you worship the very same
Father and Son with them in the power of the same
Spirit, even though you may be in very unfamiliar

cultural settings. Even when you don't understand the language in which the songs are being sung, you are able to immediately worship in spirit and truth. When you then break bread together (even though the "bread" can taste very different!), the love of Jesus is present in undeniable ways.

I think that this experience really helped my five children (now all adults who follow Jesus) as they were sorting through the deep question of whether the message of God's love they learned as kids was an invention of their parents and their local church or was really true. When they met these strangers who read the same Book and, often and amazingly, even sang the same tunes, it helped them to realize that this Jesus is relevant to people and cultures of all kinds. This kind of experience stabilized them as their faith was challenged along the way by people and institutions in our local community.

3.   What If God Visited the Earth in Person? (1:16–17)

For I am not ashamed of the good news of Christ. It is the very power of God that imparts salvation to every person who believes it; to the Jews first and also to the Gentiles. (A past history with and greater knowledge about God implies a greater opportunity to receive from him.) Through this message, God's own righteousness is revealed from heaven and imparted to people, from start to finish, on the basis of faith.

Comments ——————————————————————

Something very radical (lit.: "to the roots") occurred through the coming of God's Son, Jesus, to this world. It was an event unlike any previous act of God in the whole of human history. It was the event by which God himself came in person to the planet. God actually did what many people have half-heartedly complained about: "If God wants us to believe in and follow him, why doesn't he just appear to us and tell us in person?"

But what if a holy, just and loving God (as the Scriptures reveal him to be) really did visit us in person to invite us back into a mutual and genuine love relationship with him—to set things in motion for all the evils of this world to be resolved? How would that story go, given the voluntary nature of love and the fact that evil is not simply "out there" but "in me" as well?

Come to think of it ... this scenario would go very much like the gospel of Jesus. God foretells of his intentions in many ways over many years in preparation; intervenes and becomes like one of us; lives a perfect life; reveals his wisdom, love and power; lays down his life to absorb and absolve our personal guilt and shame; deals out a mortal wound to all evil; overcomes Satan and death; delays his final justice for this world's evils to offer his creation, over a long period of time, the opportunity to choose to love him back, before those who have chosen and cherished evil have to face the consequences; and also sets up a way of doing all of this so that those who choose his love are not able to take credit for their choice and thus fall into pride or gloating.

Finally, why might Paul, or anyone else, even be tempted to "be ashamed" of this Story? Maybe because such a radical act on God's part would necessarily expose and shake the fragile internal and external psychological and social arrangements that individuals and whole cultures (religious and otherwise) have historically made in an attempt to survive and feel okay about ourselves. Bearing such a message would inevitably involve the rising of some conflict on all fronts, because God himself has come on the scene, and he isn't necessarily buying all our human wisdom or self-righteous religions—not to mention our excessive self-indulgences. Sharing this message can get one into trouble with other people! High drama and passionate spiritual romance truly await us as Romans unfolds.

4.   The Bad Side of the Good News (1:18–23)

This may sound strange, but the good new begins with some bad news! God's awesome anger is also revealed from heaven. He is adamantly against all the ungodliness and unrighteousness of people who suppress the truth because they love sin more than truth. You see, God has partially revealed himself to every person through both his or her own conscience and creation itself. His invisible presence and moral attributes have been easily discernible from the beginning of time. The fingerprints of his divinity and eternal power have clearly branded all he has made. Therefore, people are without excuse for their unbelief in him.

All throughout world history, although people knew God was there, they neither honored his divinity nor were thankful to him. Rather, they invented their own man-centered religions and philosophies of life, thereby snuffing out the light of spiritual knowledge in their hearts. They claimed to be getting wiser, but they were actually becoming more foolish. They "remade" the invisible God, who is glorious and incorruptible,

*into gods of their own imagination—idols made in the
likeness of human beings, birds, beasts and even bugs.*

Comments ⸻

The meta-narrative of human history that we
have typically been taught is more like how a so-
phisticated belief in one God (monotheism) grew
up over many centuries out of the context of a su-
perstitious belief in many gods (polytheism). I remember being quite shocked as a young believer
in Christ as I first read the apostle Paul's overview
of humanity's story. It's more like "devolution"
than "evolution" ... on the spiritual side of things,
at least.

Several things stand out to me that challenged
my presuppositions and still challenge my soul,
because I would really like to believe better things
about us as a species. But then I simply reread stories from world history, not to mention the daily
news from around the globe, and I can't deny or
contradict what Paul states concerning the spiritual
condition of human race.

First is how connected we all are to one another
in our cultural and family contexts. We like to think
more individualistically about our lives, and we
underestimate how entwined on many levels we
are with our ancestry—for good or ill. Certainly, the
Scriptures tell us that God sees and evaluates us on
an individual basis, but we are greatly influenced
spiritually by our cultural settings.

Second is the fact that God has granted to every person who has ever lived a general revelation of the reality of his existence. This general,
or natural, knowledge of God is graciously given

to inspire us to seek more specific revelation of who has made us and has displayed his power throughout all creation. We instinctively know that "creation" implies a "Creator," and it takes a deliberate effort on our part to push this knowledge away from our consciousness. The ancient, pre-Christian philosophers (they did pretty well in many cases) understood and affirmed this. It wasn't until Descartes (1596–1650; ironically, a religious man himself) that more modern philosophy emerged and pressured us to doubt everything we instinctively know before we rebuild our knowledge base.

Third is how dishonor and ingratitude toward "the God who is there" is the genesis of our spiritual death, which then bleeds over into our whole lives and relationships. When we become so sick of being and living disconnected from our Creator and Heavenly Father, a great way to find our way home is to stop in our tracks and tell him again from the depths of our hearts that we believe he is there—that he is powerful and good—and to simply ask him to reveal to us more of who he is, what he has done and what he is doing. And, as we will discover as Romans continues, we should ponder (and come to terms with) the Person and Work of Jesus his Son.

5.   Whatever Happened to Sin? (1:24–32)

Because of their idolatry, God let the nations go their own way to pursue the unclean desires of their own hearts and even abuse his purposes for their own bodies. They sold out the truth to buy the original lie—to deify the creation, and thus defy the Creator who is to be eternally worshiped. That's really the bottom line. So God backed off and they plunged headlong into sexual perversion: women's natural attraction for men became twisted, and they turned to lesbianism. Men also turned away from heterosexuality and burned with lust for other men. They embraced unnatural sex and, as a consequence, seriously damaged their own souls and bodies.

Because they rejected the knowledge of God they once had, he allowed their consciences to become callused, and they indulged themselves in evil things without remorse. Their lives were characterized by all kinds of unrighteousness: illicit sex, wicked ways, covetousness, malice, extreme envy, murder, contentiousness, character assassination, gossip, betrayal, hatred of God, vengeance, pride, arrogance, evil innovations, disobedience to parents, ignorance, promise breaking, lack of healthy affections, stubbornness and absence of mercy. Although they know God's justice requires a spiritual death sentence for these offenses, they themselves not only do them, but also idolize others who do.

Comments —————————————————————————

Whatever has happened to sin? For Paul, it was obviously alive and thriving at every turn in this world, and he didn't pull any punches in this passage. In reality ... not much has changed since Paul's day. But it's hard for people in our culture to look with such brutal honesty into the tragic condition of humanity and human relations removed from friendship with God. We prefer to re-designate such attitudes and behaviors with much nicer tags that minimize and even justify them. Paul's above list of sins is painful to read, isn't it? It goes on and on like a downward spiral into an abyss of human brokenness and dysfunction ... (I really don't enjoy meditating on this passage.) We tend to get used to sin in our world (and in our own lives) and begin to think it is normal, rather than an alien invasion into God's good creation that has pulled us down into sub-normality. But God has never gotten used to sin ... though he is certainly not shocked or intimidated by it. Paul's purpose in exposing the darkness and sickness of humanity has a redemptive focus—he is not just being mean or wrongly judgmental. Actually, his heart was full of great love and compassion for all the people in every culture he ever encountered.

The ending of chapter 1 is focused on the spiritual plight of the whole Gentile world. But Paul is setting his readers up for a miraculous offer of a most marvelous remedy in the Person of Jesus of Nazareth. We apparently won't be willing to take the medicine until we are convinced of our disease. Yet, before Paul begins to ingeniously unveil God's surprise of a free gift of salvation and a new beginning, he must turn his attention to sins of another genre—the sins of God's own people—the sins of religion gone bad.

6.   To Whom Much Is Given... (2:1–11)

Now before you religious folks congratulate yourselves for not being guilty of what all those other people are guilty, you need to look more deeply at your own lives before you judge them and thereby condemn yourselves. You'd better be sure that you aren't actually guilty of the same root sins, because we know that God will judge us all according to the naked truth. If you are proven to be a hypocrite, how will you escape his judgment? Just because he has blessed you and shown you his rich favor in many ways, don't take these things for granted—that doesn't automatically mean that you're okay. Don't you know that God may be showing you his goodness and patience in order to woo you into repentance? Don't mistake tolerance for approval!

But in fact, you have done this very thing. Because of your hardness of heart and religious pride, you are accruing a wrath account that will come due on the day of wrath when God's righteous judgment comes down. He will give to every person what is due him or her. To the believing, who by patiently and persistently doing right, show that they are seeking the things above—glory, honor and immortality—he will give eternal life.

But to the unbelieving, who stubbornly refuse to submit to God's truth and instead embrace unrighteousness, he will dispense his hot and holy vengeance. Yes, it's true, for Jews first and also for Gentiles. (A past history with and greater knowledge about God implies a greater opportunity to receive from him. It also implies a greater accountability to him for not receiving from him—this is the great equalizer!) On that day, God will pour out trouble and torment upon every person who cherishes evil in his or her heart. Yet he will pour out glory, honor and peace on those who pursue righteousness. God has made this opportunity for salvation available to all ethnic groups, for there truly is no racism in his heart.

Comments

The passage doesn't need much commentary, as it speaks loudly for itself. After exposing the spiritual darkness of the Gentile world in chapter 1, Paul now turns to the religious but self-righteous Jewish folk—of whose ilk he had been a prime example. One thing that stands out to me in this section of Romans is how God sees down into the deep heart of matters and of every person. He is looking into human hearts, seeking to find genuinely humble, vulnerable, childlike trust in him, his Son and his Spirit ... and nothing else will do. Not careless self-indulgence. Not careful self-righteousness. Both extremes are unacceptable—and deep in our own spirits, we know the ugliness and distastefulness of both debauchery and religious pride/racism in our world.

What pleases God is a person who sincerely and repeatedly turns to him, desires to receive his truth into the depths of her/his heart, comes to trust in who Jesus is and what Jesus has done, and responds with heartfelt gratitude and affection. (And she/he later discovers all this is to be inspired by the Holy Spirit himself!) This simple foundation for getting along with God never changes—no matter how spiritually mature we might become. Authentic spiritually mature people don't attempt to measure or project their maturity—they're too caught up in the wonder of God's love, kindness, presence and service to others in his name to notice or care.

7. Many Surprises Await Us (2:12–16)

People who live in sin without being exposed to God's written law given through Moses will be condemned without reference to it. However, those who live in sin and have been exposed to the Mosaic law will be condemned on its basis. Possessing intellectual knowledge about the Scriptures will never save anyone. Salvation is only found by personally embracing and submitting to whatever spiritual knowledge God has revealed to us. When Gentiles who have never heard of the Mosaic law live by the light of conscience within them, it proves that God has written his moral law on the hearts of all people. They instinctively know when they do right or wrong. God has specifically revealed to me that he has appointed a day when he will judge the secrets of men's hearts through the lens of who Jesus Christ is and what he has done. (Imagine some of the surprises we will have.) I assure you that after that day, no one will ever again point his or her finger at God and accuse him of being unjust!

Comments —————————————————————

This little section of Romans 2 touches on the common stumbling block in people's minds regarding the spiritual fate of those who have never been exposed to the Scriptures or the gospel. Naturally, we deeply question how God can judge someone in such circumstances. Sometimes people who hear the gospel of Jesus Christ pull back from putting their trust in him to become their Lord and Savior. I faced this question head on when I first became a follower of Jesus at age 18, and as a teacher and pastor I have helped others face it along the way. Here are the simple points that I landed on in those early days of my faith that have helped me and many others come to peace on this issue.

1. God is God (not me!) and God is absolutely just and good. Our hearts can totally trust in these realities, and also trust that when all the facts of human existence are on the table in eternity's light, no one will be able to find one fault with God's ways or evaluations. I won't, and neither will you. The anticipation of one day having this fuller light gives me peace to leave eternal judgment in the hands of the only One capable of such a thing.

2. When we are personally exposed to the Person and Work of Jesus, we need to be first of all be concerned with the question, "Who do we say that he is?", not "What about all those 'poor souls' who have never heard of Jesus?" I am the first "poor soul" that I can do something about! Coming to terms in my own heart with the compelling evidence that points to Jesus being who he said he was also gives me peace. I mustn't allow—and have not allowed—such a

giant question about the possible fate of people who have never heard to keep me from receiving desperately-needed freedom from my guilt and shame, which is freely offered to me in Christ.

3. We must make room in our theology for the largeness of God's grace and the mysterious and surprising works of the Holy Spirit in drawing people to faith in Jesus Christ. God's grace doesn't begin to work upon people when they first hear about the good news of Jesus. It has already begun to work ... witnessed by the simple fact that they have been allowed to hear it. Every believer whom I have ever encountered can point back to how she/he now can see how the Holy Spirit was at work in his/her life before coming to Christ. There are marvelous accounts of how the gospel of Jesus has come to people and whole people groups who didn't seem to have the opportunity to hear about him.

A prime example of this is in the tenth chapter of the book of Acts, where a Roman centurion named Cornelius (a classic pre-Christian) had a powerful encounter with the grace of God before he was converted to Jesus. Even his prayers and acts of compassion were being accepted and remembered by the one true and living God! An amazing story unfolds of how Cornelius and his whole extended family came to faith in Jesus. It was so outside the box that it even shocked the apostles of Christ and messed with their theology. Let's be very careful about dictating exactly how God might lead a person to Jesus—some of his ways may surprise and stun us too.

8.   Circumcision of the Heart (2:17–29)

Again I address you religious Jews. You claim that you have spiritual security by your knowledge of the Mosaic code, God is on your side, you know his will and you have a superior philosophy of life based on divine revelation. You are confident that you are the divinely chosen moral governors of the earth—guides to the spiritually blind, a light of truth in the midst of the world's dark deception, instructors to the foolish, teachers of the uninstructed and the ones entrusted with the scriptural blueprints of ultimate knowledge and truth.

You, then, who presume to instruct others, why don't you listen to your own words? You preach to others to not steal, but you are thieves yourselves. You condemn adultery in others, but you're guilty of it yourselves. You say you hate idolatry, but you put many things ahead of God himself. You claim to honor the commandments of Scripture, but you dishonor their Author by violating them. Indeed, the Gentiles ridicule the precious name of the God of Israel because of you Israelites, just as the prophets of old have said.

Being Jewish has its advantages if you're not a religious hypocrite. Yet, if you are playing a religious game, do you think that God sees you as a true Jew? If a Gentile wholeheartedly embraces the truth God has revealed to him, isn't he more "Jewish" in God's sight than you, even though he hasn't embraced Jewish religious rites and customs? Indeed, such non-Jews, ethnically speaking, will end up judging you ethnic Jews who violate your own stated convictions. For true "Jewishness" is not a matter of ethnic origins, outward religious rites or scriptural knowledge. True Jewishness is a matter of the heart—a spiritual circumcision. It has to do with spiritual reality, not religious formality, and it causes a person to become a God-pleaser rather than a man-pleaser.

Comments —————————————————————————

In the fallen state of our weak, independent humanity, it seems that we tend to flesh out in two extreme ways. I think this is the point that Paul so earnestly makes as we join the last part of Romans 1 with Romans 2. We tend toward living for the thrill of pushing beyond the boundaries associated with temporary pleasures, becoming addicted to those experiences to the point that we sabotage our relationships and revert to mere brutes. Or ... we see through the ugliness of this way of life and gravitate to a moral/religious system/code that enables us to rise above living by such carnal passions. We associate ourselves with a culture that has a reputation of being connected to God and seek to overcome being unspiritual. Or ... maybe we are simply born into such a culture, and our group's accepted way of life is based on this kind of religion-based "moralism."

The classic problem with the latter condition, however, is that just as the moral character of the pagan cultures devolves over time into more twisted forms, religious/moralistic cultures and their stepchildren tend to devolve into self-righteousness, judgmentalism, externalism, image projection, cultural and ethnic pride, hatred and the hypocrisy that is encoded in denial. This is a far cry from being connected to God in a genuine, vital way.

This was the general condition of first-century Judaism, and the apostle pulls no punches as he lays bare the hypocritical morality that was present within its ranks. I think he is saying, "The flesh is flesh, whatever form it may take, and we human beings must be somehow lifted out of our 'fleshliness,' because we can't do it for ourselves. History and sociology have proven this fact." He has been writing hard to reveal that both the irreligious and the religious are in the same basic boat and in desperate need of a Savior.

This section of Romans 1 and 2 is indeed the bad side of the Good News, but it sets the stage for hearing about the most amazing divine surprise the world has ever known ... the gift of Jesus the Christ to a world that is spiraling down into the mire of humanly energized religion and irreligion.

9. A Most Critical Question: Did God Lie, If Jews Need Jesus? (3:1–4)

Now I know that you're tempted to think: "If what he's saying is true, then there has been no meaning to all it has cost the Jews for being God's chosen people. What's the advantage of being a Jew in the first place?" Actually, there are many privileges—especially the stewardship that God gave them over his message to humanity through the prophetic Scriptures. So if some Jews have been unfaithful to their divine calling, does this negate the faithfulness of God himself? No way! God is, and will always be, true even if all people were to contradict him. The Scripture says of him, "You are always right in all that you say, and you always prove your critics wrong."

Comments ————————————————————

At this point in his letter, Paul has just written many paragraphs graphically detailing the very real and deadly trouble that the souls of both Jews and Gentiles are in. The beginning of chapter 3 opens with a literary tool that he will use throughout the rest of the letter. He pens a contrary question that he knows that his previous statements will have evoked in the hearts and minds of his readers, and then goes on to give a reasonable answer to the argument of the "ghost" doubter.

In my view, this first question is the most profound and fundamental one of them all. Yet this question's profundity can easily escape us. Let me put it in other words. If a law-keeping and God-honoring Jewish person is not right with God and, in the larger context, if the Jewish people are not "saved" or "safe" by being associated with their historic/national/ethnic faith community and its beliefs, rituals and customs ... *then God has lied.* He has broken his part of the ancient bargain he made with Abraham, Moses, David and the like, since he absolutely promised that he would save their children/followers throughout the generations to come. So God is not righteous if what Paul says is true.

I believe how Paul addresses this question is the main theme of the book of Romans, as he posits a different paradigm for understanding and interpreting the meta-narrative of the Bible from Genesis forward. In the gospels, Jesus initiated this new, authoritative framework for understanding the kingdom of God and the Old Testament prophecies. And ... this claim was the primary reason, humanly speaking, why Jesus and Paul both were executed.

As followers of Jesus in our day, we need to let this sobering philosophical/doctrinal foundation of the first part of Romans sink into our hearts and minds. It's truly radical and upsets the status quo of our spiritually complacent cultures—religious and otherwise.

10. Sin More to Maximize God's Grace? (3:5–8)

I will continue to anticipate arguments based on mere human reasoning. "If our being wrong magnifies the fact that God is right, he shouldn't have any complaints, and he's unjust for judging us for our wrongs." Wrong again! God is bound by his nature to approve all that is right and to condemn all that is wrong. You might respond, "If God's truth is seen more clearly by its contrast to my falsehood and he receives more honor because of it, how can he be just if he still condemns me for being sinful?" Some have taken this reasoning to such an extreme that they recommend (and have actually claimed that we have taught!), "Let's do more and more evil, so that greater good may result." This kind of thinking is truly damnable and not even worth a rebuttal!

Comments ————————————————

Paul is beginning to ramp up in anticipation of revealing the divine logic of the gospel of Jesus Christ. Before he does, he addresses a couple more common objections of skeptics.

The first objection is about God's amazing ability to capitalize on the tragic presence of evil in the world (and in human hearts!) to show his own holiness and justice (and later, mercy) by contrast. But instead of being stunned and humbled by this divine attribute, some people, in essence, react to the gospel by saying, "Oh ... we're actually doing God a 'favor' by being the 'flawed object' of this contrast. So ... if he holds us accountable for our sins, he is unjust. If he is unjust, then he is not worthy of our worship and service. Hey, Paul ... we gotcha ... you're preaching foolish nonsense. And, if what you're saying is really true, sin isn't such a big deal anyway. So what's all your urgency about?"

The second one takes this reaction to the gospel message a step further. This argument says, "So Paul, what you're actually saying is that we might as well sin as much as we can. If God can use our sin to bring glory to himself, then let's give him some more material to work with. Cool. Ha ... now we really gotcha!" This is obviously not what Paul is saying. Just take a step back and rehearse the horrors of sin in our world and in world history—and in our personal lives and relationships—and reread chapter 1.

Still, there is an important irony here for us who follow Jesus and share the good news of his grace. If some people do not react to our message of God's grace in Christ in a similar way and accuse us saying these kinds of things, we probably aren't preaching what Paul did! God's grace is so free and freeing ... so unintimidated by the presence of evil and sin ... so capable of overcoming and negating the tragedy of our fallen existence ... so filled with a Beauty that totally eclipses all the ugliness of evil ... that a superficial reaction to hearing the Good News often causes people to conclude that sin and evil really aren't much a problem after all ... if what we're saying is true. Properly preaching the gospel has always made believers vulnerable to these accusations that twist its impeccable logic into such foolishness.

God's actual attitude toward sin and evil is revealed in the gospels. We see him come humbly into our world through Jesus to live right in the midst of the sinful age for love's sake. We see him seeking

and loving and forgiving and healing and resur-
recting the lost, the unloved, the sinful, the sick and
even the deceased. We see Jesus pressing beyond
the sin and evil in people to see and call forth who
they were really called to be ... doing all that he did
to free their hearts to embrace the dawn of new creation, which was rising upon the dusk of the old
creation to trump its darkness with a brilliant light.
God loves the sinner—his fallen image bearers.

Yet we also see the mood change in the gospels
to that of a heavy sobriety—a time of temptation,
agony, betrayal, scattering, mockery and terrible
injustice—as Jesus, at the end of three and a half
years of compassion-filled ministry, turned his face
like flint to go to Jerusalem and to deal with the
root problem of humanity. And this he ultimately
did by taking upon himself the guilt and shame of
all humanity—past, present and future—so that he
could then take it away, triumph over it through his
sacrificial death on the cross, and then finally triumph through his blessed resurrection. God hates
sin—the disease that has held captive his fallen image bearers. So ... sin is a terrible problem and nothing to be flip about. But God ...

11. All in the Same Boat (3:9–20)

*So are we Jews superior to the Gentiles? Again I
say, "No way!" I have just made it clear that Jews and
Gentiles are both in the same boat—in bondage to sin
and in need of salvation. Scripture confirms this in the
Psalms: "No one is righteous in himself—absolutely no
one. No one possesses intrinsic spiritual understanding
or intrinsic desire and power to seek after God. Everyone
has gone his own way and embraced vanity. No one is*

innately good—absolutely no one! Death and decay are within them; their words are manipulative and deceitful, like the poisonous venom of serpents. Their speech is full of cursing and bitterness. They are quick to the kill. They leave destruction and misery in their wake, and they are ignorant about healthy relationships. Nothing is sacred to them and they don't know the proper fear of God."

Now this wasn't just written about all those Gentile folks out there. It was specifically written about Jews, for it was written in the Jewish Scriptures! So all the people on the earth, Jew or Gentile, need to just shut their mouths and acknowledge their guilt before God. Therefore, no one is made righteous in God's sight on the basis of trying to obey the Mosaic law, for the law was primarily given to expose sin.

Comments —————————————————————

Paul's final paragraphs wrap up the point that he began to make in the second part of chapter 1. Righteousness is not intrinsic to human nature. The fall of our first parents has affected our basic nature. Gentile "flesh" and Jewish "flesh" are still human "flesh," and it all falls greatly short of the holiness of God. We have all sinned not only against God's standard of perfection, but, at times, against our own better judgment. Some of us display more sinful attitudes and actions than others, and some of us display more of what is "good" in humanity than others ... but still, we have all missed the mark in plenty of ways. And we all know it is true when we are honest with ourselves. Our God-given conscience informs us so.

Because our sinful nature and tendencies are so common, we often try to find ways to explain them away, suppress them, whitewash them with religion, minimize them, redefine them or mask them. We imagine, "If everyone is imperfect ... it must not be a big deal to God anyway. He ought to be used to it by now!" But then the great gospel of Jesus come along and challenges us to face the reality of being fallen. The Holy Spirit gently and firmly puts his finger on our own personal sinfulness and allows the guilt and shame to surface so that we can squarely face, not deny, our true condition. I need forgiveness for my many failures. I need a Savior ... for I cannot save myself or change my own nature.

Then the Holy Spirit goes on to convince me that a Savior is there for me, if I will only have the courage and gut-level honesty to turn and face him. Who is it? Yes, it's Jesus Christ after all. Of course it's him. I suspected that he was the real deal the first time I heard of him. The One whose name is on the lips of so many ... even if it is used as a cuss word. (Even the naughty cannot keep him off of their minds!) He died for us, he is risen, he is Lord of all, and his influence is all around us and even moving upon our souls. But will I melt or carry on in my hardness, suppressing what I know must be true? Oh, God ... help me to melt over and over again.

12. God's Ingenious Salvation Strategy (3:21–31)

However, a new day has dawned, and the righteousness of God, which transcends the Mosaic legal system, is revealed. The Scriptures themselves, written by Moses and the prophets, point us to this very truth. Now this divine righteousness is available to all people who really believe in the Messiah, Jesus, and put their trust in who he is and what he has done for them. For there is no real difference between people—all have sinned and fall far short of God's standard of perfection. Justification (God reconciling us to himself) is a free gift of God's grace purchased by Jesus Christ, whom God has clearly presented as the only righteous one; he therefore is the only worthy blood sacrifice for the sins of all people of all times, which God has patiently endured. Sacrificing his own Son was the only possible way that God could impart his righteousness to people and still be true to both his justice and his mercy.

God's ingenious salvation strategy undermines all the arrogant self-righteousness of religious people because it is not based on the principle of trying, but on trusting. We therefore conclude that people are made right with God not on the basis of religious works, but on the basis of putting their confidence in Jesus the Messiah. God isn't only the God of the Jews, but also of the Gentiles. And if he is the same and only true God for all, then he must save all by the same means—believing.

So do we nullify the value of the Mosaic law because of this? No way! In fact, its very focus is confirmed.

Comments

Imagine that the whole human race has been living perpetually in the nighttime. Some nights are darker than others, and when the full moon shines on a clear night, people think how bright it is outside. The moon is esteemed as the brightest source of natural light in the world. Then imagine that something unprecedented occurs.

One "day," while people are minding their own business, on the edge of the horizon a powerful and brilliant glow appears. Everyone's attention is drawn to the eastern sky. It intensifies over several minutes, until suddenly the people of the earth witness, for the first time in their long history, a piercing ray of the sun. They probably assume that the end of the world is at hand. Then a brilliant and massive disk of light that emits a penetrating warmth rises into the heavens. As it rises, it becomes too bright to gaze upon as it simultaneously heats up the atmosphere. The "days" of the past are now paling in comparison to this "DAY" that has suddenly dawned upon the earth. The moon, still visible in the sky, is fading from sight. Then, as normal days and nights commence, the people learn more about this amazing star and its rhythms, they realize that the moon is just a dead stone, and its only light is a reflection of the great and powerful light of the sun.

This is the word picture that comes to my mind as I think about the Big God-Story of the Scriptures, and as I ponder the history of God's dealings with humanity in the Old Testament in light of what he did by inaugurating the new covenant in Christ's blood. All that God did in human history pointed forward to the appearance on earth's stage of Jesus of Nazareth—the Christ. The Old Covenant was written on dead stones that did not change the stony human heart within the soul of God's fallen image bearers. Its light only reflected the Light of the One to come. But the new covenant was based in a Person who is the source of true light that is too brilliant to gaze into. He provides a warmth that goes deep into all of human life and existence. He made a way for God's own nature and righteousness to be "birthed" into the soul of a person, which changes the very chemistry of her/his nature. He lovingly chose to do this on the basis of his own goodness, justice and grace rather than the insufficient religious performance of any broken human being. Those who would receive this grand miracle would not be qualified by their race, religious background, level of education or social status. All that the heavenly Father would require them to do is trust the One he sent and agree in the depth of their hearts that he is the only begotten Son of God, who has been given to be the Savior of the world.

And ... this strategy is far from being anti-Jewish. That people of every race and nation are invited to receive Jesus as the promised Messiah—the Father's free gift to all humanity—is the fulfillment of what the Hebrew prophets heard from God, anticipated and foretold. God's promise to Abraham that he would be the father of many nations and a blessing to every family on the earth finds its consummation in all that Jesus was and is about.

13. Was Abraham a Jew When He Got Right with God? (4:1–5)

How was Abraham, our father according to human ancestry, made right with God? If he had been justified by his religious performance, then he would have had something to boast about—even though God would have seen right through it. For the Scripture makes it clear: "Abraham believed God, and it was counted to him as righteousness." If someone works, then his reward is not a free gift, but something he's owed for his labor. But to the one who realizes he can't earn salvation, but simply stops trying to and just trusts in the One who saves the sinful, his belief is counted to him as righteousness.

Comments ————————————————————

Father Abraham, esteemed by all, was not Jewish. The Jews, as a people group, did not exist in his day. We easily overlook this simple point. He was from a culture that had devolved into polytheism and idol worship, along with the other cultures of his world and time. But the Living God ... "I Am that I Am" ... the Omnipotent Creator of all things ... intervened miraculously in his life, spoke to him and transformed him into his friend. Abraham's life and journey was shaped by God's calling him away from his land and its culture and religion, and the earth has never been the same. Even though Abraham, in his earthly life, saw very few of the outcomes of the promises God made to him, he certainly sees them now. There is a great and profound continuity between this visible realm and the one we don't see with our physical eyes!

As the apostle Paul continues to unfold the essential elements of the Big God-Story of the gospel of Jesus Christ in the book of Romans, he reminds us of the history of God's interventions with humanity. Before he discusses the place and purpose of the law of Moses in God's economy, he goes back before the time of Moses to reinforce the fact that God's salvation methodology is rooted in a non-Jew's belief (i.e., trust and response deep in the heart) in God rather than in ritual, law-keeping and/or being born into the "right" ethnic or social group. Can God save a non-Jew? We had all better hope so ... including Jewish people ... for they would not exist as a people unless he could and did.

So ... for God to suddenly open the way for Gentiles to be "grafted in" to his covenant family, through the Messiah Jesus, is not an out-of-character thing for him to do—no, not at all. In fact, it is a logical (and prophetically oft-foretold by the Jewish prophets) extension of his eternal purposes in his dealings with humanity as a whole, well-grounded in his covenant with Father Abraham. This radical development in the unfolding story of God's salvation in the earth was something that actually was, and should have been, expected by all who took the ancient prophecy of Scripture to heart.

14. Trying or Trusting (4:6–15)

David also affirmed that God's righteousness isn't earned when he declared, "How blessed are those whose transgressions are forgiven and whose sins are covered. Blessed is the person whose sins the Lord does not count against him."

Now think about it. Is this blessing only given to circumcised Jews, or is it also available to uncircumcised Gentiles? Remember, we agreed that Abraham's faith was the basis of his righteousness. Was he circumcised or uncircumcised when this was said about him? He himself was an uncircumcised Gentile when God said this to him! Only after this was he circumcised, which was only an outward sign of the righteousness that God had already bestowed on him because of his belief. This made Abraham the father of all who believe God, even uncircumcised Gentiles. So, then, God's righteousness is available to them as well. And Abraham is obviously the father of the Jews, if indeed they walk in the same kind of faith Abraham displayed while he was still an uncircumcised Gentile. God's awesome promise that Abraham would be the father of many nations was not given to him and his descendants on the basis of religious performance, but because of the right relationship with God he enjoyed on the basis of believing God. If this promise can be earned, then faith is nullified and God "owes" salvation to people. But trying to live up to the Mosaic code actually produces greater offense and guilt in people, for where there is no clear standard, there is no clear violation.

Comments ───────────────────────────

Up to this point, Paul has been laboring in Romans to reveal how the gospel of Jesus is a great leveler for people of all races and religious backgrounds. Our human nature tends toward trying to earn God's love and acceptance based on our moral performance—this inclination comes so easily to us. We think this view of religion contains a certain basic "fairness" because we instinctively know that God is holy, and he would certainly want us to behave better if we are to approach him and have a relationship with him. It also gets drilled into us, at least in our culture, through our family, education, athletic and business systems. Bad performance brings punitive measures from the authorities, and good behavior is typically rewarded. Probably the closest thing on the human level to the kind of love that God has for us is the love of a healthy parent (or maybe especially a grandparent!). Beneath the pressure a good parent may put upon a child to perform better is an undeserved love from the very beginning of the child's life that comes from simply being family. Ultimately, parents' love for a child can tolerate a lot of misbehavior and poor performance on the part of their daughter/son without breaking the bond of affection. Some parents certainly communicate and display this unearned love better than others, and some, in their fear that their child might take advantage of this love, hardly express it at all.

But in Romans, we are talking about the relationship of a perfectly moral and all-powerful Being with human beings who are imperfect and lacking much in power. Although better behavior is commendable and ultimately an important issue (Romans 6-8 addresses this matter thoroughly), it is not the fundamental basis of establishing a life-giving relationship with God. And that is actually the main point so far ... we (whether Jew or Gentile) can't establish a friendship with God by our own efforts. No one is good enough or holy enough by himself/herself to pull this off. All of us need God to reach down to us to initiate a relationship, if one is to be had at all. This is what the gospel of Jesus Christ is all about. This is what the Heavenly Father has done for us in Christ. And ... this quality of divine love is in line with what he modeled to us in the life stories of Abraham and David (and others) recorded in the Hebrew Scriptures.

Salvation by grace through faith is at the root of the faith of all who have ever truly been God's friends. And now because of Jesus (who he is and what he has done) the opportunity for people of all nations to know God has exploded across our planet by simple agreement with this simply profound news.

15. Abraham: A Father for All Nations (4:16–17)

But trying to live up to the Mosaic code actually produces greater offense and guilt in people, for where there is no clear standard, there is no clear violation. Therefore salvation must be by grace through faith so that the promise might be divinely secured for all, Jews or Gentiles, who express the same kind of trust in God that our father of faith, Abraham, did. As Scripture says, "I have made you a father of many nations."

Comments ————————————————————

In this little section of chapter 4, Paul continues to press the point that God's salvation methodology has never been based on people trying their best to improve themselves morally. He posits a notion that he will elaborate on in Romans 7: that the main reason God gave the law to the children of Israel through Moses was never to make them (or us, or anyone) intrinsically righteous, but to diagnose and highlight the sin and brokenness that ruled in their fallen human natures. This would set them up to ultimately completely trust in God and his promised Messiah rather than in the always limited, imperfect degree of their obedience to the law. Adding to this radical reframing of understanding God's historical purposes and his dealings with and future plans for Israel, Paul reinforces that God's intention was always to include the Gentile nations in his covenant-based salvation through his original promise to Father Abraham.

Both of these fundamental notions deeply challenged the prevailing interpretations of Jewish history and theology in the first century. These ideas, based in the Jewish Scriptures, were ironically very difficult and painful for first-century Jews to accept. They struck a terrible blow to both the prideful nationalism and self-righteousness that tend to gradually creep into any culture that has a genuine history of experience with the Living God. (The very same religious traps exist in our day within "Christendom" and so-called "Christian nations".) The gospel of Jesus always strikes a death-blow to human pride in all its various forms, but not to humiliate us as human beings—rather, to open the door to an amazing grace that comes from God as a free gift to the humble.

16. Faith Is Agreeing with God (4:17–25)

He (Abraham) believed God, who raises the dead and has the prophetic power to call the things yet future as good as done. Against all odds, he continued to hope and believe that God would give him a son and make him a father of many nations. Even after he turned one hundred and both he and Sarah were beyond the age of conceiving children, he grew strong in faith without surrendering to unbelief. He kept praising God, fully convinced that God would do what he said he would. Again, it was his faith that was counted to him as righteousness.

Now this was not just true for Abraham, that his righteousness was by faith. It applies to us, who will also receive God's righteousness if we believe in him who raised Jesus our Lord from the dead. He was sacrificed for our trespasses and raised again so that we might be made right with God.

Comments ——————————————————————

Jesus said that great power is available when two people agree in prayer before God. But even greater power is available when we agree with God himself (and, most importantly, agree about who Jesus is and what he has done for us in his death and resurrection). This, I believe, is the essence of what exercising faith is. Faith has a passive side because, when it comes to miracles, only God's power can accomplish such things; we must humbly wait for him to act and move ... even upon us. But faith has an active side as well.

I heard Dallas Willard say in one of his sermons that faith is present when "my whole being is set to act as if something was so." This is how Abraham lived before God ... not perfectly, even in his case, but substantially over the course of his life. Abraham not only received God's gift of righteousness at the beginning of his friendship with God; he also walked in God's righteousness by embracing an ongoing posture of agreeing with God and acting accordingly with the strength that God provided him. It's not a bad goal to consider adopting: to seek to agree with God with my whole being, as best as I can discern his heart and mind, yet without becoming arrogant about any way in which I come to understand his truth.

Father, may I act today as if Jesus died to wipe away my guilt and shame and rose from the dead to give me the free gift of your very own righteousness. May I be conscious that Christ lives in me as I live out the life and circumstances you have arranged for each moment of the day and evening that lies before me.

17. Salvation Is a Big Word (5:1–2)

By believing in and putting our personal trust in Jesus, in who he is and in what he has done for us, we have been justified—forgiven and declared righteous by God. And because of this, we are no longer at war but at peace with him. Not only do we have direct access to God, but we are also confident that we now live in a state of being characterized by the availability of God's free and freeing grace—unmerited favor and desire and power to live for him. Even beyond all this, we have a joyfully motivating, present, earnest expectation concerning our glorious destiny—being personally perfected and living in a perfect place in the presence of God.

Comments ————————————————

Salvation is a big word; that is, it covers a lot of territory. Because we are in Christ, our past, present and future have all been absolutely revolutionized. In this little paragraph at the beginning of Romans 5, the whole landscape of our life is in view. All of the failures and sins of our past, along with the tormenting guilt and shame associated with them, have been washed away in the vast sea

of God's deliberate forgetfulness. In the present,
we have new desires ... healthy and holy passions,
encoded and embedded into our deepest heart ...
along with the power to live them out. (Not perfectly, but substantially and truly.) We now enjoy
a new state of being that is centered in the reality
of Christ living within us ... whatever our circumstances might be. His peace is ours, and a genuine interactive friendship with the Father, Son and
Spirit in realtime is our gracious inheritance and
the key to living well in this fallen world. Regarding our future, we have to use our renewed imaginations to even begin to conceive of the beauty, joy,
and complete and amazing satisfaction—spiritually, mentally, emotionally, physically, vocationally
and relationally—we will eternally know and in
which we will forever delight.

18. One Great Thing Feeds Another (5:3–5)

*Not only do we have joy because of our bright future,
but, paradoxically, we also discover joy in the middle of
the pressures and difficulties of this life. This is because
we are confident that there is divine purpose in these
things. Consider the positive character qualities that can
grow out of our trials. Patience can only be formed in us
by the temporary denial of what we would prefer, and
true spiritual maturity cannot exist without one of its
main elements—patience. Being personally transformed
through this maturation process imparts the assurance
that one day we really are going to be fully like Christ.*

*Furthermore, we know that our hope of perfection is
not a fantasy because of the reality of our encountering
God's love for us, in us and through us. All this is made
possible by the vital personal relationship we already*

freely enjoy with the Holy Spirit, who fills our hearts with God's love. So it is a glorious cycle: genuine personal growth here and now inspires confidence in our future perfection, which, in turn, inspires further spiritual growth in the present.

Comments

Joy is a bottom-line issue of the kingdom of God in our lives. In this first part of Romans 5, Paul is revealing the psychologically sound life view that underpins and informs our experience of joy in Christ. As believers, our future bliss is obvious (and worthy of regular pondering!). However, this expectation is a "living hope" (1 Pet. 1:3) that has the intrinsic power to translate down payments of this future joy into our present experience, despite any challenging circumstances in this still imperfect environment. Two primary elements converge to impart to us such joy.

First, trials, which are inevitable, are actually useful to our deepest longing and our ultimate goal: to become like Christ. We (and others) have witnessed the genuine (and also inevitable) growth in Christ-likeness experienced by patiently enduring adversity without giving up on loving God and others. (Resistance, though painful, builds muscles!) Second, in the midst of our trials and sufferings, God is with us "in the now" through the indwelling of the Holy Spirit. Mysteriously, he makes a way for hope and joy to sufficiently seep into our hearts and minds, so that we are blessed, stabilized, comforted and surrounded (often consciously) with the divine in the face of the messes and tragedies of this life. The pains are real, but so are the comfort and the joy.

This dynamic in our lives truly is a powerful and compelling witness to the reality of Christ's resurrection in the eyes of a watching world.

May we find grace to face the trials of the day with the joy of Jesus Christ pumping in our souls.

19. Higher Love (5:6–8)

Consider this strong love of God. The human race was spiritually dead—lost in sin and alienated from God. Now someone might sacrifice his life for a good friend, but for an evil enemy? Unheard of! Yet God's love is of a higher nature than mere human love. As much as he hates sin, because of his love, God found a way to separate sinners from their sin. In this love, he pursued us, and at just the right time he became one of us. Then, in our place, he received in himself his own just punishment for mankind's sins—the death penalty.

Comments ————————————————————

God's Big God–Story is deeply woven into these few verses of Roman 5:6–8. The eternal love conspiracy of the divine Trinity has thoroughly resolved the problem of evil in this world through the Person and Work of Jesus the Christ. God wants us, and he wants to be wanted by us, but our sinful nature has kept our hearts in bondage. We have been caught in a frustrating loop that is driven by the "hyphenated sins" born of sitting on the thrones of our hearts: self-centeredness, self-justification, self-reliance, self-promotion, self-absorption ... ad infinitum.

But here, Jesus has come onto the scene of human history to personally take on and dispel the heat of the sins, the guilt and the shame of all humanity in his great substitutionary sacrifice on the cross. Those who simply believe (or agree) in their hearts that he would do this for them are personally transformed. They are translated by the power of the Holy Spirit into God's "new genesis" that is now mysteriously present and growing in this world. This new creation has been destined to gain momentum and progressively eclipse the power of this fallen, old age, thus bringing a comprehensive renewal and the ultimate fulfillment of God's original design for creation when Christ returns. Isn't it astounding that a problem so difficult, heavy, agonizing, pervasive, costly and complicated ends up being resolved so simply and freely through the obedience of One Man and the exercise of childlike faith in him?

May God grant us childlike hearts of trust that vulnerably receive such great love.

20. Much More (5:9–10)

Now if in the past, Jesus shed his blood so that we could have peace with God in the present, surely we won't suffer God's wrath in the future. And if he died for us when we were God's enemies, now that he is alive again and we as his friends share this resurrection life, surely he will bring us to perfection. The most difficult and unimaginable thing has already taken place!

Comments ——————————————————

Here is the way that the NIV translates verse 10: "For if, when we were God's enemies, we were reconciled to him through the death of his Son, how much more, having been reconciled, shall we be saved through his life!"

We typically think of being saved by the death of Jesus (which is obviously a big part of the deal), but here Paul distinguishes being "reconciled" to the Father and being "saved." The former is by means of the death of the Son, and the latter is through the life (i.e., the resurrection) of the Son. We also have this "much more" term, which Paul repeats several times in this chapter. What could be classified as "much more" than being reconciled to God through the death of Christ on the cross for us?

It is this: our salvation doesn't end with the new birth, but rather is inaugurated by the new birth. Now there is a whole journey in Christ that begins in this world and will carry on into the ages to come—a journey of *life* in Christ. His death is very vital and important for us to always keep in view and proclaim repeatedly, but we do not typically speak about and celebrate enough regarding the life. His death is a doorway; his life is a destination that is associated with this very meaningful journey. Salvation is life; life is to dominate our consciousness and to inform our relationships and our pathway for all worship and service.

May the Holy Spirit make us aware today of the "much more" that God is doing in our lives this day. He is further conforming us to the image of Jesus, and he is involving us in his plans and purposes for the people and work he puts in front of us.

21. Simply Enjoying God (5:11)

And so, not only do we have joy because of our glorious future and because our present sufferings have meaning, but we also simply enjoy God. Our Lord Jesus Christ has made this personal fellowship with God possible through his sacrificial death for the forgiveness of our sins.

Comments ————————————————————

Paul concludes this first section of Romans 5 about the sources of joy for living in this age by coming to the bottom line of joy. Our greatest blessing is having a real-time, interactive friendship with the most amazing Being in the universe ... the Maker of Heaven and Earth. We celebrate our absolute pardon for all our failures and sins, and for the free gift of righteousness that is also ours because of Jesus. We marvel at the expectation of a future that is beyond our wildest imaginations in terms of its beauty and satisfaction. But, along with these joys, the Holy Spirit has equipped us with the capacities of both soul and body (software and hardware!) to walk with God as his friends, and to experience the transcendent and undergirding joy of knowing his genuine companionship ... even though our feet still get dirty while treading this fallen world.

May we draw near to the Father, Son and Holy Spirit by faith each day and open the windows of our beings to God-joy.

22. Something More Original than Sin (5:12–14)

Sin entered into the world through Adam's fall, and death was the consequence. Moreover, death spread to all mankind, for all became sinners themselves—through both natural birth and by personal choice. (Sin was in the world before God gave the law to Moses, but sin remains nebulous if there is no clearly-revealed standard.)

But even though sin itself was not clearly defined from the time between Adam and Moses, its consequence, death, still had dominion over mankind—even over people who did not commit the same transgression that Adam did. He was given a role in influencing humanity that can only be compared with Jesus Christ himself.

Comments

As Paul continues his version of the meta-narrative of God's story, he compares and contrasts Jesus with Adam. This is fitting given Paul's awareness that, through the events surrounding his first coming, Jesus has inaugurated the new creation, or the New Genesis, that the earth has been longing to witness. Adam and Jesus are the "first Adam" and the "last Adam" (Jesus "terminated" Adam's fallen race in his death on the cross) ... the "first man" and the "second man" (Jesus "raised" humanity in his resurrection and ascension; cf. 1 Cor 15). Adam and Jesus are the heads of the only real two "races" in the earth, despite all our international variety and color! It's also not insignificant that Jesus, as the eternal Word, was instrumental in the first genesis, which is strongly reassuring to us regarding the Father's plan to mitigate what went wrong with our first parents when they were tested.

It is important to note that sin is pictured in Scripture as an alien invasion of God's good original creation, which has tragically affected both the earth and the heavens ... the visible and the invisible realms. This understanding undermines the common gnostic notion that the material realm is evil and the spiritual realm is holy. (A personal confession: I really hate Gnosticism and its effects on unsuspecting believers, who are continually beat up by its modern forms in the church world.) The downside of the fall is obvious as we simply rehearse human history; read our daily world news; and take an honest look at our own personal, historic struggles, temptations and failures. And then, of course, there is death ... a harsh reality we tend to face squarely only during funerals. As much as people may argue about whether sin is a real issue in human life, death always brings us back to the reality that something terrible has happened to all creation. The only word I can think of for the popular denial of sin in our culture is ... well ... *ridiculous*.

The upside of this tragedy is that there really is something more original than sin in this world! It is the goodness of God's original design, which has been horribly marred, but is still powerfully on display and is a conduit of great provision and joy for human life, despite our first parents' garden rebellion. Furthermore, God hasn't given up on his original design. The new creation, rather than completely destroying the original, assimilates and incorporates the remnants of its goodness and renews its sacred purposes. The ultimate form of God's intentions for the universe is not to enshrine an eternal, ethereal realm of disembodied spirits and endless church services! Rather, I deeply believe, he desires one of physical substance, unimaginable Trinity-worship, purpose, noble work, meaningful peer relations, ongoing development, exploration and discovery ... a new heavens and a new earth ... without any brokenness to interrupt God's (or our) total satisfaction.

23.   How Do You Like Them Apples? (5:15–19)

But if you think Adam's sin had impact, consider the impact of Christ's free gift! If the first man's action resulted in sin and death spreading to so many people, the action of this Man not only negated sin and death, but also imparted righteousness and eternal life to people. Consider this contrast further: Adam's one sin resulted in many sins and a corresponding judgment from God. This is natural. But the free gift bought by Christ captured all of that sin and condemnation and transformed it into righteousness. This is supernatural! Yes, one man's sin was powerful enough to cause death to have dominion, but the gift of Jesus Christ was even more powerful. Through him, people can receive what they don't deserve—God's unmerited favor and an overcoming, transcendent life. To sum it up in other words, one act of disobedience resulted in sin and judgment coming upon all mankind; even so, one act of obedience resulted in righteousness and a higher life being made freely available to this whole sinful, condemned human race. If the first thing seems unfair, the second certainly is!

Comments ─────────────────────────────

Truly, Adam's choice was sweeping and powerful in its effects on all his descendants. Yet Paul's point is that Christ's work was "much more" powerful in nature. Whenever I read this passage, I always think of an analogy. Imagine how one rotten apple, given just a bit of time, can easily spoil a whole barrel of unspoiled apples. But can you imagine placing a perfect apple into a barrel of rotten apples and, after a bit of time, finding that all of those apples have been restored to a perfect state? In the first case, you would lament the power of natural corruption, but you would not be surprised. In the second case, you would absolutely stunned at an unprecedented miracle that you would want the whole world to know about! So it should be regarding the life and ministry of Jesus the Christ and his effect upon fallen humanity.

It's humbling to admit that there are massive forces at work in our world that have deeply affected and do affect our lives ... forces way beyond our own personal will, as critical as our choices are. The "force" of Adam's ancient choice, the "force" of our Creator bringing each of us into this world via our parents mating, the "force" of the Heavenly Father's grace toward us in Christ and the "force" of the Holy Spirit drawing us to Jesus Christ are four of these most powerful realities.

God delights in being our Savior (it's just who he is and what he does!) and all he asks for is our humble cooperation and a lifetime of thanks and loving him back. All the rest of our spiritual formation develops from these reasonable responses.

24. Grace Trumps Law (5:20–21)

In addition, it may seem strange, but God purposefully instituted the Mosaic legal system to flush the sinful nature out of hiding, which resulted in more sinning. Yet this all the more magnified God's sin-conquering grace. (I'll expand on this theme later.) Before Christ, sin ruled and death was dominant, but now through Jesus our Lord, grace rules—enthroned by the dominating righteousness that leads to eternal life.

Comments ——————————————————————

Paul does elaborate on this mysterious and outstanding purpose of the Mosaic law in God's economy in chapter 7. Jesus and the apostles point out that the law does have other purposes than to highlight and expose the sinful nature of human beings. But I'll wait to comment more on this until we get to chapter 7.

What stands out to me from this final paragraph of chapter 5 and so beautifully sets up the theme of chapter 6 is that Paul sees God's grace, which has been offered freely to us all in Christ, as more powerful than our sins, as powerful and intimidating as they can be. We (and the Holy Spirit within us) are in an ongoing battle with the flesh, but it is not a battle between two equals. Because of Jesus and our faith in him, we have been translated into a whole new realm of life ... even here and now in this fallen, evil age.

This is maybe the greatest mystery of the kingdom of God: the new genesis, inaugurated by Jesus. It has been birthed in the midst of our sick, broken world, like a seed of life that has germinated deep in the soil where there is no light. And we have been assimilated and sucked up into that higher life, like inanimate minerals that are transformed by and literally become a part of a plant and its life.

It seems to me that Paul's fundamental point in equipping us to rise above the power of sin in a practical and daily way begins with our need—we have to deeply grasp the reality of how we are now living in a different environment than we did before being born of the Spirit, and we must be fully conscious of this radical change 24/7. We are now breathing air (receiving grace) from highest heaven by means of the real connection between heaven and earth provided by the Holy Spirit—the Spirit sent to us from heaven, who is truly above, beneath, around and ... yes ... within us. To attempt to take the other practical steps of overcoming without internalizing this primary point is a recipe for defeat (and maybe a good explanation for why believers live, and have lived, in such defeat both today and throughout history). But not you ... and not me ... not today! Instead, may we be alive to God, breathe in the presence of his kingdom all about us and carry his joy.

25. Looking for Loopholes? (5:20–6: 2)

In addition, it may seem strange, but God purposefully instituted the Mosaic legal system to flush the sinful nature out of hiding, which resulted in more sinning. Yet this all the more magnified God's sin–conquering grace. (I'll expand on this theme later.) Before Christ, sin ruled and death was dominant, but now through Jesus our Lord, grace rules—enthroned by the dominating righteousness that leads to eternal life.

Now I know what you're tempted to think: "If this is true, then we might as well sin more so that God's grace can continue to be magnified." Right? Wrong! You see, we live in a whole new era, and new dynamics are now at work. For us, to deliberately live in sin is out of the question because we are actually dead to the whole dominion of sin.

Comments ————————————————————

Paul touches on an important natural response in people's hearts and minds to God's amazing grace. (This grace boldly stares our sin in the face, is not shocked or dissuaded in the least and totally moves in to trump all our guilt and shame.) I think it's awesome that Paul gives voice in his letter to such natural thinking, and the fact that he brings it to light only causes the authenticity of the gospel to rise.

When the absolutely free nature of God's gift of forgiveness and new life for us in Jesus hits our hearts, shortly thereafter, we begin to wonder about the future sins and failures we are certain to experience. We wonder if God will not hold them, along with our past compromises, against us. What will actually motivate us, or "others" to whom we preach (after all, we don't like to make the inner conversation about such dark thoughts too personal!) not to give in to temptations to sinful self-gratification? Don't we also need some extra terrifying threats to hover over our heads and keep us in line on a moment-by-moment basis? (The serious warnings of the New Testament are reserved for people who are in danger of rejecting faith in Jesus.)

Instead, Paul comes at countering such dark thoughts from a different, refreshing angle. He doesn't argue for restricting our freedom to keep us in check, but instead argues for us to embrace and enjoy an even greater awareness of our freedom. So free are we, in fact, that we are now dead to the tyranny of sin. The apostle doesn't urge us to fearfully obsess, "How can I not sin?" and/or "What if I lose my salvation?" like we easily might lose the key to our car. Rather, we are to calmly reason, "Why would I really want to continue to give myself to sin?" and then make our daily choices by remembering the answer, which turns out to be a no-brainer. Sin, of course, is not satisfying to the human soul (though, assuredly, it continually seems as if it were!), and this is why we turned away from it to Jesus in the first place.

26. A Whole New Power Supply (6:3–7)

You have got to realize that as many of us who have been baptized into Jesus Christ have identified with him in his death and also in his burial and resurrection. Our baptism is like a burial of our old "sin and death" life that Jesus embodied on the cross. And just as Jesus was raised from the dead by the power of God, so also in baptism we are raised up for the purpose of living by means of a new power source.

For God's intent in our dying and being buried with Christ is not to leave us lying powerless in the grave, but also to raise us with Jesus to live a transcendent life in him. Our old "sin and death" life was put out of commission through a mysterious co-crucifixion with Jesus. As a result, a life lived under the compulsion of our lower passions has passed away with a vengeance, and such selfishness is no longer our master. We are dead and therefore liberated from the mandatory control of sin.

Comments ───────────────────────

In our ongoing struggle in dealing appropriately with our flesh (a rather complex word and subject), it is vital that we begin at the right place.

Something radical happened to our fallen human
nature some 2,000 years ago, long before we were
born. Jesus Christ appeared on the scene of human
history, died and rose again so that we would be
able to personally and freely receive the gift of a
new nature that is in harmony with the Trinity. Our
battle with temptations and sins must begin by
believing that Jesus has totally overcome sin and
death on our behalf through what he has already
accomplished.

A clearly defined pathway leads us out of a life
that is limited by self-concern and our attempts to
transform ourselves into better persons. It begins
by pausing long and hard enough to soak deep
into our heart the good and great news of who Jesus is and what he has done for us. By this, a quiet
strength seeps into our souls that then empowers
us to successfully engage the battle to discover our
truest self and, thereby, progressively grow into
loving God and others well.

27. Changed from the Core (6:5–10)

For God's intent in our dying and being buried with
Christ is not to leave us lying powerless in the grave,
but also to raise us with Jesus to live a transcendent
life in him. Our old "sin and death" life was put out
of commission through a mysterious co-crucifixion with
Jesus. As a result, a life lived under the compulsion of
our lower passions has passed away with a vengeance
and such selfishness is no longer our master. We are dead
and therefore liberated from the mandatory control of sin.

But, as I said, we didn't just die with Christ, we have
been catapulted into life with him: Jesus only had to die
once, and he vanquished death once and for all through

his resurrection. He died for sins just once, but he lives perpetually for his Father's pleasure.

Comments ————————————————

I believe that one of the deepest longings of a human spirit is to be transformed into a better person. Most people try to make this happen at points in their lives. Most of us fail to see transformation to any significant degree through our self-help strategies and programs. Many people give up on trying to change for the good at all and then dive more deeply into expressions of human depravity. One of the great attractions of the gospel of Jesus is the embedded hope and promise of radical, personal transformation. Only, in the case of the gospel, the help we receive is not essentially self-help as we commonly understand the term (though we ultimately do participate cooperatively and meaningfully in the process). It is the help that occurs through a powerful, gracious and undeserved divine intervention ... acts of the very Holy Spirit himself.

The New Testament speaks of this transforming experience with God in the stark terms of a necessary personal "death" and subsequent "resurrection" that is not, first of all, physical. Rather, it has to do with our core nature, or the condition of our heart. We must somehow both "die" and be "raised" for this core change to actually occur. However, the active principle, or the animating force, of this change is not based on us "killing" and "raising" ourselves, but on accepting for ourselves the vital identification with Jesus Christ that God has amazingly arranged for us. What Jesus accomplished once and for all in his historical death

and resurrection is relevant to our personal transformation, because the power of the Holy Spirit
rests and remains all over the message. That power
is released upon and within us in realtime when we
simply believe in and humbly surrender to Christ
as our Lord and Savior. After all, Jesus is dead no
longer, but is alive and still acting in our world to
perform this miracle of new birth in the lives and
hearts of those childlike enough to accept this free
gift.

Though this beginning can seem more or less
dramatic in the way it actually takes place in the
various stories of individuals, it is quite dramatic
in the invisible realm nonetheless. And it is the only
sufficient, effective foundation for the kind of real,
lasting personal transformation for which we long
for and journey toward in Christ.

28. It's All Downhill from Here (6:11–14)

*Now you've got to get this! Knowing this truth is a key
to your liberation. What happened to Jesus has happened
for you and to you. You are dead to sin's loveless lordship
and fully alive to God's loving fatherhood because of
what the Lord Jesus did for us. Even during this earthly
life, you can now say no to the enticements and impulses
of your lower passions—so just do it! You are not to
submit to the selfish demands and compulsive cravings
of your physical drives. Courageously resisting sin is
another key to your victory. No longer turn over your
human powers to become weapons of unrighteousness
and thereby continue in sin. Rather, consciously and
deliberately surrender your powers of both mind and
body to God, and he will possess and use them as weapons
in his powerful hands for his noble purposes. After all,*

you are alive for his pleasure. Now knowing the truth and resisting evil are vital measures, but incomplete. Passionately pursuing God is the third key to living above the dictatorial power of sin. Remember, sin is no longer your master, because you have passed through the night season of religious externals into the brilliant day of grace—may your eyes adjust to the light!

Comments ───────────────────────

We have the firm foundation of knowing deep in our heart that we have been translated out of the environment of our old "sin and death" life into a new atmosphere that is infused with the fresh air of heaven itself (*breath* and *spirit* are the same word in both Hebrew and Greek), and that we are truly and already integrated into the new creation that Christ has inaugurated. We are therefore able to deal with the ongoing realities of the world, the flesh and the devil from an entirely new vantage point. So much of the daily battle to overcome turns on the hinge of maintaining the awareness, or the alert consciousness, that we have been graciously born anew on this higher ground. The higher hill is our hill; we have a new and righteous heart; two thirds of the angels didn't fall; the Trinity is fighting with us and for us and our victorious destiny is secure in Christ. Besides, we are built for the battle, and the fight is the noblest one ever fought.

Today ... and each hour of this day ... we can rise up and calmly say no to sin; live in an opposite spirit from the world around us that is fueled by "the lust of the eyes, the lust of the flesh and the boastful pride of life" (1 Jn. 2:16; in other words, imagining ourselves to be independent from God and his grace); firmly tell Satan to "get behind" us when he confronts us and, by the power of the Holy Spirit, live in an interactive friendship with our Papa that is characterized by a running dialogue in the course of both our activities and leisure. Then ... we can sleep enfolded in the Father's mighty arms and rise to do the same tomorrow.

We need to overcome and re-engage our lives from a Christ-centered angle that is grounded in the ancient wisdom of his first apostles, whom he formed into authentic geniuses of human life under God. May the Lord help us to make a clean break from any of our past failed strategies to do so.

29. Our Body Is Our Friend (6:13)

No longer turn over your human powers to become weapons of unrighteousness and thereby continue in sin. Rather, consciously and deliberately surrender your powers of both mind and body to God, and he will possess and use them as weapons in his powerful hands for his noble purposes. After all, you are alive for his pleasure.

Comments ───────────────────────────

If we read Romans 6-7 only on a surface level, it is easy to get the impression that Paul tagged the human body as the source of our moral/spiritual struggles. The thought that the body and its needs are intrinsically evil and opposed to spirituality is ancient, powerful, popular and very damaging to biblical spirituality, as though we'd be better off to escape this "prison" of the soul. It is also quite natural for us to think this way, and this is why Gnosticism and the dualism that undergirds it regularly crop up in various forms throughout history within religious movements (including the church world—and especially in revivalistic environments). Our physical drives are an easy target for angry, ambitious or bored preachers. False guilt is a powerful lever that can be, and has been, used to pressure people into responding extravagantly to their persuasive appeals for surrender, service, time or money. (We have enough real guilt to deal with in our lives ... who needs false guilt thrown in to confuse the issue?!)

For years I have been laboring to help believers acquire a healthy, scriptural view of the body and how its proper use fits into the overall process of becoming more like Jesus Christ (who, even still, has a body himself). Through a redemptive lens, we can overcome any past intimidation that our bodily drives/passions held over us and come to see how the body is actually our friend, not our enemy, in sanctification. As Paul implies above, its members can and must become weapons of righteousness instead of weapons of unrighteousness.

30. Incarnational Spirituality: Alive for God's Pleasure (6:12–13)

Even during this earthly life, you can now say no to the enticements and impulses of your lower passions— so just do it! You are not to submit to the selfish demands and compulsive cravings of your physical drives. Courageously resisting sin is another key to your victory. No longer turn over your human powers to become weapons of unrighteousness and thereby continue in sin. Rather, consciously and deliberately surrender your powers of both mind and body to God, and he will possess

*and use them as weapons in his powerful hands for his
noble purposes. After all, you are alive for his pleasure.*

Comments

Following are some simple ways to think about
the physical side of our lives:

1. I find it is more helpful to think in terms of the
    visible and the invisible, when it comes to the
    duality that exists between the heavens and the
    earth, rather than the spiritual and the natural—
    overdoing the latter easily leads to dualism.

2. It has always been tempting for religiously-
    inclined people to imagine that the spiritual
    realm is holy and the natural realm is unholy.
    But Scripture makes it clear that both the invis-
    ible and the visible realms were created by God
    as good, and both realms have also been af-
    fected by rebellion and sin. Christ came to bring
    and ultimately apply his salvation and justice
    to both realms—thereby redeeming/renewing
    the whole of God's good creation and securing/
    fulfilling the amazing, eternal destiny of human
    life under and with God.

3. Sin in human nature goes deeper than sins of
    the body, right to the core of the heart, soul and
    mind ... the actual fountainhead of sin. But sin
    has certainly taken advantage of our physicality
    and very often uses the physical needs/drives
    as a base of operations for its expressions: food,
    drink, sleep, sex, strength, speech, wealth, beau-
    ty, companionship and the like. None of these
    things are sinful in and of themselves, but they

are often conduits of sin in human life. Almost every sin of the body is simply a God-ordained human need/activity taken beyond its proper bounds or expression.

4. The body, through Christ, becomes holy, sanctified and a temple of the Holy Spirit himself.

5. In following Jesus as disciples, we are called not to suppress our physical drives, but, rather, to subordinate them to the dominion of the Holy Spirit. We can thereby enjoy the physical side of life through its proper expressions, which are defined and protected by the boundaries set for them by God's word and wisdom.

6. Spiritual disciplines (solitude, silence, prayer, fasting, secret giving, contemplation, study and the like) are useful in training our bodies to co-operate and integrate with the Holy Spirit (I call them "humility drills"). We are to engage in them regularly, gracefully, rhythmically and temporarily. (Extreme asceticism is actually counter-productive to becoming more like Christ by the power of the Spirit ... though it appears very holy.) They are not meritorious in nature or signs of our spiritual maturity to flash around for others to admire—and this is the constant danger associated with using them.

7. The Holy Spirit wants to use our bodies/physical life as a vessel of his life and power. This is a manifestation of the incarnational nature of true biblical spirituality, which is modeled by our Lord Jesus: our simple presence, our speech,

our gaze, our smile, our touch, our hospitality, our sleep, our work, our marriage and family life, our talents, our art, our science, our money, our menial services, our property and the like.

Let's ask Christ to be the Lord of our body—to make us a mobile fiery and living sacrifice, useful in this broken world to bring a taste of heaven's love, grace and power here and now, to the people he brings our way today and every day.

31.   All Ready to Live a Life of Love (6:15–18)

Now if you're still tempted to think I am recommending that we still live in sin because of the compensating nature of God's grace and that we are no longer pressured to live up to a complicated external code, you have really missed the point! If you're looking for an excuse for sin, then your wrong understanding of God's grace is already betrayed. This issue I'm talking about is a matter of the heart and its motivating passions. All of us are love slaves. Either we love sin and serve it, or we love God and serve Him. Now, you used to love sin but, thank God, he opened your heart to believe and obey the good news of Jesus, which was preached to you. Now you have been freed from the mastery of sin and have become love slaves of righteousness.

Comments ────────────────────────────

Here Paul makes a life of devotion to God seem so simple, and in one way it is. "His yoke is easy and his burden is light" (Mt. 11:30). Still, we have to deal with some complicating factors on the journey into becoming fully like Jesus. It is no small matter for our whole being to become truly integrated into the kingdom of God. There is no substitute for time and cooperative experience with God when it comes to achieving a life of mature love. I haven't met one person who has "arrived" yet. (I have met some who seem to emote the attitude that they have ... but to me, this always comes across as spiritual bravado in contrast to reality.) The apostles didn't teach that believers, new or old, reach a place of actual sinless perfection in this world, though some texts might seem to indicate this if viewed in isolation from other texts. (The right hermeneutic principle is that a correct doctrine is established by examining, collating and integrating all the texts of Scripture on any given subject.)

The simple side of overcoming sin is to recognize that something at the core of a believer's being has been miraculously transformed because of what the Trinity (working in concert) has done for her/him. God has infused hatred of sin and love for him into the heart, or essential human nature, of a believer and has displaced the old heart of stone with a new heart of flesh (Ezek. 36:26). Whatever ongoing struggle believers may have with inner sinful passions, desires or attitudes (and associated behaviors), they must uncover the starting point for winning the battle(s): that deeper within them are a ready desire and power to love and serve God, which he has freely given to them as a gift in Christ. The risen Christ is living within us by the Holy Spirit, and he is now intent on progressively living and demonstrating his life through our lives.

This, I believe, is the essential, clear point that Paul is making in the passage above.

32. I Can't Even Relate (6:19–23)

I keep repeating myself because these concepts are so foreign to us and we so easily lose our grasp of them. Just like you used pour your energies into loving unclean things in unclean ways, now put your new energies into loving and serving what is right and pure. Before, you couldn't even relate to what was holy. Now, you look back on your shameful and fruitless old life, realizing that it only leads to death.

So now, in Christ, we can't even relate to living in sin because we are love slaves of God. We enjoy the fruit of living whole and holy lives, which leads to everlasting life. For death is the paycheck for sin, but God's free gift is eternal life through Jesus Christ our Lord.

Comments ───────────────────────────────

We don't often hear the truth about who we really are, what has actually happened to us and what kind of amazing resources are now available to us in Christ from the daily newspaper, the nightly news, the popular culture media, or from most of the people in this world—even those in our church communities. From where on earth can we hear this amazing news repeated? How can it be reinforced in our inner beings? It seems that Paul understood that this great news tends to be elusive and needs to be repeated to us in various ways for it to really sink in. In this chapter, he just keeps laboring and laboring on behalf of his readers in his jealousy for them to internalize such truth and never let it go.

By the grace of God, we were mysteriously included in and identified with the death, burial and resurrection of Jesus (the book of Ephesians adds his ascension as well). This has forever changed our essential nature, as well as our relationship with and basic posture toward this world, our old self and the spiritual powers of evil. As Peter states in his epistle, God, by his power, has provided everything that we need for both life and godliness through giving us intimate, experiential knowledge of Jesus Christ (2 Pet. 1:3).

The only ways (literally speaking) that I have experienced the ongoing reinforcement of these truths in my heart and mind is by regular meditation on the New Testament Scriptures, the whispers of the Holy Spirit to my soul, and being around friends who also believe and know these things— and who make a concerted effort to encourage me over and over again. It's important to hear these things preached in public and pondered in solitude ... but, for me, it has also been vital to have a circle of friends who know me well and who have, face to face, thought deeply and pondered out loud with me about these truths and their applications. A meaningful connection with a few true friends is often the missing, divinely-designed context within which these biblical truths find the right kind of soil to be rooted, cultivated and nurtured into maturity.

If you don't have this kind of circle of friends, ask God to provide. Then go and sincerely offer yourself as this kind of friend to a few others you seem drawn toward and see what happens. Father, I ask You to lead my friends into these relational circles of Christ's love.

33. Keep It Together (6:20–23)

Before, you couldn't even relate to what was holy.

Now, you look back on your shameful and fruitless old life, realizing that it only leads to death.

So now, in Christ, we can't even relate to living in sin because we are love slaves of God. We enjoy the fruit of living whole and holy lives, which leads to everlasting life. For death is the paycheck for sin, but God's free gift is eternal life through Jesus Christ our Lord.

Comments ─────────────────────────

In Romans, Paul expounds on the nature and scope of salvation in God's kingdom. The term *salvation* covers a lot of territory ... it's a large word in theology. In evangelicalism, we have often reduced the word and the concept to refer to the crisis experience of being born again ... and there is certainly a lot to say about personal justification. However, "salvation" in Romans relates to everything from the fulfillment of God's covenant with Abraham, to the vindication of God's integrity, to the historical Person and Work of Jesus, to the future, full, complete release of all creation from the effects of the fall in Eden when Christ returns.

On the personal level, salvation involves not only the crisis of regeneration, but also refers to what the theologians have tagged as *sanctification* and *glorification*. In the New Testament, sanctification is used in two primary ways: it means "to be set apart for God" and/or "to be made holy." Given these two uses of the term, there is a proper sense in which sanctification both precedes and follows justification ... and there is a seamless connectivity between them. Again, we have too often separated justification and sanctification in our teaching and understanding, but they are deeply wedded ... and our ultimate glorification in Christ is also connected to them both, to the point that, in God's sight, it is a done deal.

Here at the end of Romans 6, we see that personal justification naturally bears the fruit of sanctification in our lifestyles and relationships. In our quest to become like Christ, we must continually connect justification and sanctification and not allow them to become separated in our thinking and teaching. They are in a symbiotic relationship, and they fuel one another. Moreover, "holiness" (the same word as *sanctification*) must not be divorced from "healthiness" or "wholeness." These concepts are also connected linguistically to the word for salvation. Many holiness groups and movements throughout history have focused on getting their followers to adopt a rigid set of beliefs and behaviors without reference to becoming whole people or engaging in healthy relationships. But this kind of conformity does not do justice to the kind of abundant life that Jesus came to bring us. And this kind of religious conformity will not be powerful enough to give to a watching world the kind of compelling witness that is worthy of the truly good news of Jesus.

May God give us the grace to become the whole and holy people ... grace that flows freely from the amazing miracle that has already occurred deep in our heart through Jesus Christ by the power of the Holy Spirit.

34. Remarried to Resurrection (7:1–4)

Let me draw an analogy that you Jews will understand from your knowledge of the Mosaic legal system. As general principle, a law remains in force as long as a person is alive. For instance, a wife is legally bound to her husband until he dies. After he dies, she is obviously free from her marriage commitment to him. However, if she is joined to another man while her husband is still alive, she is guilty of adultery. But again, if her husband dies, by law she is free to marry another man without being charged with adultery.

Now here's the application, dear friends. Again, you need to grasp the awesome impact of both the death and resurrection of Jesus. You have died to the Mosaic law through your identification with the crucified Christ (on the cross, he embodied this law, which was your first "husband"); so that you can be honorably "remarried" to another Man—the resurrected Christ. Now you are free to bear the good fruit of being intimately joined in spirit to him.

Comments ———————————————————

Paul uses another analogy as he continues to

reinforce the radical change that has happened in the cosmos, the human story, and in the very core nature of a person who has truly placed his/her faith in who Jesus is and what Jesus has done. Various ways in various passages in the New Testament describe this change in dominions or eras ... grace vs. law, new creation vs. old creation Christ vs. Adam, Spirit vs. flesh, new covenant vs. old covenant, faith vs. works ... but they all refer to the same basic shift, though sometimes from different angles.

Jesus' death and resurrection are sometimes juxtaposed in Romans, as in this passage. In his death, Jesus dealt conclusively with the sinful Adamic nature and also the law (given through Moses) that the sinful nature was bound under and to. Then, in his resurrection, Jesus opened the way for our fallen nature to be miraculously transformed and made new by the power of the very same Spirit that raised him from the dead. The Spirit is also able to liberate us from any paralyzing sense of obligation to earn God's love and favor by living up to a complicated, demanding external code.

The risen Christ actually lives within us as our closest companion, our friend and the pilot of our lives. He is not our co-pilot—rather, we are now sitting in the "second seat" of our lives ... living in concert with and interactive response to the resurrected Lord, who is pleased to express himself through the practical, daily life that he has given each of us to live. Something shifts deeply within us when we become continually conscious that he is alive in us and we are alive in him.

35. The Law Is a Setup (7:5–7)

When we were living in our natural state, God's moral standard provoked our sinful passions, which used our bodies as a base of operations to produce bad fruit. But now that we are spiritually alive in Jesus, we are set free from trying to live up to an external code without an internal transformation and motivation. Before, we were held in bondage—spiritually dead. Now, we can serve God in this new way because we have spiritual life dwelling inside of us. I know what you're tempted to think: "If this is the case, the Mosaic law is to be equated with sin." Right? Wrong!

Comments —————————————————————————

As Paul unfolds God's Big God-Story throughout Romans, he faces the major challenge of helping his readers understand that God has not failed or lied in regards to the promises he made to the Old Testament patriarchs and to Jewish people in general, but that the gospel of Jesus the Messiah is the climactic fulfillment of those very promises. He takes pains to expose that everyone, whether Jew or Gentile, needs the personal redemption that the Father has provided for us in Christ. Simply being born a Jew and sincerely attempting to keep the law of Moses is not sufficient for the kind of spiritual life that God had always had in mind and has now made accessible for us all to receive. The Holy Spirit, through the gospel, provides a new understanding ... the revelation of a mystery that had been hidden in past times regarding how the various pieces of God's dealings with humanity in history fit together.

Paul especially must reveal how this very large piece of Israel's story—the law given through Moses—fits into the big picture of God's salvific purposes. He makes it clear that law keeping was not the basis of Father Abraham's righteousness, but, rather, that his belief in God was. And beyond this, this covenant of faith became the historical root for the flower of God's righteousness, which bloomed in Jesus so many centuries later. If seen in the context of the larger story, the gospel is a logical, though admittedly dramatic and surprising, extension of God's promise to Israel (and the whole world) through the patriarchs. So, to expand the analogy, the law of Moses then can been seen as the essential, long, plain "stem" of the plant upon which the flower is set ... and, thereby, the flower is enabled to show forth its beauty to all creation.

The law of Moses was useful for various purposes in the bigger story. One of these purposes was and is to create an ironic but essential dynamic: the good, holy law of God, when we deliberately engage with it, diagnoses and exposes sin in fallen human nature by coaxing it out of hiding. The Father in heaven has always intended to use this irony to set people up to receive the good news of Jesus the Messiah. "For the law was given through Moses, but grace and truth came through Jesus Christ" (John 1:17). More to come ...

36. Nothing Shocks God (7:7–11)

I know what you're tempted to think. "If this is the case, the Mosaic law is to be equated with sin." Right? Wrong! First of all, this code clearly defined sin from God's perspective. For instance, I didn't know about the evil nature of covetousness until I was taught the Ten Commandments. Before we are educated concerning God's moral standards, we obviously have many ethical blind spots. But secondly, this law created another more subtle, ironic dynamic. When we do become exposed to the knowledge of good and evil, our rebellious hearts spring into action and conceive new ways to sin. (Once I learned about lusting, the latent and hidden lust in my heart went into overdrive.) You see, the problem is not in the commandments; it is inside of people's hearts.

When I was more ignorant of good and evil, I thought everything was fine. But when I learned more, sin awakened within me, overpowered me and wiped me out. The knowledge of God's commandments, which I stockpiled to equip me for the moral battle, was the very ammunition that sin stole from me and then loaded into its weapons to destroy me. I didn't realize that it had been hiding in the munitions depot the whole time!

Comments ———————————————————

In Romans 7, Paul speaks in detail about the emotional and psychological processes that we, in our weak humanity, experience in relation to law, ethics, temptation and giving in to sin. One of the amazing things that stands out to me as I read this passage is how God is not shocked, scandalized or intimidated by the sins of humanity ... far from it. He knows the condition of our hearts so much better than we do, and because of his grace, he wants us to see more clearly how we tend to minimize, suppress, hide, redefine and put "cosmetics" on our brokenness and rebellion. Have you ever raised a beloved two-year-old?! It seems that, left to ourselves, we are stuck in the terrible twos, spiritually speaking. Our Father in heaven loves us so dearly, but he calls us to face our failures and limitations head on: "Denial ain't just a river in Egypt!"

Paul posits the concept that God instituted the law through Moses, among other reasons, to function as a compassionate diagnostician. The law ferrets out the disease (that which is robbing us of true peace) that has permeated our nature, life and relationships. He has used this tool across the span of history and cultures to prepare people to receive the free gift of salvation he has extended to us in Jesus the Christ. Because our inner nature is bent toward doing our own thing rather than minding God, and because we justify ourselves in our independence from him in so many imaginative, self-deceptive ways, he gave us his law to expose to ourselves the mess that our inner being is in. Sin is so bad that God had to come in person to the planet to deal with it in a comprehensive, conclusive way by means of an ultimate, personal sacrifice. To cover it up is not the solution to its presence or effects in this world.

God's law provides the necessary dynamic relief, or contrast, so that we can perceive how far short of his beauty we fall when left to our own wisdom and strength. We must humbly acknowledge our moral and spiritual brokenness and gratefully agree to believe in God's miraculous provision for us in Jesus Christ, because his sacrifice is the only sure foundation for the new life that he longs to freely dispense to any person who will simply receive it like a child.

37. Religion Is Frustrating (7:13–25)

Now don't get me wrong. God's commandants are

right, fair and good. So are God and his moral laws to blame for my spiritual death? No! Never! Again, the problem is the sin hiding within us. God wanted to expose its presence, power and pervasiveness, and allowed it to even use his holy commandments to reinforce to us how evil it is. God's moral law itself is spiritual, but the problem is in us—left to ourselves, we are sinful and our hearts are in a terrible bondage.

Allow me to narrate the frustrating experience of trying to live up to God's moral standard by our own strength and willpower, without the energy of the Holy Spirit flowing through us.

"What I do, I hate. What I want to do, I don't. What I hate, I do. By wanting to do right, even though I don't, it proves that I value the rightness of God's standards. This reveals that there is something within me blocking me from being who I really am—it's sin. I realize that my inner longings are somehow short-circuited, because the performance of the good that I would like to do eludes me. For the good that I want to do, I don't do. But I actually do the evil that I don't want to do. So I conclude that the deepest part of my being is not controlling me, but a foreign power called sin has invaded my life. I have discovered a principle of human nature: when I set out to do good, an evil within me sabotages my efforts. A deeper part of me would love to obey God's moral law, but another parasitic force uses my bodily members as its host and controls me. A civil war rages between my moral values and the sinful passions that operate through my body. And sin is winning the war! I am truly a miserable person! Who can liberate me from this living death? Thanks be to God, Jesus Christ will!"

So friends, this is the awful dilemma of anyone who tries to serve God apart from the Holy Spirit's presence and power living in and flowing through him—his mind agrees with God's moral law, but another part of him is in bondage to sin, and he is unable to live up to its standard.

Comments ——————————————————————

I don't believe that Paul is here illustrating the normal Christian life. Rather, I think it is a reference to "Everyman" ... though, certainly, he must have experienced this frustrating dynamic along the way in his spiritual journey. It is unquestionably a description of a person who has been somehow awakened spiritually, to the degree that she/he believes in God and has a sincere desire within to please him ... and this is a good and noble thing. Many would say that this stage of spiritual life seems to be a necessary phase that we go through on the way to true spiritual maturity, which marks us with a deep personal conviction that efforts made in our own strength (flesh) to please God are not sufficient and are ultimately self-defeating. Jesus and the apostles did teach the truth of such self-defeating fleshly efforts in many places. In their writings, both Kierkegaard and Nouwen both articulate something akin to this as a common spiritual pathway. I do believe they were onto something and I will expand on this in the next installment.

38. Our Own Zeal Sometimes Gets in the Way (7:21–25)

I have discovered a principle of human nature: when I set out to do good, an evil within me sabotages my efforts. A deeper part of me would love to obey God's moral law, but another parasitic force uses my bodily members as its host and controls me. A civil war rages between my moral values and the sinful passions that operate through my body. And sin is winning the war! I am truly a miserable person! Who can liberate me from this living death? Thanks be to God, Jesus Christ will!"

So friends, this is the awful dilemma of anyone who tries to serve God apart from the Holy Spirit's presence and power living in and flowing through him—his mind agrees with God's moral law, but another part of him is in bondage to sin, and he is unable to live up to its standard.

Comments ————————————————————————

Many people have gotten uptight about whether the person to whom Paul refers could be a genuine Christian or not. The person obviously could be religiously inclined but not genuine. However, I really don't think that this is the main issue. Many true followers of Jesus have testified of having gone through phases in their post-conversion journey that were characterized by an ongoing struggle with fleshly habits and addictions and cycles of moral defeat.

That's why I posit the notion that this whole Romans 7 dynamic is about rising above religious willpower (human zeal!) and the desire to externally perform "up to code" ... irrespective of being the mere will power of an unconverted or converted person. It's about transcending what has become known as performance orientation. This normally doesn't happen in our souls without some deep, painful self-realizations over time through life experience. In the New Testament, Peter is the classic study on this as he struts his stuff to Jesus, hears

Jesus prophesy both his future sin of betrayal in the courtyard and its later positive outcome, experiences deep contrition and brokenness over his spiritual pride and lack of love, and then is restored and re-commissioned by Jesus on the beach after his resurrection.

So ... let me take the principle in Romans 7 to this deeper level and more subtle application. From my observations over thirty-five years as a spiritual counselor (and from my own experience), I am convinced that most believers do experience phases in which we serve God out of our own human zeal and enthusiasm, which does seemingly propel us forward in God for a season. Only later do we rudely discover that this motivating force resulted in degrees of self-righteousness, legalism, judgmentalism, lack of love and mercy and, thereby, spiritual defeat. (And, of course, these features are what merely religious people are infamous for!) Then, out of our disoriented awareness that we have to somehow discover a better source for our spiritual life-flow, because our past religious efforts didn't actually please God, the pendulum naturally swings to the other extreme: we finally are forced to relax the religious muscles that we have been tensing for so long.

At this point in this divine breaking process, the deepest part of us still longs to please God and avoid sinning. But we suddenly discover that we don't possess the willpower within us to perform as well on the external moral/spiritual front as we once had. God wounded our spiritual pride (the more deadly sin that had been very active and hiding in our hearts) by setting us up for a strategic religious failure. (In some of my writings and sermons, I have referred to this as an apparent "divine betrayal barrier," which we each must confront and cross to become the proven spiritual dads and moms that God longs for us to become.) So we end up, as genuine believers, experiencing something very much like the Romans 7 treadmill for a time ... or times. With seasons under our belt marked by two starkly contrasting spiritual dynamics, we progressively realize that neither basic posture is what Jesus truly came to offer us. Then, we are much more ready to consistently enter into and live in the joy and liberation of Romans 8.

Sometimes I really wish coming into spiritual maturity didn't have to be such a long and challenging journey. How about you? But then I think about how I really don't have anything better to do with my allotted years of earthly and imperfect life than to discover in every season how the Father is slowly conforming me, more and more, into the image of his Son through both blessings and trials ... and then trying to learn to cooperate with him more fully.

39. The Enlightened Sinner (7:21–25)

So I find this law at work: When I want to do good, evil is right there with me. For in my inner being I delight in God's law; but I see another law at work in the members of my body, waging war against the law of my mind and making me a prisoner of the law of sin at work within my members. What a wretched man I am! Who will rescue me from this body of death? Thanks be to God—through Jesus Christ our Lord! (NIV)

Comments ————————————————————

The most stark, vivid "Romans 7" season in my life happened between the years of sixteen and eighteen. At sixteen, I had experienced a supernatural conviction experience while sitting in a conservative Baptist church service in the northern suburb of Detroit, where I had grown up. My older brother, Mark, had become a believer through their influence and had challenged me to come to this church with him. It's a long story, but it's enough to say here that the Holy Spirit spoke directly into my heart about my sinfulness and lost state.

Even though I didn't really want to believe I was in such a corrupted state, I somehow knew in my heart how true it was. But I decided to run away from Jesus Christ. I thought that I would like to make myself more presentable to him after making some personal reformations. And that is what I attempted to do for two years! Only ... I failed more miserably on the moral front the harder I tried to be good. I was what the Puritans referred to as an enlightened sinner. My conscience was very sensitized toward good and evil, but I was progressively losing personal power to resist temptations and to even live up to my own standards ... not to mention God's.

God used this terrible season of internal agony and "civil war" to prepare me for the amazing conversion encounter that I had with Jesus at age eighteen. I was so ready to surrender to him by then. I felt very much like I had been dragging "the body of death" (v. 24) around with me that Paul so eloquently pictures above. The historical background for the word picture that he apparently had in mind when he wrote this passage is recounted below.

> "Near Tarsus, where the apostle Paul was born, a tribe of people lived who inflicted a most terrible penalty upon a murderer. They fastened the body of the victim to the killer, tying shoulder-to-shoulder, back-to-back, thigh-to-thigh, and arm-to-arm and then drove the murderer from the community. So tight were the bonds that he could not free himself, and after a few days the decay in the body of death spread to the living flesh of the murderer. As he stalked the land, there was none to help him remove the body of death. He only had the frightful prospect of his own slow, gangrenous death."[1]

"What a wretched man I am! Who will rescue me from this body of death? Thanks be to God—through Jesus Christ our Lord!" Come on ... Romans 8!

40. Aerodynamics Over Gravity (7:22–8:2)

A deeper part of me would love to obey God's moral law, but another parasitic force uses my bodily members as its host and controls me. A civil war rages between my moral values and the sinful passions that operate through my body. And sin is winning the war! I am truly a miserable person! Who can liberate me from this living death? Thanks be to God, Jesus Christ will!

(So friends, this is the awful dilemma of anyone who tries to serve God apart from the Holy Spirit's presence and power living in and flowing through him—his mind

---

1 Eby Preston, "The Ashes of a Red Heifer," Kingdom Bible Studies, http://www.kingdombiblestudies.org/ashes/ashes1.htm

agrees with God's moral law, but another part of him is in bondage to sin, and he is unable to live up to its standard.)

But things are very different for those who are in Christ—they have a real choice. They are enabled to walk in the Spirit's power and not just their own. Therefore, they have been liberated from the endless guilt trip associated with human religious performance and its impossible demands. For the law of life in the Holy Spirit has been instituted in Christ, which supersedes and transcends the law of sin and death—like aerodynamics over gravity!

Comments

Oh, that divine interruption, "but"! Here, it is in my paraphrase, but it is in the original in various New Testament texts that communicate the same point. God has done something for humanity in Christ that most of us have not yet comprehended, internalized or lived out in practice. Who can liberate us from the dreaded Romans 7 treadmill driven by our religious will power? Who can empower us to face the presence of sin in this world and in our own lives, and then beat up the bully who has intimidated and dominated us for so long? Thank God, Jesus Christ will ... by the power of the Holy Spirit!

It is also clear that Paul is not primarily speaking about living in this kind of freedom only after this earthly life is over. Certainly, we will not see the fullness of the effects of the liberation he has purchased for us until he comes again. However, the apostle is referring to an experience of the richness of Christ and his Spirit in this world ... in this age ... in this soul and body ... whereby we can substantially live in freedom from the mandatory dominion of sin that Romans 7 describes in such gory detail.

On the practical level, a mystery needs to be unraveled for us to achieve the liftoff that Paul holds out to us. We have to emotionally distance ourselves from our intimidating, past failed experiences to obey God and even to walk in the Spirit, into the truth of what Jesus has already done for us and in us ... in order to tap into the realm of grace of which the apostle is speaking. We need to discover more deeply in our heart of hearts who we are in Christ so that we find the solid higher ground on which we can confront the bully, thereby gaining an unfair advantage. When we know who we really are in Christ, it is not a battle with one stronger than us, or even between two equals. It is a unfair battle between Christ within us and something that he has already trumped and judged.

41. Christ in Us (8:1–4)

But things are very different for those who are in Christ—they have a real choice. They are enabled to walk in the Spirit's power and not just their own. Therefore, they have been liberated from the endless guilt trip associated with human religious performance and its impossible demands. For the law of life in the Holy Spirit has been instituted in Christ, which supersedes and transcends the law of sin and death—like aerodynamics over gravity! What the Mosaic legal system could not do because the people under it were infected with sin, God himself did by sending his Son from heaven to live as a man and personally identify with human weakness. Then, because of our serious sin problem, God fully vented his righteous anger against sin as Jesus, bearing all the past and future sins of humanity, bled and died on the cross.

Now the moral essence of the Mosaic code can actually be fulfilled in Christians whose power center is the Holy Spirit within them, instead of their own mental, volitional, emotional or physical powers.

Comments ────────────────────────────

The Father has always known that only Christ could, and can, successfully live the Christian life! Think of the joy that he and his glorified Son felt after the work of redemption was done and the Spirit could then be sent to literally indwell those who simply opened their hearts to agree with the good news of it all. Contemplate the divine plan (and may we never outgrow the wonder and awe that attends such awareness) of how Jesus conclusively dealt with the entirety of human guilt and shame in his substitutionary death. Think of how he inaugurated the new and living way of experiencing human life by his powerful resurrection and glorious ascension. Savor the realization that the Father set his love upon you long before you were aware of or wanted him; drew you to faith in Jesus by the magnetic personality and power of the Holy Spirit; and transplanted a new heart deep within you that yearns to know, worship and serve God above all else.

In his wisdom, God has chosen to allow the gravitational pull of sin's presence to remain for a while longer in his creation. Until Christ returns, this pull will always be there, exerting its force and pressure upon our lives. (Kind of a bummer, eh?) It is a power to which we, as believers, are free to turn and succumb. Temptation and sin have enough strength to bring us down if we try to overcome either one by self-reliance.

But another amazing power is at work in this world ... and alive in our souls ... as well. It is the power of Christ's resurrection life. By this power, we can defy gravity and "walk on the water" of this fallen age ... but only as we keep our eyes on Jesus and don't try too hard to measure or boast to others about how spiritual we are. Only Jesus Christ himself really knows how far we have developed into his likeness, only he is the true measure of our new life and only he is our boast.

The most holy people I know are more aware of their weaknesses than they are impressed by their own strengths, and they are able to take God and his great kingdom seriously without taking themselves too seriously. They are not sanctimonious in the attitudes they emote. They are not uptight around earthy people, and they are able to perceive what these may become. They are not uncomfortable in their own skins. They are not bound by a multitude of behavioral rules. They are free spirited, constrained by love, bold, authentic, tender, tearful, transparent, good listeners, humorous, unselfconscious, happy for others to be the center of attention, not defensive, quick to repent when they are wrong and even more humbled when they are praised. Father, help us to walk in Your love by a true fellowship with Your indwelling Spirit. And ... make us more like Your Son in every way each day.

42. God Did It (8:3–4)

What the Mosaic legal system could not do because the people under it were infected with sin, God himself did by sending his Son from heaven to live as a man and personally identify with human weakness. Then, because of our serious sin problem, God fully vented his righteous anger against sin as Jesus, bearing all the past and future sins of humanity, bled and died on the cross. Now the moral essence of the Mosaic code can actually be fulfilled in Christians whose power center is the Holy Spirit within them instead of their own mental, volitional, emotional or physical powers.

Comments ————————————————————

The effort to obey the law of Moses could never be sufficient to make a person righteous or holy in the sight of God. Moreover, God never intended it to do so. Our Father in heaven knew all along that we needed more than a magnificent, but impersonal, code to form us into the kind of people he longed for us to become ... people who would become fit to live in harmony and friendship with him. He saw that the very core of our being was shut down by the heaviness of guilt and shame.

He made historic preparations that were endorsed as divine through powerful interventions and that inspired ancient prophecies. Then he chose to come in person to fulfill the prophecies and to once and for all effect the change in human life that we so desperately needed. He did this by sending his only begotten Son to become like us so that we, by the grace of God, could become like him. He did this by leading his Son to a cruel and bloody execution to pay the terrible debt of the sins of the world that he himself did not owe. He did this by raising his Son from death and bringing to birth the new beginning ... the new genesis ... the new creation ... that paved the way for the reconciliation of heaven and earth. He did this by offering his salvation to us as a free gift, and by that qualifying us by that to become living temples of his very Holy Spirit, who comes to indwell the souls and bodies of those who simply believe and humbly receive.

We are not alone, left to ourselves, or left to our own resources in responding to this high calling to live as friends of the Father and his Christ. his Spirit has come within us to be the new "power center" of our humanity. We willingly offer all our other powers in joyful subordination to this blessed Holy Spirit. He then subtly takes the helm of our lives, progressively refines and integrates our human capacities under his gentle dominion and empowers us to bring great pleasure to the Father's heart through the enjoyment of being his.

Oh, Holy Spirit, come and fill me anew with the love of God ... and all that this inevitably involves.

43. Understanding "Flesh": It's Kind of Complicated (8:5–8)

For those who live according to the flesh set their minds on the things of the flesh, but those who live according to the Spirit set their minds on the things of the Spirit. For to set the mind on the flesh is death, but to set the mind on the Spirit is life and peace. For the mind that is set on the flesh is hostile to God, for it does not submit to God's law; indeed, it cannot. Those who are in the flesh cannot please God. (ESV)

Comments ———————————————————

The word flesh in Scripture is used in a variety of ways, and so can be easily misconstrued. It can mean humanity, a physical body, the entirety of a person's life, a corpse, a relative, food, and human—though not necessarily sinful—weakness. Remember, "God became flesh"! And in Luke 24:39, the risen Christ describes his glorified human body: "See my hands and my feet, that it is I myself; touch me and see, for a spirit does not have flesh and bones as you see that I have" (NASB). In Paul, especially in Romans and Galatians, flesh also is very much linked to sinful human nature.

In A. R. G. Deasley's excellent article on flesh, he makes the point that Paul uses the word "flesh" in two distinct ways in his writings. Of the first way, he states, "The term acquires the transferred sense of that which is frail and provisional (1 Cor 1:26; Gal 1:16; Ph 3:3). As transient, it is not the sphere of salvation, which is rather the sphere of the Spirit. This does not imply that flesh is evil per se: life 'in the flesh' is normal human existence (Gal 2:20), but it is still merely human. This picture accords generally with that of the Old Testament."[1]

Of the second, he points out that Paul builds upon the first definition and states,

> The uniquely Pauline understanding begins from the idea that flesh, as weak, becomes the gateway to sin (Rom 8:3; 2 Cor 12:7; Gal 4:14). Still more, as the arena in which sin entrenches itself it becomes the instrument of sin (Rom 6:12–14) to the extent that it becomes sinful itself (Rom 8:3), and so an occupying alien power (Rom 7:17–20). The accompanying war Paul describes as a struggle between flesh and Spirit (Rom 8:5–17; Gal 5:16–24). The seriousness of the struggle is indicated by the fact that the mind–set of the flesh leads to death (Rom 8:6), and that those living in the flesh cannot please

1   A.R.G. Deasley, "Flesh," in *Baker's Evangelical Dictionary of Biblical Theology*, ed. Walter Ewell (Grand Rapids, MI: Baker Books, 1996), http://www.biblestudytools.com/dictionaries/bakers-evangelical-dictionary/flesh.html.

God (Rom 8:8). Accounts of this conflict are most vivid in contexts where Paul is describing the demands of the law on the one hand (Rom 7:4, 7–11; Gal 5:2–5), and its impotence to enable the believer to meet them on the other (Rom 8:3; Gal 3:10–12). Flesh, however, is not intrinsically sinful, and may therefore be the scene of sin's defeat. This it became through Christ's coming and crucifixion in the flesh (Rom 8:3). Those who identify themselves with him by faith likewise crucify the flesh (Gal 2:20; 5:24) so being emancipated from the power of sin in the flesh (Rom 6:14; 8:9).

Wow ... it takes some thinking to sort the application of *flesh* through properly. Wherever the word is used, a careful examination of the context is essential. Because of how Paul links flesh to sin in certain passages like the one above, and because of its other meanings in the Bible, it has been easy for casual readers of Scripture to get a negative moral perspective about the physical, material or visible realm, as supposedly in strict opposition to the spiritual, immaterial and invisible realm. This has opened the door throughout church history to an unbiblical philosophical dualism and its stepchild, religious Gnosticism, which are terribly counter-productive to a healthy spiritual life in Christ. (See readings 29 and 30.)

44. A Temporary Human Experience? (8:5–8)

For those who live according to the flesh set their minds on the things of the flesh, but those who live according to the Spirit set their minds on the things of the Spirit. For to set the mind on the flesh is death, but to

*set the mind on the Spirit is life and peace. For the mind
that is set on the flesh is hostile to God, for it does not
submit to God's law; indeed, it cannot. Those who are in
the flesh cannot please God. (ESV)*

Comments ————————————————————————

It's easy to see how it can be challenging to
get our minds around the exact meaning of Paul's
use of *flesh* in Romans and Galatians. It's easy to
get confused about the kind of flesh that is sinful,
useless and worthy only of "crucifixion" or "mor-
tification" and the kind of flesh that is not sinful
... merely human. The notions implied by a saying
of Pierre Teilhard de Chardin, popular among believers and teachers, reflect this challenge. Maybe
you've heard it before: "We are not human beings
having a spiritual experience; we are spiritual beings having a human experience."[2]

The good thing about this statement is that we
are, indeed, spiritual beings. The point that messes
with the hearts and heads of believers is that we
are not going through a temporary human experience, as though being human is something horribly less than God intends for us. (Well ... someone
better inform Jesus about this, because he is, and
now eternally will be, a human being!) Jesus came
to restore divine dignity to being a human, and too
many of us are falsely ashamed that we are such.
We aren't comfortable in our own skin. Statements
like the one above pressure and tempt us to deny
our humanity and to pose, mostly in silly ways to

2   Pierre Teilhard de Chardin, "Pierre Teilhard de Chardin: The
    Phenomenon of Man," Wikiquote, http://en.wikiquote.org/
    wiki/Pierre_Teilhard_de_Chardin

the watching culture, as supra-human, religious, disembodied spirits. This thinking is the seedbed of Gnosticism among Christians throughout the centuries.

One unforeseen, terrible result of this kind of denial is that many believers don't learn how to steward their human desires, drives and needs—food and drink, sleep, sex, money, companionship, power, clothing, work, recreation, retreat and the like—because they are quasi-ashamed that they aren't spiritual enough to sufficiently ignore these things. Many pretend that these "fleshly things" aren't important to our lives under God. (Christians have much to learn from the Jews in this regard.)

To take it to the next level, spiritual leaders will often create the image that they live above such "fleshly things," and many of them suppress vital aspects of their humanity in their zeal to be and appear to be extraordinary. However, over time, they begin to hide from others the outlets they create to express their humanity, because they must protect the image that they project but that they cannot actually live up to over the long haul. This shame-based secrecy opens the door for their personal lifestyles (whatever that means!) to become laced with unhealthy sinful expressions, crazy perversions and excesses that come rushing out from their depths because their submerged humanity has been screaming out for some air to breathe. When their repressed humanity finally breaks the surface, they are unable to breathe normally ... they must gasp. At some point, this terrible noise unavoidably attracts the attention of others, and another "Christian leader" scandal hits the news.

I have seen too much of this through the years, even in my own communities of faith that have been full of zealous (often over-zealous) Christ followers. This is what has stoked my fire on the subject and causes me to approach passages like the one above with careful thinking and writing, lest they be misunderstood and misapplied once again. So ... what "walking in the flesh" and "walking in the Spirit" means practically will continue to be our subject for several more readings.

45. Synchronization (8:5–8)

For those who live according to the flesh set their minds on the things of the flesh, but those who live according to the Spirit set their minds on the things of the Spirit. For to set the mind on the flesh is death, but to set the mind on the Spirit is life and peace. For the mind that is set on the flesh is hostile to God, for it does not submit to God's law; indeed, it cannot. Those who are in the flesh cannot please God. (ESV)

Comments ——————————————————————————

Paul contrasts two possible "power centers" that believers are free to choose to live from: the flesh or the Spirit. I do not buy the popular notion that believers actually have two natures ... honestly, I think this is a source of much confusion and spiritual defeat. The new birth in Christ has provided for us a new nature that is essentially holy because it is in union with the Holy Spirit himself. The Trinity now lives within us! (And if this realization isn't the key to a genuine Christian life, I don't know what else could be. What could possibly trump this reality?)

However, getting God "in" our lives is one thing; letting God "out" through our lives is quite another. We are free to either progressively learn to yield ourselves to the Holy Spirit's quiet and humble lordship over our human powers and capacities. Or we can lose our practical synchronization with the Person of the Spirit within us and revert to living out of our flesh ... a false self, if you will. It is no longer our true nature, but it huffs and puffs and poses as though it were. Our old self can intimidate us and deceive us into believing that Christ has not essentially transformed us. On the practical, moral and performance level, a true believer is capable of having (at least in unholy spurts) as vile of attitudes and behaviors as any other human being.

In the passage above, the apostle refers to a central, practical method and means by which we can cooperate with the process of manifesting the life of Jesus through our lives. First and foremost, authentic spirituality has to do with a focus and inclination in our thinking ... setting the mind (as a contrast to our actions), which then naturally leads to changes in our behaviors. I like to think of it in terms of "minding" the Holy Spirit, akin to how we speak about children minding their parents. It's interesting to me that "minding" and "obeying" are linked in a common idiom in our culture. Are you and I "minding" our Father these days?

Elsewhere, Paul refers to this as the renewing of our mind (Romans 12:1–3) and ... even more intriguing ... as the renewing of "the spirit of our mind." I guess thinking is a spiritual matter after all! Meditate a bit on the passage below and see if you can discern the basic framework for understanding the nature of the battle between our new (true) self and our old (false) self. Hint: it is not a battle between two equals!

> *But you did not learn Christ in this way, if indeed you have heard him and have been taught in him, just as truth is in Jesus, that, in reference to your former manner of life, you lay aside the old self, which is being corrupted in accordance with the lusts of deceit, and that you be renewed in the spirit of your mind, and put on the new self, which in the likeness of God has been created in righteousness and holiness of the truth.* (Ephesians 4:20, NASB)

46. Discerning Truth (8:5–8)

Those who live out of the selfish compulsions of their lower passions have a corrupt mindset, but those who live by the Spirit's power have a renewed mindset. Note the stark contrast: to be selfishly minded is death in the making, but to be spiritually minded is life and peace. The selfish mindset is at odds with God, for it is not submitted to his moral standards and it cannot be by its very nature. So, no matter how hard they might try, people who live by human energy alone cannot please God.

Comments ────────────────────────

I think of the word *praxis* as I seek to work through the paraphrased exegesis and its application. (I do have a very personal stake in this effort too ... that's why I've called this book a devotional paraphrase.) Here is its primary definition from an online dictionary: "Praxis: n. Translating an idea into action; 'a hard theory to put into practice.'"[3]

Praxis also carries the connotation that in order to practice a theory well, there is a need for an experiential knowledge that somehow comes from personally touching or being touched by that theory. Philosophically, *praxis* is linked to a wisdom that goes beyond the possession of raw knowledge. In Hebrew, *wisdom* is linked to *taste*. It is impossible to teach other people what something tastes like ... they must taste it for themselves. Spiritual wisdom is caught more than taught. Wisdom takes on a texture and a flavor that makes an individual person beautiful when it is genuinely integrated into her/his life.

I find profound paradox at the heart of every major doctrine of Scripture. This can qualify good theology as a hard theory. I see this truth reflected in Job 11:5-6, even though it came from the lips of Zophar, who was falsely accusing Job: "But would that God might speak, and open his lips against you, and show you the secrets of wisdom! For sound wisdom has two sides...."

Sound wisdom has two sides, or is double. The challenge to one who would be wise is to find the radical middle that brings the two sides together without doing damage to either.

It seems that God intends for us to wrestle personally with difficult concepts like: What does it actually mean for us to walk in the Spirit and not walk in the flesh? How can this (or even ... should this) be measured or evaluated in our lives? God apparently wanted Jacob (a man who tended toward deceit) to wrestle with him. Jacob did, out of his passion to receive God's blessing and partnership; in

3 "Praxis," DIE.net, http://dictionary.die.net/praxis

the process, he was personally converted and was renamed Israel (prince of God), though he ever after walked with a limp. This Bible story seems like a parable of life to me. Wrestling has always been a way that fathers and sons have bonded.

I would go further and suggest that one of the most vital functions of the church, or body of Christ, is to create environments where believers read Scripture aloud and wrestle with its intended meaning and applications (another reason for smaller communities of some kind or another to be the backbone of a healthy church). Some of the most important transformations and spiritual experiences have come into my life through this practice with my friends in Christ.

Too often believers want to have preachers and teachers just tell them what to do without having to grapple with God himself (it does seem a bit overwhelming!). But our Father is intent on having each of us touch him ... and be touched by him ... in person during the process of trying to understand what he wants from our lives. The paradoxes of theology are resolved in our minds and hearts only through "meeting God" in person.

When it comes to discerning what it means for us to walk in the Spirit and not walk in the flesh, we must integrate both objective and subjective sides of the matter. In my history, I have leaned too often to the objective side and not been at peace with the subjective side. But this approach has led to further frustrations in my spiritual life. Now that I am older ... and, I hope, wiser ... I am more reconciled to the subjective side. I see how important it is to seek and find truth with capacities that include, but go beyond, my cognitive abilities. An over-reliance on our rational abilities, which our western educational systems have historically promoted, has led to much legalism and to what lies beneath it: dysfunction in our interpersonal relationship with God and others (i.e., a lack of authentic love!). In light of the bigger context of Romans 7 and 8, I believe this capacity of bringing these two sides of our being into a dynamic balance is a very real part of being "renewed in the spirit of our mind" (Eph. 4:23) and with possessing a renewed mindset.

We are called, challenged, invited and empowered to love God with all our heart, soul, mind and strength. To love God with all our mind, then, must mean to love him with both of its sides—left and right!

47.   Rewired for the Spirit's Flow (8:8–10)

So, no matter how hard they might try, people who live by human energy alone cannot please God.

But now you are obligated to live life not out of your lower passions, but by the Holy Spirit's impulses, if indeed he really dwells inside of you. And if he doesn't, then you haven't yet become a true Christian. However, if Jesus lives within you, then the controlling energy of sin that previously used your body as a conduit has been short-circuited, and you've been "rewired" so that his Spirit's life can now flow through you as a current of righteousness.

Comments ────────────────────────────

God never intended that the human being would live independently of his life and Spirit. He sent his Son Jesus Christ, who did all that he did, so that the Spirit of God could come live within any human soul who would put her/his personal trust in him. A life of holiness is not so complicated and burdensome ... not weighed down by multitudes of rules, regulations and taboos. If God has gone to such lengths to indwell us, genuine holiness, of course, intrinsically has to do with an interactive relationship between the Trinity and ourselves.

The objective side of holiness functions like boundary markers that keep us from self-deception. In Galatians 5, Paul states that the "works of the flesh" (v. 19) are obvious, as is the "fruit of the Spirit" (v. 22). The New Testament clearly identifies the things that are out of bounds and in bounds. However, the fact that certain people may keep themselves from going out of bounds behaviorally is not necessarily an indication that they are involved in the passion of the game. This is where the subjective side of a truly holy life comes to bear.

Are we engaging in realtime with the Father, Son and Holy Spirit? Are we seeking? Are we listening? Are we responding? Are we trusting? Are we fighting? Are we enduring? Are we risking? Are we forgiving? Are we moving forward? Are we sacrificing for love's sake? Are our hearts and heads in the game? Are we minding the Coach who lives in and whispers his instructions to our souls? Real holiness is all about the realtime, miraculous, indwelling, loving dominion of the Holy Spirit over all our human powers—which were originally, divinely designed to be fabulous and essential servants, but terrible masters, of the spiritual life.

48. "Minding" the Holy Spirit (8:5–7)

Those who live out of the selfish compulsions of their lower passions have a corrupt mindset, but those who live by the Spirit's power have a renewed mindset. Note the stark contrast: to be selfishly minded is death in the making, but to be spiritually minded is life and peace. The selfish mindset is at odds with God, for it is not submitted to his moral standards and it cannot be by its very nature.

Comments ————————————————————

Just one more thought now on setting our minds on the things of the Spirit or, as Paul says in Colossians 3:2, setting our minds "on things above, not on things on the earth." I like to refer to it as "minding" the Holy Spirit, which is a nice word play that brings the focus of our thinking together with a heart of obedience. The bottom line is that many believers become overly mystical and lean toward Gnosticism when they imagine what this really means for our daily lives. Paul is not referring to a concerted effort to try to figure out what is going on in the angelic realm or *trying hard* to listen for voices from the invisible realm. (Sometimes we actually do get glimpses into and tokens from this realm, mostly serendipitously … though we can create an atmosphere around our souls that makes us susceptible to hearing God in a subjective way.) It's not a way of being that removes us from engaging with life upon God's earth. In fact, setting our minds on the things of the Spirit has tremendous practical applications for our lives and relationships here and now. And … actually doing it each day on earth is vitally connected to our eternal rewards.

Being spiritually minded is primarily about living out of a quiet and confident communion ... a friendship ... with the Trinity who indwells us, and about seeking to have our minds renewed so that we more and more come to view what is happening within us, around us and in our world from divine perspectives ... viewpoints and associated feelings and responses that are informed by the Word and the Spirit. It's a discovery of what a human life on earth looks like that bears the fruit of the Spirit: *love*, and then joy, peace, patience, kindness, goodness, faithfulness, gentleness and self-control ... and that is empowered to live and minister in the power of the Spirit's imparted gifts and grace. This life, of course, also implies clearly saying no to the sinful works of the flesh that are so obviously manifesting all around us in this fallen world.

True spirituality finds its source of life and wisdom in the highest heaven, but it is embodied in Christ followers, whose feet gratefully walk out our connection with God here on the earth that he has promised to renovate fully one day. We are invited to be his humbled, emboldened agents here and now for the honor of Jesus the Christ.

49. Death and/or Life? (8:11–13)

If God's Spirit who raised Jesus from the dead dwells in you, God will take possession of your weak and mortal body by the Spirit and make it his living vessel. Therefore, dear friends, we live with a holy indebtedness—not to live for our selfish pleasures, but for the pleasure of our gracious Master. For if, after all this, we stubbornly continue to live selfishly, death, in one form or another, will encroach upon us: but if we ruthlessly put to death our old selfish tendencies and lustful habits by the Spirit's power, true life will flourish and endure.

Comments ————————————————————————

It's like we simply need to continually choose what is going to die in our lives: our extreme, stubborn self-centeredness and all that flows from that basic orientation ... or our experience and enjoyment of abundant life in Jesus Christ and of the love, peace, joy, meaning and adventure that goes naturally with this quality of life. Either way, one way of being must die and the other way will automatically live. In Christ, the Father has provided all we need to genuinely walk in the freshness of life in the Spirit. Now he is inspiring us to simply cooperate by believing that it is true and by subordinating our energies to the Person of the Holy Spirit, whose presence dwells in our deepest parts and then moves outward to our very physical being. If we respond to this kind of divine initiative, the Holy Spirit will respond to our response and faithfully do his part. He will even help us to respond ... he is, after all, called The Helper!

Paul later calls this latter kind of cooperative response to God's grace and mercy our "reasonable service" (Rom. 12:1) of worship. Good theology makes great sense, and a wholehearted response of gratitude, love and service on our part is truly a brilliant investment.

50. Already And Not Yet (8:14–17)

Genuine children of God are characterized by their commitment to following the leadership of the Holy

*Spirit. And this makes the Christian life adventurous—
not enslaving or intimidating, but an intimate association
with God as a loving Papa. Our intimacy with the Holy
Spirit makes God's fatherhood real to us. Now if we are
his children, then we have an inheritance from God;
in fact, we share in the very same one that Christ has
received. But don't forget, of course, that we must endure
our share of suffering for Christ if we expect to be exalted
with Christ.*

Comments ————————————————————————

An effective appetizer is meant to stimulate our
hunger, not satisfy it. This is a good analogy for the
tension we experience, by God's design, between
the overlap of the old creation with the new. God
allows us to experience enough reality of his presence and the "powers of the age to come" (Heb.
6:5) here and now that we become extremely dis-
satisfied with the best that this age has to offer our
souls. A genuine and undeniable kinship with the
Trinity and the many blessings associated with a
life of passionate worship and meaningful service
deeply reorients our hearts. We become able to persevere through the complications and setbacks of
life in this fallen age, in which not everything is going well and nothing is going perfectly. It also enables us to wait joyfully and patiently as we long,
for the "full meal deal" that is yet to come.

We have a sure promise of a full future inheritance, which instills spiritual hope into our
hearts and minds, and we also can experience a
substantial down payment of that inheritance in
our earthly journey. The New Testament teaches
what has been called a "realized" eschatology

(the doctrine of matters regarding the end of this age), without teaching ... as many do today ... an "over-realized" eschatology that leads to an unhealthy triumphalism and an idealization of the church and the Christian life. This error of emphasis also leads many into a deep disappointment over the course of a "long obedience in the same direction," as Eugene Peterson long ago described the life of a disciple of Jesus.[4]

An "under-realized" eschatology will certainly not do either. This opposite error of emphasis has led to a denuded spirituality in church circles that is stripped of joy, power, divine presence, purpose, hope, faith, love, zeal and the like, and that has left a dutiful, religious drudgery and boredom in its wake ... no expected divine responses to our responses to his divine initiatives.

The properly blended eschatology of Romans 8 (the premier chapter in Scripture on the subject) is a framework for a spiritual life that can provide us with a divinely-designed "vehicle" outfitted for riding the bumpy, curvy roads of this life's cross-country race ... a powerful and reliable engine, an aerodynamic body, tires that hug the road in all weather conditions, and great shock absorbers ... along a route with filling stations strategically placed by our wise, loving Papa along the course.

51. Papa (8:14–17)

Genuine children of God are characterized by their commitment to following the leadership of the Holy

---

4 Eugene Peterson, *A Long Obedience in the Same Direction: Discipleship in an Instant Society* (Downers Grove, IL: InterVarsity Press, 2000).

Spirit. And this makes the Christian life adventurous—
not enslaving or intimidating, but an intimate association
with God as a loving Papa. Our intimacy with the Holy
Spirit makes God's fatherhood real to us. Now if we are
his children, then we have an inheritance from God;
in fact, we share in the very same one that Christ has
received. But don't forget, of course, that we must endure
our share of suffering for Christ if we expect to be exalted
with Christ.

Comments ————————————————————

The matter of knowing God as "Father" or
"Papa" is very central to a healthy spiritual life.
Most of us naturally project aspects of the relationship we had or have (or didn't!) with our earthly
fathers onto our conception of God ... we see him as
kind, engaged, affectionate, wise, available, good,
sensitive, firm, legalistic, tough, distracted, harsh,
unjust, abusive, absent, negligent, unaffectionate ...
you can add to the lists. (It's a good exercise and
discussion for a small group of friends.) Often, a
combination of the good and the bad characteristics become imprinted on our souls in regard to
our thoughts and feelings about fathers. Dads have
great power in the lives of their kids.

Thankfully, much has been said and written
over the last twenty-five years in the church world
about how to process, pray and break through so
that we can receive the good that our fathers gave
us—yet not confuse, deep in our hearts, our heavenly Father's nature with that of our dad's. I find
it interesting that, long ago, the writer of Hebrews
was in touch with this very issue:

Furthermore, we have had human fathers who

corrected us, and we paid them respect. Shall we not much more readily be in subjection to the Father of spirits and live? For they indeed for a few days chastened us as seemed best to them, but he for our profit, that we may be partakers of his holiness. Now no chastening seems to be joyful for the present, but painful; nevertheless, afterward it yields the peaceable fruit of righteousness to those who have been trained by it. (Hebrews 12:9–11)

The main point that the author of Hebrews makes about God's fatherhood and our lives in this passage (and also the final sentence in the Romans 8 paragraph above) relates to how we process trials, adversities and sufferings. As a spiritual director, I have found that many of us have great difficulty holding on simultaneously to our image of God as a loving Papa and his allowance of difficulties and negative situations to intrude upon our lives. This seems to me like one of the greatest challenges in our spiritual lives ... how well do we process legitimate sufferings in our hearts, emotions, minds and relationships? Are we able to hold on to our strong belief that God is good when life becomes so difficult to endure?

May the Holy Spirit himself help us all to know God's loving fatherhood in the midst of our fallen world and challenging life circumstances.

52. The End Arrived Early (8:18–23)

My evaluation is that our present sufferings are not even worthy to be compared with the beauty and perfection that will ultimately be produced in us. Actually, the whole created order is unconsciously longing and inaudibly crying out for the perfection of believers. All creation was cursed through Adam's fall, but God promised that he would one day liberate it from its bondage to fully share in his children's uninhibited freedom. The various kingdoms within creation, up to this present time, are groaning and travailing with spiritual labor pains. Even though we have the hefty down payment of perfection through the gift of the Holy Spirit, we similarly groan within ourselves, because we still have to wait for the fullness of our salvation— the resurrection. The kingdom of God is here, but not fully.

Comments ────────────────────────────

The gospel of Jesus Christ is all about the climactic act of God, which was wondrously, mysteriously introduced into the middle of the grand drama about heaven and earth that spans the ages. This unique plot line sets his story apart from so many of the stories we have written for ourselves. Normally, the end comes at the end. But in this case, "The End" appears in the middle of the drama and secures the hope of a perfect outcome for God's good, original creation. God himself, the author of the story, becomes the central character by taking on human flesh in the divine Person of his Son. He enters human history to deal conclusively ... through his life, death, resurrection, ascension and subsequent gift of the Spirit to his followers ... with the problem of evil and all its tragic effects upon the entire creation.

The "not worthy" comparison to which Paul refers in this passage reminds me of the words of Jesus in John 16:21: "A woman, when she is in labor, has sorrow because her hour has come; but as soon as she has given birth to the child, she no longer remembers the anguish, for joy that a human being has been born into the world" (NKJV). All creation is pregnant with the new creation inaugurated by the first coming of Christ, and sorrows and pains are associated with the tensions of our condition. In watching my wife, Terri, go through five pregnancies and deliveries, there is no doubt in my mind that there are both physical and emotional paradoxes of pregnancy at every stage. This is because there is also a kind of strong hope and joyful expectation with pregnancy, to which few things can be compared. Even beyond the pregnancy ... Paul pictures us and all creation in labor. (Admittedly, 2,000 years is a long gestation!) Eugene Peterson captures this so well in his Message translation of verses 22–25:

> All around us we observe a pregnant creation. The difficult times of pain throughout the world are simply birth pangs. But it's not only around us; it's within us. The Spirit of God is arousing us within. We're also feeling the birth pangs. These sterile and barren bodies of ours are yearning for full deliverance. That is why waiting does not diminish us, any more than waiting diminishes a pregnant mother. We are enlarged in the waiting. We, of course, don't see what is enlarging us. But the longer we wait, the larger we become, and the more joyful our expectancy.

53.   The Three Groans (8:24–27)

Hope, our expectation of a heavenly future, is an essential part of God's plan for our salvation. If we had total fulfillment of our salvation here and now, then this hope would not be necessary. But as it is, we are called to wait with patience and hope in our hearts for the fullness yet to come. In the meantime, the Spirit helps us in our human frailty—we don't even know how to pray or what to pray for. But the Holy Spirit, living within us, prays through us with deep sighs and longings that go beyond our ability to understand or articulate. And God, who is ever searching human hearts, picks up on the Spirit's signals because he is praying within us in perfect harmony with the Father's will.

Comments

There are actually three "groans" mentioned in this part of Romans 8. The first two were mentioned in the last installment. Creation is groaning ... we ourselves are groaning ... and here the Holy Spirit is also groaning. So, at least we are in good company. With all of the reality, assurance and in-breakings of God's presence and kingdom we can know in this world, it is still far from the perfection and beauty we will one day enjoy when the new creation swallows up the old one entirely. (Yes ... resurrection life can digest all the troubles, pains, failures, tragedies, setbacks, injustices, sins, disappointments, burdens, sicknesses, heartbreaks and the like ...)

Our heavenly Father uses the pressures and imperfections of this life as constant reminders that we have not been essentially designed for this world as we know it. "We were meant to live for so much more," as the popular band Switchfoot has reminded us in one of their songs.[5] Try as we

---

5   Jon Foreman and Tim Foreman, *The Beautiful Letdown*, Switch-

might to think and believe and work as though it is so, we always come away with our inner groan intact. Many teachings, movements, cultural trends and fads and gurus of various sorts try to entice us to imagine that if we follow them and/or their advice, then this deep, pervasive groan will be lifted from us. But it is there by our Father's design and purpose, and only the return of Jesus will see its displacement. A healthy longing and expectation for his return is essential to a vibrant, biblical spirituality here and now. This kind of strong hope does not make us "so heavenly minded that we are of no earthly good," but rather keeps us "so heavenly minded" that we are empowered to be of earthly good ... day by day by day. In the midst of this emotional and spiritual tension, a mysterious power may seep into our souls that may also motivate us to seize the day. Today is the only day we have to live within.

Let us not be afraid to face and embrace the groaning within us ... it will lead us to a healthier frame of heart and mind. We may even discover that we're praying more often and better than we thought.

54. Two Great Intercessors and Us (8:26–27)

In the meantime, the Spirit helps us in our human frailty—we don't even know how to pray or what to pray for. But the Holy Spirit, living within us, prays through us with deep sighs and longings that go beyond our ability to understand or articulate. And God, who is ever searching human hearts, picks up on the Spirit's signals because he is praying within us in perfect harmony with the Father's will.

foot, Columbia Records.

Comments ────────────────────────────

We encounter much spiritual resistance in this age in our experience of learning to pray well. First of all, we are aware of how small, powerless, uninformed and insecure we are compared to our Creator. (What could we possibly say to him that would matter in the least?) Then, there is his invisibility (which can certainly challenge good communication!), our consciousness of our sins and the shame associated with them, the demands of our busy lives, and our physical weariness. We've all also had experiences with seemingly unanswered prayers, which can easily jade our zeal to pray again. Then, of course, there are the preemptive strikes upon us from every angle by a host of invisible, evil powers, who are actually threatened by the words we might speak into the heart of an all-powerful, living and responsive God.

Still, Scripture reveals throughout its pages that our Heavenly Father invites, commands, longs for, listens to and answers the prayers of children, women and men just like us. At times, we read about the great miracles that God performed in response to the prayers of ordinary people. We wonder if God might have us pray such prayers that evoke the display of his glorious power and might.

I take courage in that the disciples of Jesus asked him to teach them how to pray. Prayer is an art that we must learn, and effort and extensive practice go in to mastering any art. The beginning steps of learning an art are typically the most challenging for us. We do not know what heights we may attain in prayer (for anything is possible with God and to those who believe him), but we can definitely begin (or begin again) to pray. When I scan the Scriptures for insight on how to begin to pray, I land on two passages. The above verse, Romans 8:26, is one of them. The other is a few verses later in 8:34: "Who is he who condemns? It is Christ who died, and furthermore is also risen, who is even at the right hand of God, who also makes intercession for us."

As I consider the beginnings of prayer, I think first about the two expert intercessors who have been assigned to me. This is not essentially different than Jesus inferring, in John 15:16, that he himself is our "advocate" (which John confirms in his first letter) by referring to the Holy Spirit as "another helper" or "advocate" who will be given to us. Actually, the first steps to an effective prayer life seem to be humbling myself to a point to where I am not ashamed to say that I do not know how to pray well, and then receiving the truth that Jesus is praying for me in heaven and the Holy Spirit is praying within me and for me here on earth. And they, I hear, pray quite well! Even my groans regarding the things within and around that weigh me down and burden my soul count as prayer, if I become more aware of the partnership I share with the Spirit of God within me.

55. The Good, the Bad and the Beautiful (8:28)

We are confident that God is weaving all things in life together, both the good and the bad, into a beautiful whole on behalf of those who love and trust him—for they have been apprehended for his transcendent purposes.

Comments ————————————————————————

No doubt, the first part of this paragraph of Romans 8—verse 28—is the most famous verse from the chapter, at least in our generation: "And we know that God causes all things to work together for good to those who love God, to those who are called according to his purpose." This verse is so full of comforting reality that it simply leads me to childlike prayer.

Heavenly Father, you are truly amazing. You are so great and good and powerful. Were you really there, peering in on my life before I knew you, already purposing to redeem both the providential gifts you gave me from my mother's womb and also my foolish choices along the way? Thank you for not being intimidated by my sins. Thank you for pursuing me and seeing beyond my resistance toward you. Thank you for being so creative and resourceful. Thank you for your love and ability to cause good to trump evil ... you make light to shine out of the darkness. Thank you for your powerful hands, which work and shape the clay of this earth into vessels that you can use for your noble purposes. Allow me to be one such instrument and do my part in your grand drama.

I do love you, Father ... and your Son ... and your Holy Spirit. Help me to love you more and more as the years progress.

56. Transcendent Life (8:34–39)

Who can now bring an accusation against those whom God has chosen to be his? He has already declared them not guilty, but righteous. Who can now condemn them? Jesus Christ died and rose again for their sake—he is their advocate before God, and God has agreed with him up front! What can separate us from the reality of the love of Jesus? Can pressure or troubles, persecution or rejection? Can natural disasters or loss of possessions? How about dangers or even physical death? No, these are the very kinds of experiences that Scripture teaches children of God to expect in this fallen world—"For your sake we are constantly handed over to death, we are like sheep headed for the slaughter house." Indeed, these are the kinds of evil events we encounter but over which we prevail because of our confidence in God's goodness and love toward us—no matter what things look like. I am convinced that neither death nor life; angels, authorities, nor demons; the present or the future; life's peaks or valleys; nor any created being can isolate us from God's love, which flows down richly to us through Christ Jesus our Lord.

Comments

The answers to the question, though meant to be rhetorical, about who can accuse or condemn us, are (1) the devil, (2) ourselves and (3) the fallen authorities of our earthly cultures. But, then again, who really are any of these beings compared to Jesus and our heavenly Father? The Father has given all authority in heaven and on earth to Jesus, and he is the true Judge of all. And it just so happens that the Judge ... is in love with us! The Judge took upon himself our sin, guilt and shame and resolved them forever through his death, resurrection and ascension. Case closed.

And what, then, can separate us from the love of Jesus? Nothing now, actually ... which is the apostle's point. But our doubt about his love for us ... influenced by the refuse, and its stench, of living in this fallen age ... can definitely do a number on our enjoyment of this love. Our doubts and fears can cloud our sense of our Father's love. Paul is jealous for us to overcome this doubt and fear.

When things do not go well in this life for me, I am tempted to immediately imagine that God has changed his attitude toward me and has now decided to punish me for my failures after all, as though the gospel was some kind of a bait-and-switch political deal. This is because I know that God is all-powerful and that he intervenes, even miraculously, in this world to bless his children, answer our prayers and accomplish his will. So ... when (not if!) something bad happens to me or mine ... God must surely now be upset or angry with me. When I first came to faith, I subconsciously imagined (and hoped) that accepting Jesus meant that nothing bad would or could happen to me.

However, these imaginations are overly simplistic equations of spirituality and life. And life's violation of these equations is at the root of my doubts about God's goodness and love toward me. I crave an ironclad code to live by as a basis for my spiritual security. I secretly and silently demand that God follow this code that I have scripted for him. (This is the subterranean fountainhead of all legalism—it is a control issue.) A part of me does not like the fact that he is a "living" God and that a personal relationship with him is at the heart of the faith Jesus Christ has come to bring to the world ... not a predictable and static religion. I do not like living in the tension of having a relationship with an all-powerful, loving God who does indeed care for me and hear my prayers ... and who does, at times, even miraculously intervene to undo evil situations ... but who also continues to allow evil events to happen all around me. I tend to equate "God" and "God's love for me" with "life in a fallen age." I do not like the basic paradox of my faith.

It is this temptation to doubt the goodness and love of God that Paul indirectly addresses in the grand passage above. I believe that overcoming the doubt of our Father's love for us, in the midst of a life in which not everything is going well and nothing is going perfectly, is the essence of "the good fight of faith" (1 Tim. 6:12). We are called to take a bold, and sometimes lonely, stand ... with the adverse winds of this age blowing in our faces ... and lean into it while we declare to the whole cosmos our unyielding belief in the truth of the last paragraph of Romans 8: "God is good. God is good. God is good. God is good. Life can be hard, but God is good. And ... absolutely nothing can separate me from his love for me through Jesus Christ my Lord!"

57. A Broader Concept of Suffering (8:35–39)

What can separate us from the reality of the love of Jesus? Can pressure or troubles, persecution or rejection? Can natural disasters or loss of possessions? How about dangers or even physical death? No, these are the very kinds of experiences that Scripture teaches children of God to expect in this fallen world—"For your sake we are constantly handed over to death, we are like sheep headed for the slaughter house." Indeed, these are the kinds of evil events we encounter but over which we prevail because of our confidence in God's goodness and love toward us—no matter what things look like. I am convinced that neither death nor life; angels, authorities, nor demons; the present or the future; life's peaks or valleys; nor any created being can isolate us from God's love, which flows down richly to us through Christ Jesus our Lord.

Comments ————————————————————

A final thought on the eloquent, inspiring end of the eighth chapter: I think it is very important for us to broaden our understanding of suffering for Christ in this world. Many passages in the New Testament speak of the comfort, the reward and the transcendent meaning of suffering nobly and well as a follower of Jesus. Many believers tend to think that only being ridiculed or persecuted for our faith rates as true suffering for Jesus. As a counselor, I have discovered that people often do not categorize their trials in life as legitimate sufferings ... and this tends to cut them off from vital biblical truths that speak profound comfort and grace to their pain.

However, this passage truly broadens the playing field of what Paul considered as legitimate sufferings for Christ. Disasters, troubles, loss, dangers, setbacks, disappointments, rejections, demonic assault, approaching death ... all these common experiences of life can rate as legitimate sufferings for the sake of Christ, if we will simply count them as such and continue to grow in love despite them. We can redeem our sufferings and the resulting brokenness if we commit our souls to our faithful heavenly Father in the midst of them and endure them for his honor. This does not mean that we should not pray fervently to him to change these situations. Jesus prayed this way in the garden of Gethsemane, and he is our model.

If we do not recognize the pains of living in a fallen world as legitimate sufferings, then we will tend to deny them in unhealthy ways and develop strange ways of coping with them. My good friend, Bob Edwards, has said that if we don't process our pain in fellowship with God, it will come out "sideways." I have learned a lot from Bob about sufferings ... and joy, and life, and the love of God and the love of people.

ROMANS CHAPTER NINE

58. Paul's Greatest Burden (9:1–3)

I tell you as sincerely before God as I can, and the Holy Spirit moving within my conscience affirms the truth of this, that I am carrying a continual and heavy burden in my heart for my own Jewish people. I would even accept eternal rejection from Christ if somehow I could change places with them.

Comments ――――――――――――――――――――

Generally speaking, Jesus and his apostles deeply upset the spiritual and political status quo of both the Jews and the Gentiles of their day ... of this, there is no doubt. Jesus and many of his apostles gave up their lives in violent deaths because of this fact. Paul would say in another place that the gospel is a "stumbling block" to Jewish people and "foolishness" to the Greeks (1 Cor. 1:23). But in reality, the coming of Messiah Jesus into this world was the greatest and climactic act of divine love, mercy, reconciliation and justice the world would ever witness. Beautiful and terrible irony has always been at the dramatic heart of God's big God-Story.

Jesus and his apostles claimed to understand and

were sent to reveal a new, divinely-inspired viewpoint on God's history with his creation, with Israel and with all the nations. The Father entrusted them with spiritual authority and gave them the added benefit of clear prophetic hindsight. They would labor to show and teach how God clearly established the groundwork for this new view in the Scriptures, and that the gospel and the new covenant were and are a logical extension built upon that foundation. In fact, Jesus was actually present in that history. He was the chief cornerstone of the foundation of the "house of God" and the grand drama related to this divine family heritage, which would play out in human history and destiny through his gospel.

Beginning in chapter 9, Paul elaborates on a theme that he began to speak of in chapter 3. This theme, far from being parenthetical in Romans, is at the heart of this amazing epistle, and we will pick this theme up in the next installments. But before we go there, we must pause profoundly to catch the dear apostle of Christ's breaking heart, which undergirded the strong words and challenging worldview he laid out to both the Jews and Gentiles of his day and ours.

He states, "I could wish that I myself were accursed, separated from Christ for the sake of my brethren, my kinsmen according to the flesh." This speaks for itself (if we dare to even speak it) ... especially knowing how deeply Paul knew and loved Jesus from the first day he met him on the Damascus road. In our zeal to share the good news of our Lord with the people the Father puts in our lives, may his Spirit capture our hearts with the same depth of compassion, humility and self-sacrifice. It is this kind of love that will give weight to our words and claim of personally knowing God through Christ Jesus the Lord.

59. Living in the Bullseye of the Old Testament Prophets (9:1–5)

I tell you as sincerely before God as I can, and the Holy Spirit moving within my conscience affirms the truth of this, that I am carrying a continual and heavy burden in my heart for my own Jewish people. I would even accept eternal rejection from Christ if somehow I could change places with them.

They are the Israelites—God's historic chosen people—who were entrusted with the message of salvation, the manifest presence of God, the divine covenantal agreements, the written law, the awesome prophetic promises of God and the responsibility of being God's true priests in the earth. The great spiritual patriarchs are their ancestors and, in his humanity, Jesus the Messiah (who is also fully divine), came from their lineage. He has authority over all things. He really does!

Comments —————————————————————

In order to reset the context for Romans chapters 9–11, the details around which there is considerable honest debate (and not a few irrational and fear-based reactions) in the body of Christ, we really should digress. We must look again at what Paul briefly spoke about in chapter 3 and some of the selected comments I made about the passages—which we will do in the next reading.

Keep in mind that Paul viewed himself and the other apostles as standing in the same Spirit and

... because of the "event" of Jesus Christ in their day ... standing in the bullseye of the trajectory line from the previous generations of Hebrew prophets. The apostles of Jesus were the new Jewish prophets on the scene of human history, chosen and sent by God, who had the distinct honor of authoritatively proclaiming the central focus and fulfillment of the ancient words of their predecessors. As you think back on the lives and ministries of the ancient Hebrew prophets , they were very often, like the apostles, resisted and persecuted by the religious and political authorities of their day for their witness and message. The irony, which Jesus pointed out on more than one occasion, is that the Jewish people generally came to venerate their own prophets only after their forefathers' initial rejection of them. So ... the apostles of Jesus were standing in good company and were similarly treated.

And let us never forget the tears of the heart that Paul continually shed over the tragedy of anyone rejecting Jesus as the Messiah and their personal Lord and Master. Hating or resenting our fellow humans (including those who may choose to reject our Lord and the gospel) in any way is never an option for one whose heart has been captured by Jesus ... he who was a friend of sinners and laid his life down for us all. May we too embody this apostolic heart of love, mercy and patient hope of redemption.

60. "Reframing" God's History with His People (9:4–5)

They are the Israelites—God's historic chosen people—who were entrusted with the message of salvation, the manifest presence of God, the divine covenantal agreements, the written law, the awesome prophetic promises of God and the responsibility of being God's true priests in the earth. The great spiritual patriarchs are their ancestors and, in his humanity, Jesus the Messiah (who is also fully divine), came from their lineage. He has authority over all things. He really does!

Comments

So ... we need to connect the dots between chapter 3 and chapter 9 in order to regain Paul's train of thought. Many of Paul's first-century Jewish kinsmen were of the persuasion that if the message he was preaching was true, then God was, at best, unfaithful to his covenant with Abraham ... and, at worst, an outright deceiver. However, Paul (and Jesus himself) challenged the traditional presuppositions beneath the popular theological paradigms of the applications of God's covenantal promises to Israel. They also revealed (unveiled) the true essence and administration of his promises ... things that had been shrouded in divine mystery throughout the centuries until the appointed time ... the time of Christ's appearing. So ... a refresher from two earlier readings:

From reading 9:

Now I know that you're tempted to think: "If what he's saying is true, then there has been no meaning to all it has cost the Jews for being God's chosen people. What's the advantage of being a Jew in the first place?" Actually, there are many privileges—especially stewardship that God gave them over his message to humanity through the prophetic Scriptures. So if some Jews have been unfaithful to their divine calling, does this negate the faithfulness of God himself? No way! God is, and will always be, true even if all people were to contradict him. The Scripture says of him, "You are always right in all that you say, and you always prove your critics wrong."

Comments ————————————————————————

In my view, this first question is the most profound and fundamental one of them all. Yet this question's profundity can easily escape us. Let me put it in other words. If a law-keeping and God-honoring Jewish person is not right with God and, in the larger context, if the Jewish people are not "saved" or "safe" by being associated with their historic/national/ethnic faith community and its beliefs, rituals and customs ... then God has lied. He has broken his part of the ancient bargain he made with Abraham, Moses, David and the like, since he absolutely promised that he would save their children/followers throughout the generations to come. So God is not righteous if what Paul says is true.

I believe how Paul addresses this question is the main theme of the book of Romans, as he posits a different paradigm for understanding and interpreting the meta-narrative of the Bible from Genesis forward. In the gospels, Jesus initiated this new, authoritative framework for understanding the kingdom of God and the Old Testament prophecies. And ... it was the primary reason, humanly speaking, why Jesus and Paul both were executed.

As followers of Jesus in our day, we need to let this sobering philosophical/doctrinal foundation of the first part of Romans sink into our hearts and minds. It's truly radical and upsets the status quo of our spiritually complacent cultures—religious and otherwise.

Comments from reading 12:

And ... this strategy is far from being anti–Jewish. That people of every race and nation are invited to receive Jesus as the promised Messiah—the Father's free gift to all humanity—is the fulfillment of what the Hebrew prophets heard from God, anticipated and foretold. God's promise to Abraham that he would be the father of many nations and a blessing to every family on the earth finds its consummation in all that Jesus was and is about.

61. Ishmael and Esau Were Also Sons of Abraham (9:6–13)

But just because the Jews, generally speaking, are not presently right with God, it does not mean that God's word has somehow failed. For just as not all ethnic Jews are the true "Israelites," neither are they automatically the children of God simply because they are the natural descendants of Abraham. Ishmael was Abraham's natural-born son too, but the promise of salvation wasn't to him; it was to the supernatural-born son, Isaac (and his descendants). This is a historic scenario with spiritually symbolic meaning—namely, the true children of God who are the heirs of the promise of salvation are not qualified to be so through their natural birth, but through the divine promise of a supernatural birth.

For this is the nature of God's saving promise: "At this time I will come, and Sarah (not Hagar) will have a son." This same spiritual principle was repeated in the next generation as a confirmation. God's promise was not even given to all the natural-born children of Isaac, but only through his son Jacob. This was to prove the point that salvation never was, and can never be, dependent on ethnic origins or human religious performance, but on God himself and his sovereign purposes and choices. For before Isaac's twins were even born and able to perform any works—good or bad—God said to their mother Rebecca, "The elder shall be subservient to the younger." This fulfilled the Scripture, "I have chosen Jacob and not Esau."

Comments ───────────────────────────────

Here Paul is expanding on the primary foundational point of his revelation regarding the Big God-Story of the Scriptures and how the new covenant in Jesus is a logical, though admittedly surprising, extension and fulfillment of God's promise to father Abraham. It was a new "old thought." The apostle John said it this way in 1 John 2:7–8, "Brethren, I write no new commandment to you, but an old commandment which you have had from the beginning. The old commandment is the word which you heard from the beginning. Again, a new commandment I write to you, which thing is true in Him and in you, because the darkness is passing away, and the true light is already shining" (NKJV). The adding of the law through Moses, with all its regulations and cultural distinctives, kept the nation cemented together through the centuries and prepared her as a "womb" for the personal coming of the Messiah. But the law did not negate the essential nature of God's election and choice of human beings for the experience of his salvation.

In chapter 2:28–29, Paul said it this way: "For he

is not a Jew who is one outwardly, nor is circumcision that which is outward in the flesh; but he is a Jew who is one inwardly; and circumcision is that of the heart, in the Spirit, not in the letter; whose praise is not from men but from God" (NKJV). This circumcision of heart finds its ultimate expression by what Jesus and the new covenant are all about. Being, or becoming, a true "Israelite" was never about race or human bloodlines ... it is, and has always been, about personal and living faith in God and his word. This was first of all proclaimed to the Jews and then also to the Gentiles (Rom. 2:9–10) because of God's intent to spread the good news of Jesus, his Son, to the whole world and every people group within it. Abraham was called to be a "father of many nations" (Gen. 17:4–5) ... and this has now become a reality by the grace of God in Christ.

62. Mystery Fuels Our Hearts (9:14–20)

Again, I can anticipate what you may be tempted to think: "God is unjust for saving people on the basis of his choice to show mercy rather than on the basis of their own efforts." Right? Wrong! God made this point clear even in Moses' day when he said, "I will have mercy and compassion on whom I choose to show mercy and compassion." Our salvation therefore does not depend on our willpower or our frantic efforts to earn it, but on God's willingness to show mercy. This truth is again reinforced in Scripture when God said to Egypt's Pharaoh, "I have raised you up to your office of power to reveal my superior power. This will be a showdown that will make me famous among all the nations of all ages." God has the power at his command to soften or harden people's hearts for his own righteous and higher purposes.

Now your natural mind will react by suggesting, "If no one can resist God's will, then how can he justly find fault with us weak human beings?" Here's my response— it's an illegal question for any of us to ask! We must refuse to attempt to explain the mystery of the interplay between the sovereignty of God and human responsibility in a way that is totally satisfying to us. God has intentionally left this philosophical stumbling block in our path to keep us mindful that we are his creation, not vice-versa. We're dealing with the all-knowing, all-powerful, infinite Creator of all things here! How could we, or why should we, expect to fully comprehend his infinite mysteries with our finite minds? Doesn't he have the right to withhold some secrets from us to keep us humble and worshipful? A world full of morally fallen people is bad enough; what if we all possessed omniscience too? As part of his "job description" as God, can't he do with mankind what he thinks best for the universe?

Comments

We long to personally connect with Someone who is greater, better, more powerful, wiser, more loving, more just and more intelligent than we are. God has "put eternity in our hearts" (Eccl. 3:11). And knowing him is the essence of life. Though we can truly come to know him through Jesus Christ, the Scriptures and the Holy Spirit's work within us, truly we do not know everything about him. That will be the stuff of infinite ages to come. The mystery of God messes with our minds, but it fuels our hearts. This is why Father has left us truths about him and his eternal kingdom that hold great mystery and tension at their center.

For too long the church, under the cultural

pressure of modernism, has been progressively embarrassed and almost ashamed about the great mysteries of our faith. Ironically, now the Western cultural winds have shifted and people are starving to touch and be touched by ... guess what? ... mystery—so much so, that they often open their minds so widely that their brains fall out! We owe an apology to our secularized culture for caving to the pressure in decades past to denude our faith of the greatest mysteries the world has ever known.

To bring it down to the personal level, I like to say to myself and others, "Is it all right with you if God is and does certain things that I can't fully explain in a philosophically pleasing way?" Indeed, if I (or we) could, I would be highly suspicious that I had made a god after my own image, rather than finding myself in a love relationship with the living God. So it is with this great mystery Paul touches on in Romans 9: the interplay between the sovereignty of God and the responsibility of human beings before him. Great theologians have disagreed on the details of explaining this biblical truth in tension, and they always will. As best I can, I choose to take to heart in the present moment the various passages that emphasize one side here and another there ... like a little child who doesn't need to understand and explain as much as she/he needs to connect and relate. God is sovereign and we are responsible ... go and deal with it. Or better said, let it deal with you!

63. Paralysis By Over-Analysis (9:20–24)

We're dealing with the all-knowing, all-powerful, infinite Creator of all things here! How could we, or why should we, expect to fully comprehend his infinite mysteries with our finite minds? Doesn't he have the right to withhold some secrets from us to keep us humble and worshipful? A world full of morally fallen people is bad enough; what if we all possessed omniscience too? As part of his "job description" as God, can't he do with mankind what he thinks best for the universe? But here are just a couple of little thoughts that help put the matter in perspective! Just maybe, we need to note God's patience with rebellious and sinful humans who provoke him to anger, since he has always had the justifiable reasons and power to totally wipe us out at any time. Just maybe, we need to gratefully acknowledge God's rich, undeserved mercy and his wisdom in choosing some people from among both Jews and Gentiles to receive his salvation, rather than always throwing our impotent philosophical arguments at him about why he shouldn't be the way he is or do the things he does.

Comments ————————————————————————

It is good for our souls to contemplate (and it is also good for our minds to be blown away by) the greatness of God. It is good for us to wrestle with the concept of God's choice being the only sure foundation for the salvation of humanity ... and for our salvation. As I look back on my God-story, he plainly took the initiative toward me and helped me to open my heart to Jesus Christ. I am convinced that I chose him because he first chose me. How about you? No one comes to him without the divine drawing influence of the Holy Spirit upon our broken hearts. This truth of God's gospel of grace is truly a humbling one for us to receive. But our pride needs to be broken anyway ... right?

It is good and right that we cannot take credit for saving ourselves, though we are involved interactively with the Trinity in the process. Because we are, we sometimes are tempted to think that we had more to do with the spiritual initiation of it all than we actually did.

However, if we attempt to intellectually over-analyze the philosophical implications surrounding God's sovereignty, a terrible irony can kick into gear. We can move from awe, humility, wonder and childlike receptivity to spiritual paralysis. We imagine that we cannot take any initiative (that will matter) toward God by our choices. We can very easily gravitate toward spiritual passivity and wrongly sacrifice the dignity of the gift of will and choice that our Father has given us. When spiritual life is boiled down to the practical level (which we need to do at the proper times), we must highlight, to ourselves and others, the vital importance of choosing Christ, choosing to walk in the Spirit, choosing to say no to the dominion of our lower passions, choosing to love God and others ... etc.

It is in the choosing of the right ... the choosing of the light ... that we will be most often and passionately convinced that the Spirit of God has been invisibly, subtly and humbly helping us make such choices, which led us (and continue to lead us) out of darkness. This is the clear implication of what Jesus said to Nicodemus at the end of their famous interchange in John 3:21: "But whoever lives by the truth comes into the light, so that it may be seen plainly [i.e., usually afterward] that what he has done has been done through God" (comment added).

64. The Remnant of Israel (9:25–33)

God spoke through Hosea the prophet: "I will transform rejected and unlovely people and make them my accepted and loved ones, so that where I used to say to them, 'You are not my people,' now I will say to those very same ones, 'You are the children of the living God'" (Hos. 1:10, paraphrased). *Isaiah also prophesied about Israel: "Although the numbers of Jews are as many as the grains of sand in the sea, only a remnant of them will truly be saved. For the Lord will fulfill his prophetic declarations concerning both his righteous judgments and his salvation in the earth, and he will do it swiftly at the appointed time"* (Isa. 10:22–23, paraphrased). *Isaiah prophetically said of this remnant: "Unless the Lord who rules creation preserves a faithful remnant of Jews, our whole nation will be swept away in judgment like Sodom and Gomorrah were"* (Isa. 1:9, paraphrased). *So here's the great, ironic mystery of history. The Gentiles, who were not seeking salvation from the God of Israel, stumbled upon it by simply believing in the Messiah Jesus. But the Jews, who have worked so hard to earn salvation, have stumbled over God's salvation plan and have therefore failed to find it. Why is this so? Because the Jews have gotten caught in the trap of self-righteousness and their pride has blinded them from simple faith in God, which is the basis of salvation. As God prophesied through Scripture, "Behold, I have strategically placed my Messiah as a rock in the path of the Jewish people which scandalizes and offends all who are religiously or ethnically proud. But whoever believes in him will not be disappointed"* (Isa. 8:14, paraphrased).

Comments —————————————————————

Paul uses three examples to Old Testament

prophecy (and there are others like them) to reinforce one of his main points in Romans: the Jewish Scriptures themselves point to the fact that God
would one day fling open the doors of his salvation
far and wide—that he would call all the nations to
receive the Messiah and enter into the covenant relationship that he has always had with his people
through Abraham. Jesus and his apostles made it
clear time and again that this decisive hour in the
Big God-Story of human history had now arrived;
all people, Jews and Gentiles, were equally invited
to turn around spiritually and put their personal
faith in Jesus the Christ. God had personally come
to earth in Jesus to put things right, to show forth
his mercy and to display his justice.

All the first Jesus followers were Jews, and they
clearly viewed themselves as the first fruits of the
believing remnant prophesied by the ancient Jewish prophets. The fact that the majority of the first-
century Jews did not embrace Jesus as the promised
Messiah did not dissuade them in the least from this
conviction. Rather, they humbly viewed the tragic
unbelief of their fellow Jews (and the subsequent
joyful reception of Jesus by many Gentiles and their
inclusion in the now-fulfilled Abrahamic covenant)
as a further confirmation of their own prophets'
warnings ... the rock that the builders rejected had
indeed become "the chief cornerstone" (Ps. 118:22)
as David had foretold. Thousands of first-century
Jews did follow Jesus (and thousands more have
come to faith in our generation alone). So instead
of thinking that God was untrue to his promises to
save Israel, we can reframe the way we look at this
history to realize that God was, in fact, more than
faithful and true to his promises.

A further irony has been created so many hundreds of years later. The people involved in Christendom have been and are now perched on a spiritual precipice similar to the Jews of the first century. Many people who have experienced certain rituals of initiation and embraced certain social conventions by being born into a "Christian" culture populate the church world. But these things alone have never been the essential basis of entering into and enjoying a covenant with the living God. There must also be, beneath all this, a genuine, personal, heart-felt conversion to Christ, which provides an individual with a miraculous spiritual birth and a new heart for the Spirit's home, so that one longs and chooses to follow Jesus Christ as Lord and Master of one's whole life.

Religious self-righteousness and spiritual pride can creep and settle in over generations (even within a few years!) to effectively cut people off from an interactive relationship with the Father, Son and Holy Spirit. These people are placing their spiritual security in the outward forms of faith, rather than in the heart of the matter. This kind of religiousness is undoubtedly the kind of thing that Jesus, if nothing else, came to overturn.

ROMANS CHAPTER TEN

65. The Boxes of Self-Justification (10:1–8)

Dear brothers and sisters, I long with all my heart and pray to God for the Jews to come to faith in Jesus. I have to give them credit; they have a zeal for God, but they are unenlightened. Since they are ignorant of God's righteousness and are trying to establish their own, they have not submitted themselves to receive the truth about the righteousness of God. This good news of Christ puts a final end to people ever thinking that they have to earn God's righteousness by their efforts.

Long ago Moses described the dynamics of the kind of righteousness that is earned: "The person who tries to earn righteousness must be totally consistent." But the righteousness based on believing God has a different dynamic according to the Scripture: "You don't need to ascend into heaven." (Neither can you make the Messiah come down from heaven.) "You don't need to descend into the grave." (Neither can you raise Messiah from the dead.) Only God could do such things. But what does it say? "God's salvation, which we preach to you, is within your reach—it's very near. It's in your mouth and in your heart." He has already accomplished it for you; just believe it!

Comments ——————————————————————

Self-justification is, and has always been, a powerful force in human nature ... and it shows itself in many forms. It is rooted in our attempts to avoid the thoughts, emotions and consequences of both guilt and shame. These too are powerful forces in human life ... and our attempts to handle them impel us to all sorts of strange gyrations.

In the insightful book *The Anatomy of Peace: Resolving the Heart of Conflict,*[1] the authors identify four "boxes" in which we tend to place ourselves rather than squarely facing our weaknesses or failings: the "I'm-Better-Than" box, the "I'm-Worse-Than" (ironic) box, the "I-Deserve" box and the "I-Must-Be-Seen-As" box. We climb into (or just live within) these boxes for fear of having our failures exposed. These boxes are all about us saving our sense of pride by erecting a defensive shell to wrongly protect our fragile egos. (I personally prefer a box fort with two connecting rooms!) Oh, the wars—personal ones, all the way to international ones—that have been waged throughout history because of these forces.

The gospel of Jesus provides us with a simple way off this dizzying merry-go-round of living a life of self-justification that saps so much of our energy. Here is the reality. We aren't intrinsically better or worse than anyone. We don't actually deserve anything except—and I say this with tears in my heart—God's judgment. Finally, only God sees us for who we really are ... and that's what truly

---

1   The Arbinger Institute, *The Anatomy of Peace: Resolving the Heart of Conflict* (San Francisco: Berrett-Koehler Publishers, 2008), 104-106.

matters, because we can't ultimately control how other people may perceive us, and how they do won't matter in the end.

The horrific price we pay for this ... and I say this with my tongue clearly in my cheek ... is to humble ourselves like children, agree with God and simply trust in Jesus Christ—in who he is and what he has done. The miracle of God's love, peace and joy then comes upon us by the power of the Holy Spirit.

66. Salvation Is Nearby (10:6–13)

But the righteousness based on believing God has a different dynamic according to the Scripture: "You don't need to ascend into heaven." (Neither can you make the Messiah come down from heaven.) "You don't need to descend into the grave." (Neither can you raise Messiah from the dead.) Only God could do such things. But what does it say? "God's salvation, which we preach to you, is within your reach—it's very near. It's in your mouth and in your heart." He has already accomplished it for you; just believe it!

If you will confess with your mouth Jesus as your Lord, believing in your heart that God raised him from the dead, you will be forgiven and declared righteous by God. For it is by believing in our hearts and verbally affirming our faith in Jesus that we receive God's free gift of salvation. Remember, the Scripture says, "Whoever believes in him will not be disappointed." God is loving and generous, and he is the Lord of all ethnic groups. He will respond to the penitent cry of absolutely anyone who will call on the name of Jesus Christ, and he will save them from their sins.

Comments ————————————————————————————

So ... this is the golden nugget of the gospel of Jesus. An old righteousness (eternally old!)—God's righteousness—has now come near and become astoundingly accessible to all people groups and each individual, because he has brought it to us in Person. It's the only righteousness that will do. Ours is like filthy rags, until he clothes us with his ... until his becomes personally ours when we trust Jesus from the depths of our heart.

Our salvation simply isn't about our power, goodness, good works, talent, greatness, accomplishments, sensitivity, social status, wealth, religious background, race or gender. True salvation for the human being is totally tied to the Father sending his Son, Jesus, into this world. Jesus showed us the Father's nature and will in his earthly life and ministry. Jesus bore the guilt and shame of the sins of all humanity and died on the cross. The Father raised Jesus from death to life on the third day by the power of the Holy Spirit. Our essential spiritual transformation, even these many years later, is activated very simply: God did this for us in Jesus. We believe it, we openly confess it to God himself and any who might hear our voice, and the miracle occurs. God's own righteousness ... God's very eternal life ... is infused into our souls by the same power that raised Christ from the dead.

Whatever heights of spiritual life you have scaled or aspire to mount, please never forget or neglect the Rock from which true spiritual life is hewn. Come back to him again and again and again ... come daily ... come hourly ... come moment by moment by breathing out subterranean prayers as you take on the tasks, endure the trials and drink in the simple joys of life ... and lean into the Righteous One who is the very source of your life.

67. Simply Christian (10:14–18)

But how will they be able to call on him if they don't know what to believe? And how will they know what to believe if they don't first hear the good news? How can anyone hear the good news without hearing it through a preacher? And how can anyone preach the good news without being commissioned by God to do so? But he has commissioned people to preach it, as the Scripture says: "How beautiful are the messengers who bring to others the good news of peace and the joyful report of God's good gifts for people!" But not everyone who has heard it has welcomed the good news. As Isaiah laments, "Who has believed our report?"

So then, faith happens in response to truly hearing the word of God. So I ask you, "Has God's word really gone forth?" Yes, it has! As the psalmist points out, "all creation resonates with God's message to all the peoples of the earth."

Comments ——————————————————————

This section of Romans 10 reminds me of a book written by the brilliant historian/theologian and Anglican bishop, N. T. Wright, called *Simply Christian: Why Christianity Makes Sense*.[2] God is using him in a wonderful way to engage our postmodern and post-Christian culture with the essence of true faith. He is generous, wise, engaging and compelling. The well-known author of vampire fiction,

2   N.T. Wright, *Simply Christian: Why Christianity Makes Sense* (New York: HarperOne, 2006).

Anne Rice, came back to faith in Jesus by reading his books. I even saw him recently on the political satire, *The Colbert Report*, which was really hilarious. He is sneaking into all kinds of venues ... major universities included.

In the first section of this book, the kind and erudite bishop posits that there are four basic universal longings of the human heart that anyone can identify with: relational connection, beauty, justice and spirituality. He compares these longings to an echo of a voice that is reverberating throughout history and creation. In the second section of the book, he presents Jesus as the original "voice" who created the echo and then, in his incarnation, put a face to the voice. Jesus then personally took away the guilt and shame of all humanity ... only to rise again to impart new life to the earth. The third section of the book is all about the people of God, who have been ushered into the reality of the new creation inaugurated by Jesus, and their journey to reflect his love, beauty, justice and reality to God's broken but beloved world.

The witness of creation testifies of its Designer through a gracious, general, divine revelation that the content of the gospel of Jesus more fully and specifically reveals, explains and confirms. God has ordained these two witnesses, and they are necessary in order for the whole world to come to know the love of God and return to him in loving friendship. A story is told about the great American lady, Helen Keller, who was deaf, blind and dumb, and thereby totally cut off from communications with everyone and everything around her. When she finally learned to communicate through the extreme and patient efforts of Annie Sullivan, her teacher, and she first heard about Jesus Christ, she said this: "I already know him; I just didn't know his name. Thank you for telling me his name."

What an honor it is to tell the people of the world (both the people God brings our way and also sends us to) about the love of God in Jesus. Let's unashamedly tell of his love, beauty, justice and nearness.

68. Divine Irony (10:19–11:5)

But did God give fair warning to the Jews about this irony of the Gentiles receiving something from God that they would reject? Actually, he did! He prophesied through Moses, "I will make you jealous by blessing the outsiders, and I will make you angry by blessing those who are ignorant." Again, he clearly spoke through Isaiah, "I will be discovered by those who aren't seeking me and I will reveal myself to those who didn't even ask." But about the Jews he sighed, "I have been stretching out my helping hands to a nation who just take me for granted—familiarity has bred contempt!"

So has God rejected the Jews wholesale? No way! I myself am a Jew, a natural descendant of Abraham from the tribe of Benjamin. No, God has not given up on his chosen people. Remember the lesson of Elijah who miscalculated the number of faithful Jews in his own day and complained to God in prayer, "Lord, they have killed all the prophets and torn down all your altars. I am the only faithful one left in the land and they are now trying to kill me!" But God corrected his limited view by answering, "I have reserved for myself seven thousand people who have not compromised their faith to worship Baal." In the same way today, there is a remnant of believing Jews who are a testimony of God's gracious choice.

Comments ————————————————————

Here at the end of chapter 10 and throughout chapter 11, Paul comes back around to address the vital question/theme that is woven into the fabric of his entire letter: If the life and message of Jesus the Messiah implies that Jews are not automatically in a right relationship with the God of Abraham, Isaac and Jacob by being faithful to their religious traditions, then God must somehow be unfaithful to his own scriptural promises to the Jewish people, or an outright liar ... which is unthinkable and unbelievable blasphemy.

Yet, throughout Romans, Paul has gone to great lengths to reframe these promises. He has reminded his readers of very specific prophecies from the Jewish Scriptures (like the two above that came through Moses and Isaiah) that warned the Jewish nation of the peril of not recognizing the Messiah when he would actually arrive on the scene. His point is that the Person and Work of Jesus fulfilled the very Scriptures that had been neglected and edited out of the minds of the Jewish leaders— and, therefore, of the Jewish nation—by the time of Christ's appearance. The message of Jesus is anything but either unscriptural or anti-Jewish. He is and was the hope of Israel, and thereby of every person, people group and the whole of God's creation.

Truly being Jewish, or being a part of biblical Israel, as Paul has emphasized in this incisive letter, is simply not about ethnicity. It is about, and was always foreseen as, a divinely sovereign and grace-based supernatural birth that results in a spiritual heart transplant for anyone who truly believes in Messiah Jesus. Besides, just to remove two more obstacles to faith, a remnant of ethnic Jews have always believed in and followed Jesus. That, by itself, ranks as a sign of God's faithfulness to his prophetic promises to the ancient patriarchs and king David. Furthermore, a powerful case can be made that some prophecies are yet to be fulfilled about many more ethnic Jews coming to embrace Jesus as Messiah, and who will, through faith in him, return to the commonwealth of Israel before the second advent of Jesus. Even in our own generation, many thousands of ethnic Jews all over the world have come to faith in Jesus.

69. Jesus Integrated the Puzzle (11:5–10)

In the same way today, a remnant of believing Jews exist as a testimony of God's gracious choice. Now, we've got to be consistent in our thinking. Salvation by grace and salvation by works are, by definition, mutually exclusive. We can't have it both ways. On this issue it's all or none. So yes, what I am saying here is that the Jews, as a whole, have not obtained what they have been seeking, but a divinely-selected remnant of Jews have now obtained it through Messiah Jesus. The rest of the nation has become spiritually blinded. The prophetic Scripture confirms this: "God has given them a spirit of slumber. They have eyes, but cannot see, and ears, but they cannot hear." David also prophesied this: "May their fellowship circle be deluded by a false security as a judgment for their hardness. Let their eyes be blinded and their ability to walk uprightly be taken from them."

Comments ────────────────────────────────

Throughout Romans, Paul has been reframing the Big God-Story of international history and the history of Israel through the lens of hindsight provided by the Person and Work of Jesus Christ and his gospel. New realities and spiritual dynamics in both heaven and earth were inaugurated when Messiah came, bled the ground red and rose again ... prophecies came to pass, paradoxes were resolved, mysteries were unveiled and choices of human hearts took on new weight. God, in Christ, had come in person onto the scene of the human drama to show a newly-integrated picture of a puzzle. This puzzle had only been understood in its bits and pieces before Jesus fulfilled all that the Hebrew prophets foretold. Honestly, wouldn't we expect some new insights into the Scriptures if God were to come among us and explain them himself? And so ... he did.

> *"Long ago, at many times and in many ways, God spoke to our fathers by the prophets, but in these last days he has spoken to us by his Son, whom he appointed the heir of all things, through whom also he created the world."* (Hebrews 1:1–2)

Paul has been laying out some heavy news regarding the spiritual condition of both Jews and Gentiles who are without Christ. For some, what he has been saying about Israel seemed blatantly contrary to the promises God made to their nation in the past. An implied, generalized accusation hangs over the apostle: if what he is saying is true, then God himself is a deceiver. This, of course, is nonsense. This categorization allowed many Jews (and Gentiles) to scoff at the gospel and quickly dismiss it as an error. (Isn't it amazing how a little strategic spin on "truth" by the reorganization of "facts" can lead whole people groups astray?)

In the passage above, Paul quotes Deuteronomy 29 and Psalm 68 to defend his points biblically. Aspects of Psalm 68 that refer to the sufferings of the Messiah Jesus on the cross may be cryptic in nature. But the reference to Deuteronomy 29 and the larger context of both chapters 28 and 29 go right to the heart of the covenant that God initiated with Israel after he delivered them from slavery in Egypt.

People in that culture clearly understood the sovereignty of a conquering king and his right to dictate the terms of the national covenant, which contained both the blessings of cooperation and the curses of non-cooperation. Nothing is cryptic about Deuteronomy 28 and 29, except how they would actually play out in the distant future—in the Big God-Story of the Messiah's coming and the implications of his gospel for all the nations of the earth. (By the way, the use of the word *gospel* in the New Testament was borrowed from the Greek world. This word was used to refer to the messengers, or "evangelists," who were personally sent ahead of a king to announce his imminent arrival to the cities he intended to visit in person. The gospel wasn't primarily "good" news ... it was, even more essentially, "big" news.)

And the LORD will bring you back in ships to Egypt, a journey that I promised that you should never make again; and there you shall offer yourselves for sale to your enemies as male

and female slaves, but there will be no buyer.
(Deuteronomy 28:68)

This little sentence above hints at the danger of a future situation, in which the nation would be capable of violating God's will to the point that it could appear that he was not being faithful to his promise to save the nation. This is the stern, sober warning embedded in the covenant promises outlined in the context of Deuteronomy 28–29. For Jesus, Paul and the apostles to declare that the warnings of Moses had come to pass in their generation can never be construed as anti-Semitic or unbiblical. Just read again what Moses himself prophesied:

> *And if you faithfully obey the voice of the LORD your God, being careful to do all his commandments that I command you today, the LORD your God will set you high above all the nations of the earth. And all these blessings shall come upon you and overtake you, if you obey the voice of the LORD your God ... But if you will not obey the voice of the LORD your God or be careful to do all his commandments and his statutes that I command you today, then all these curses shall come upon you and overtake you.* (Deuteronomy 28:1–2, 15)

> *But to this day the LORD has not given you a heart to understand or eyes to see or ears to hear.* (Deuteronomy 29:4)

When the writers of the New Testament quote an Old Testament verse, it is often like an icon on our computer screen that we need to activate, which opens up a new window of text that sheds more light on the text we are presently reading. I believe that Paul's quote in Romans 11 of Deuteronomy

29:4 should obviously lead us back to the whole context of Deuteronomy 28–29. And these passages give prophetic insight into and biblical context for the main points that Paul goes on to make in Romans 11.

> *And the next generation, your children who rise up after you, and the foreigner who comes from a far land, will say, when they see the afflictions of that land and the sicknesses with which the LORD has made it sick—the whole land burned out with brimstone and salt, nothing sown and nothing growing, where no plant can sprout, an overthrow like that of Sodom and Gomorrah, Admah, and Zeboiim, which the LORD overthrew in his anger and wrath—all the nations will say, "Why has the LORD done thus to this land? What caused the heat of this great anger?" Then people will say, "It is because they abandoned the covenant of the LORD, the God of their fathers, which he made with them when he brought them out of the land of Egypt, and went and served other gods and worshiped them, gods whom they had not known and whom he had not allotted to them. Therefore the anger of the LORD was kindled against this land, bringing upon it all the curses written in this book, and the LORD uprooted them from their land in anger and fury and great wrath, and cast them into another land, as they are this day." The secret things belong to the LORD our God, but the things that are revealed belong to us and to our children forever, that we may do all the words of this law.* (Deuteronomy 29:22–29)

In the time of Jesus, much of the Jewish leadership and nation put their trust in their many religious and cultural traditions, thereby becoming self-righteous. Others had compromised and mixed their faith with the corrupt Roman culture. Others had turned to violence in seeking to establish the kingdom of God, and still some created an ascetic counter-culture in the wilderness to await a divine intervention. These biases blinded them and kept them from receiving God's sent One, and even from understanding the prophecies or heeding the clear warnings of their own patriarchs and prophets.

But many others—both Jews and Gentiles—welcomed, believed and received Jesus for who he was and is. They began a revolution that was paving the way for the renewal of all creation through the salvation of God in Christ Jesus the Lord.

70. The Father Trusted in His Son Alone (11:11–15)

Then have the Jews spiritually stumbled never to rise again? No way! In fact, through their fall, a door of salvation has opened wide for the Gentiles in order to strategically provoke the Jews to jealousy. And if, through their failure and loss of spiritual status, the nations of the world have been so richly blessed, what will their restoration bring to the earth?

Now I address you Gentiles, given the fact that I, as a Jew, have been specifically called to be a divine messenger to the Gentiles and therefore have special insight into this issue. I long that my work among the Gentiles might stir some of my Jewish people to a jealousy that will set them up to be saved. For if their temporary rejection has led to the reconciling of the other nations to God, their future return to God will invoke nothing less than resurrection power!

Comments ─────────────────────────

A main point that Paul makes in Romans 11—
that the Jews (generally speaking) as a people group
did not receive Jesus as Messiah ... and that this
choice opened the doors spiritually for the Gentile
world to accept him and be grafted into the ancient
Abrahamic covenant—only makes sense if we capture the intrigue and drama of God's Big God-Story
that Paul has been rehearsing.

The Father originally intended for the entire
Jewish nation to serve the other nations as a kingdom of priests and to extend the gracious blessing
of Abraham to the world. Yet, they institutionalized,
formalized and nationalized their spiritual life,
thereby effectively reducing the kingdom of God
in such a way that it walled off the Gentile nations
from coming to the living God. God, in response,
chose only one tribe of the twelve to embody the
priesthood. He didn't ultimately put his hope in
the "seeds" of Abraham to fulfill the promise, but
rather progressively focused in on the "seed" of
Abraham ... the promised Messiah ... the Faithful
Israelite who was to come.

God placed his salvific stock in a second Adam,
a covenant mediator greater than the angels, a
prophet greater than Moses, a general greater than
Joshua, a king greater than his father David and
a priest greater than Aaron or Levi. His dealings
with Israel would center on preparing a cultural/
historic/national "womb" from which the Messiah
would come forth. He would also provide a prophetic backdrop that would give the nations with a
convincing reason to believe when his Day would
come. God would incarnate his very Word, who

co-created the heavens and the earth, into human flesh in order to win the day for broken, wayward humanity. The Author himself became the lead character of the salvation story. There was and is no other human being worthy to take the book of human history and destiny and open its seals.

However, Paul is quick to also remind us that the story is not over yet and that powerful divine promise still hovers over the heads of the Jewish people. Another thrilling twist in the plot of the grace of God is at work among the nations before the end times. The Jewish nation, ethnically speaking, will be substantially, mysteriously stirred to a spiritual jealousy through the compelling witness of both their separated brothers and the Gentiles, who have become united in truly following Messiah Jesus. A remnant of ethnic Jews (who will further confirm the fulfillment of the divine promise to Abraham) will come to faith in God's chosen Messiah—Jesus of Nazareth—and be grafted in again to the rich, eternal covenant of God's grace. (The fact that they are still a people group at all, after having no homeland for so many centuries, is already a powerful divine sign and wonder in the earth.)

Those of us who have come to faith in Christ should take courage and heart from the fact that in our generation, more Jews have come to Jesus—along with the millions of Asians, Africans, Indians, Arabs and many indigenous people groups of the earth who have also come to him (despite the rise of post-Christian culture in the West)—than at any other time in history. The harvest fields are ripe, and Christ Jesus will receive the reward of his suffering and see the ramifications of his resurrection. The Father will himself see to this (Ps. 2; 110).

71. The Ancient Olive Tree (11:16–21)

This is an unchangeable spiritual principle: If the representative token of something is holy, so is the whole. And if the root of something is holy, so are its branches. So if some of the Jewish branches have been broken off from God's spiritually rich olive tree and its holy root system, and this has made a way for some branches from the wild and uncultivated olive tree of the Gentiles to be grafted into it, then you Gentiles had better not be arrogant toward the Jews. Just remember, you're not supporting the root, it's supporting you! But you might be tempted to think, "Hey, they've been broken off to make room for us." Yes, they were broken off for their unbelief and you are secured by your faith. So don't become proud, but fear the Lord. If God didn't spare the natural branches that fell into unbelief, do you think he will do less to the unnatural branches that fall into it?

Comments ————————————————

Paul is painting a word picture here that captures the essence of God's Big God-Story. In God's economy of his historical callings and dealings with humanity, He has essentially made one dominant and everlasting covenant (the rich, ancient and well-planted "olive tree") with us ... though its outworking over the centuries has had nuances and admittedly surprising, progressive features. This belief is grounded in the way that Jesus and his apostles authoritatively rehearsed, interpreted and utilized Old Testament Scripture. The covenant that God cut with Abraham—a non-Jew and the father of true faith—is central to this paradigm. Certainly the law that God gave through Moses can be viewed as another covenant, but our understanding of its purposes must be nested into the larger, Abrahamic meta-narrative of redemption. (Galatians 3 and 4 deal with this head on, as does Romans 4.) This also holds true for our understanding of the covenants that God made with Adam (in the original creation mandate), Noah (in the aftermath of the flood and reaffirmation of the creation mandate) and David (in God's promise to have one of his "sons" sit on his throne forever).

The fact that the Jews of the first century (and for many centuries since) have generally rejected Jesus as the promised Messiah—and have thereby been cut off from the historic, divine covenant—does not negate God's faithfulness to his word. Nor does it halt his relentless forward march to spread the fame of his name and accomplish his will in the nations of the earth.

The apostle then goes on to make two main points. First, the Gentile believers must be mindful not to become proud about their new status in Christ and come down wrongly on the Jews as a people. This, sadly, seems to have happened all to often throughout the history of Christendom ... and has left an understandably bitter taste in the mouths of Jewish people regarding the gospel of Jesus. We who follow Jesus should repent for this spiritual arrogance and lament that we have not well represented the beauty of our Lord to them. Gentiles owe the Jews a debt of gratitude and respect because God has grafted us, the unnatural branches, into the covenant that they historically enjoyed with God and worked and suffered to preserve. Our faith has rich and powerful Hebrew roots.

Second, Paul laments that the natural branches (the ethnic Jews) have been lopped off from their own olive tree because of their active unbelief in Christ. He gives a sober warning that seems to apply in our day to people groups and Gentile nations that have enjoyed the personal, family and cultural blessings that flow down from a wide historic reception of the gospel of Jesus. If an extended family of peoples rejects their faith in Jesus, they will likewise be cut off from the divine covenant and the attending blessings that once ruled over their lives and society. To me, this appears to be happening in a widespread way here in Western culture.

And remember, it's not the end of the story for the Jews. They have an ongoing part to play in God's Big God-Story. Divine jealousy still hovers over this people for the sake of their spiritual fathers and mothers and, of course, the glory of God's Son!

72. Wild and Natural Branches (11:22–36)

Do you see the balanced personality of God, both his goodness and his severity? He dispensed severity to those who were unbelieving, but he has shown you his goodness. And he will continue to do so if you persevere in your faith. Otherwise, he will also cut you off. Likewise, if the Jews repent of their unbelief, they will be grafted in again, and God is able to do it. For if God is able to graft wild unnatural branches into a domesticated olive tree, surely he can graft the natural branches back into their own olive tree.

I am laboring this point because I don't want you to be uninformed about this divine mystery and thereby fall prey to spiritual pride. So here it is again: a partial spiritual blindness has befallen the Jews until the fully appointed numbers of Gentiles are saved. At that time, the Jews will turn wholesale to Messiah Jesus, as it is written: "The Deliverer will come out of Zion and turn Jacob away from his ungodliness. For this is my covenant with them—I will take away their sins." So, in relation to the good news, they are presently your enemies. But in the larger prophetic picture, they are a chosen people who are favored by God because of his unconditional promises to their fathers. And God will not and cannot renege on his sovereignly-given gifts and callings.

Just as you, who at one time did not believe God, have now obtained mercy through their unbelief, even so they, who do not yet believe, will receive mercy through the mercy shown to you. For God has allowed all to experience the agonizing desolation of unbelief so that he might reveal his mercy, in no uncertain terms, to all people. So in the end, unbelief in some leads to mercy for others, which in turn leads to the mercy that finally destroys all unbelief and causes mercy to triumph over all!

Oh, the depth of the richness of both the wisdom and knowledge of God! His judgments are inscrutable and his ways are unfathomable. "For who has known the mind of the Lord? Who has counseled him into the right way?" Or "who has met God's needs in a way that God now owes him something?" For ultimately from him, and through him, and back to him are all things. To him be eternal honor. Yes, indeed!

Comments ————————————————————————

The Story kind of speaks for itself above. Paul

concludes this powerful chapter by again putting the questions surrounding the Jews and Gentiles, and their spiritual journeys, into the context of a historic, mysterious meta-narrative, which he claims has now been made clear through the coming of Jesus Christ ... and through his fulfillment of the Old Testament Scriptures.

The Story is significantly about the grandeur of God himself, who is the One who has been guiding human history along with his invisible hand. It's an account of his power, justice, holiness and the spiritual weakness of humanity when left to ourselves ... and of his kindness and love ultimately sweeping in to rescue us through Messiah from our unbelief in his wisdom, goodness and nearness. Mercy triumphs over justice, not only in our personal lives, but in the narrative of history.

It's a bit hard for us to air drop into the same level of thought and emotion that swirled around this thorny issue that Paul has been attempting to address in Romans. But, if we immerse ourselves deeply enough in the Scriptures, we are able to come to the place that we can identify from the heart with the massive historical/theological dilemma that the apostle is unraveling and the great mystery that he is revealing through the gospel of Jesus.

I can't say it better than my friend, Michael Flowers, who stated it in one of his personal emails to me ...

> From a Pauline perspective (early church), "Christianity" as a new religion did not cross his mind. Paul had come to see that in Jesus the fulfillment of all the promises of God in

the Old Testament had been inaugurated in Jesus the Messiah. The walls of ethnic exclusivity had been kicked down by the power of the resurrection, announcing the invasion of the New Age of the Kingdom into the present. His Jewish Eschatology had greeted him in person, on the Damascus road. Therefore, a Christ–less Judaism would be viewed as a thing of the past, an expression languishing within the pages of the Old Covenant, awaiting a fulfillment that had already occurred in Jesus the Messiah.[1]

... or the way that Eugene Peterson translates Ephesians 3:4–6 in the Message:

> As you read over what I have written to you, you'll be able to see for yourselves into the mystery of Christ. None of our ancestors understood this. Only in our time has it been made clear by God's Spirit through his holy apostles and prophets of this new order. The mystery is that people who have never heard of God and those who have heard of him all their lives (what I've been calling outsiders and insiders) stand on the same ground before God. They get the same offer, same help, same promises in Christ Jesus. The Message is accessible and welcoming to everyone, across the board.

And all this leads Paul, and us, to two divinely strategic responses that are captured in the final paragraph: humility and awesome worship. May we simply take our place ... on our face.

---

1   Michael Flowers, email message to author, July 16, 2009.

ROMANS CHAPTER TWELVE

73. Where Is God's Temple on Earth? (12:1–2)

In the light of these magnificent mercies of God, I appeal to you, dear friends, to offer your entire being, including your body itself, to God as a living sacrifice. This is holy and acceptable to him—and, actually, living a life of worship is the only reasonable response to who he is and what he has done. Don't let the value system of fallen humanity mold or dictate your life or lifestyle. Rather, cooperate with God's agenda to transform you through the spiritual renewal of your thinking, so that you may be able to discern the will of God, which is truly good, always acceptable and entirely perfect.

Comments ───────────────────────────

Paul has completed laying out his inspired overview of the life, teaching, ministry, death, burial, resurrection and ascension of Jesus as Lord and Christ, and has put all this into the divinely re-contextualized kingdom construct based upon the now-fulfilled messianic prophecies of Scripture. It was no small task, and its implications are revolutionary for human life on this planet. In the remaining chapters, Paul begins to tease apart some

169

of the important, practical implications of "Jesus is Lord" for our lives, lifestyles and relationships.

The coming of Christ caused a fundamental shift in what the temple of God is all about. This "new temple" imagery is a major theme of the New Testament apostles and is woven into the fabric of their writings. Christ inaugurated a new way of worship for the people of God that is "in spirit and truth" (Jn. 4:23), not focused upon ritual or confined to geography . Jesus did more than hint at this in his interchange with the woman at the well in John 4.

The "tabernacle/temple" matters related to the manifest presence of God in this world and the proper way for the people of God to truly connect/ commune with him in acceptable worship. On a practical level, manifest presence was significantly tied to divinely ordained priesthood and sacrifice. Jesus was himself the embodiment of the presence of God like no other tabernacle in the history of Israel. "The Word became flesh and 'tabernacled' [lit.] among us" (Jn 1:14). Christ himself, along with his body and the church, is the new temple of God. Also, he is the "high priest after the order of Melchizedek" prophesied in Psalm 110:4, which signaled a massive shift in the nature and dynamics of the divinely-ordained priesthood. Moreover, he himself became the once and for all substitutionary sacrifice ... the Lamb of God who took away the sins of the world in his death on the cross and his subsequent resurrection and ascension.

Here in the beginning of Romans 12, Paul dials up the image of temple worship and draws us into our proper role in the acceptable worship of the Living God through Jesus Christ. Worship begins on an intimately personal level.

74. Believing Rightly → Living Rightly (12:1)

In the light of these magnificent mercies of God, I appeal to you, dear friends, to offer your entire being, including your body itself, to God as a living sacrifice. This is holy and acceptable to him—and, actually, living a life of worship is the only reasonable response to who he is and what he has done.

Comments ————————————————

Chapter 12 is the beginning of the application section of Romans. It is quite common in Paul's epistles for him to first expound on believing rightly and then lead his readers into living rightly in that light. Our core beliefs truly do affect our daily choices.

As those who have been swept up into the new creation in Christ, a new temple/priesthood/sacrificial paradigm has been inaugurated. (The Book of Hebrews elaborates on this.) The once and for all sacrifice of Jesus, who decisively carried away all the guilt and shame of humanity in his death on the cross, trumped the past need for a stone temple, human priests to serve as mediators, and animal sacrifices. Now each believer has become a temple of God (not made with hands), a priest of God and, on the basis of Christ's death, a living sacrifice to God.

Human beings, redeemed by Jesus, have been transformed into temples of the Holy Spirit. Our entire lives (spirit, mind and body) also have become mobile, fiery altars where the very presence of God intersects with the passionate, intentional consecration of all that we are, all that we have and all that we do.

God goes with us into all of life, and we are his agents and ambassadors. In our waking and sleeping; our work, rest and play; our public and private lives (whatever that means!); our thoughts, words, prayers and songs; our eating and drinking; our dealings and inter-personal relationships ... we are living a life of worship before the Living God. ("Worship" is much more than attending gatherings to sing, pray, confess, give, read Scriptures and receive instruction, as vital as those things are.) No more dead sacrifices are needed to take away sins ... just a host of living sacrifices whose human lives substantially, though not perfectly, bear and reflect the restored image of God in the midst of a broken, fallen world.

75. What on Earth Is "the World"—Part 1 (12:2)

Don't let the value system of fallen humanity mold or dictate your life or lifestyle. Rather, cooperate with God's agenda to transform you through the spiritual renewal of your thinking, so that you may be able to discern the will of God, which is truly good, always acceptable and entirely perfect.

Comments ————————————————————

These sentences capture something essential about and basic to the life and lifestyle of an authentic follower of Jesus. We are called to take our cues for life on earth from the invisible realm of highest heaven, where Christ's reign as King of both heaven and earth is unquestioned. We know that it is only a matter of time before the just reign of the True King is fully applied to the kingdoms and peoples of this world. He is presently reigning, but is "in the midst of [his] enemies" (see Psalm 110:2 again), and is mercifully providing them with the opportunity to turn to him and be saved.

The cultures in which we live exert a powerful pressure on us to conform to images, beliefs and ways of being and relating that are in conflict with the lordship of Jesus the Christ. A kind of detachment from this present age is fundamental to true spirituality. The center of our truest self is not bound to the fallen nature of this world, and so we are free to resist the pressure to conform to the animating "spirits" of earthly cultures ... things like the well-known seven deadly sins.

Pride is excessive belief in one's own abilities that interferes with the individual's recognition of the grace of God. It has been called the sin from which all others arise. Pride is also known as vanity.

Envy is the desire for others' traits, status, abilities or situation.

Gluttony is an inordinate desire to consume more than what one requires.

Lust is an inordinate craving for the pleasures of the body.

Anger is manifested in the individual who spurns love and opts instead for fury. It is also known as wrath.

Greed is the desire for material wealth or gain, ignoring the realm of the spiritual. It is also called avarice or covetousness.

Sloth is the avoidance of physical or spiritual work.

But as we will see, detachment from the fallen cultures of our world is not an end for genuine spirituality, but rather a beginning that properly positions us to be effective ambassadors of the Living God and his great love to the people all around us.

76.   What on Earth Is "the World"—Part 2 (12:2)

Don't let the value system of fallen humanity [lit. "the world"] mold or dictate your life or lifestyle. Rather, cooperate with God's agenda to transform you through the spiritual renewal of your thinking, so that you may be able to discern the will of God, which is truly good, always acceptable and entirely perfect.

Comments ————————————————————————

"The world" is a challenging phrase to properly understand in Scripture ... have you discovered this too? The apostle John said, "God so loved the world that he gave his only Son ... " (Jn. 3:16) and later said to Christ-followers, "Do not love the world ... " (1 Jn. 2:15). This simple juxtaposition captures the essence of this challenge. How believers have handled this paradox has had huge implications for the lives and the sense of mission of many individuals and communities of faith throughout the centuries. Helpful sayings and word pictures have been used in an attempt to help believers to navigate this tension: We are not "of the world," but we are called to live "in the world." The Church is like a great ship that is in the water ("the world"), but it must not allow the water into the ship if it is to accomplish its purpose. But the application of ideas takes some deeper thought, study, prayer and fellowship (with the Holy Spirit and our friends in Christ) to properly work out in our lives.

In the previous reading I mentioned the concept of an essential detachment as a beginning point for a healthy understanding of biblical spirituality. This world (which is akin to this age) is not the source of our life. Rather, the Holy Spirit vitally connects the core of our being to the invisible realm of highest heaven, where Christ is seated and reigns over heaven and earth at the Father's right hand. Neither do we allow the cultures of this world to define the essence of our value system or our worldview. Our lives are grounded in the transcendent, eternal kingdom of God. And Scripture holds out to us a range of heart-beliefs and spiritual disciplines that, when embraced, continually reinforce this reality to our souls, minds and bodies.

Yet many believers and movements, usually out of a noble quest to be or become "holy" and not be "worldly," have taken this kind of detachment from the world to unbiblical extremes. Humorous, bizarre and tragic stories have emerged out of these religiously-overcharged subcultures. Fundamentalism and what I call "revivalism" have typically promoted a too-negative view of the world (and thereby model an extreme detachment). Liberalism has typically reacted to this and denigrated any kind of detachment from the world in an attempt to not be "religious … like those fundamentalists." I am convinced the Holy Spirit is working in our day, as only he can do, to powerfully promote a kingdom spirituality that permits us to drop out of the traditional, worn-out, reaction-charged, funda-mentalist/liberal debate. Reacting to human beings has never been a key to discovering true spiritual-ity in Christ.

I have coined a phrase that I like to use to help my fellow pilgrims who long to find a kind of Christ-centered spirituality, which provides a framework for holding onto and living out this paradox in our relationship with and view of this world. Here it is: We must be detached from this world in order to be engaged with this world without becoming entangled by this world.

As Romans 12 and 13 unfold, I think we'll find some practical wisdom from the apostle Paul that reflects this way of thinking, being and relating.

77. Blessing the "Unblessable" (12:2)

Don't let the value system of fallen humanity [lit. "the world"] mold or dictate your life or lifestyle. Rather, cooperate with God's agenda to transform you through the spiritual renewal of your thinking, so that you may be able to discern the will of God, which is truly good, always acceptable and entirely perfect.

Comments ————————————————————

We are called to follow in the footsteps of Jesus, the Prince of Life. I believe that we are to model his example of detachment/engagement with the broken, sin-laden cultures around us without be-coming entangled by the evil one and his ancient evil ways. We can all plainly see that Satan is hav-ing his way in this world quite significantly. Jesus came as a human being to face this enemy of all that is whole, right and good. In his incarnation, Jesus left the perfection of highest heaven and willingly entered this fallen age that is so full of lust, pride, greed and unbelief. He came because of love. And he came to bring full renewal to his Father's good (yes, his very good, originally) creation ... to swallow it up into the new creation that his coming inaugurated and brought to birth. All of the sin, guilt, fear, shame, hatred, injustice, racism, tragedy, brokenness, relational breakdown, despair, sickness, doubt, hardness and disappointment of this old creation are digestible in the iron stomach of the Risen Lord of the new creation. In his resurrection, he overcame death itself ... a foretaste of the final eschatological meal yet to come!

Jesus certainly wasn't into sin, but neither was he scandalized or intimidated by sin. He wasn't afraid of being spiritually polluted by befriending and touching folks. He saw beyond the sins and weaknesses of ordinary people and loved them where and as he found them. He saw what they might become by putting their faith in him. Besides ... there are no sinless people for us to love in this world! He came to rescue us all from the death that was already present and at work in our hearts. He gave us all sorts of reasons to trust in him and love him back. He was free in his spirit to be vulnerable with, make friends with, build bridges toward, show compassion and respect to, make promises to, forgive, touch and be touched by, heal, serve, affirm the good within and have parties with the people all about him ... even, and maybe especially, the people of other cultures than his own. He blessed all sorts of people whom the religious establishment of his day considered "unblessable" by God.

This radical attitude also gave him the spiritual and moral authority to expose and stand up to the evil spirits and arrogant bullies (especially the religious ones) who were drunk on their power over people.

So also we are free in Christ to now live "incarnationally" and engage the cultures of our world in the same attitude and by the agency of the same Holy Spirit, who is also working through us. Those who have been born again can see the kingdom of God that is all around us, and witness it seeping and sometimes suddenly breaking into the imperfect cultures of our world. Though our conscious goal is not to be seen as culturally relevant, we likewise must not be seen putting culturally ignorant and/or insensitive communication barriers in the way of people, which automatically hinder their ability to hear and connect with the good and great news of our Lord Jesus. Rather, we should do all that we can to break down those communication barriers (obviously, without compromising the trans-cultural and eternal values and essentials of God's kingdom) so that the message can more effectively find its way into people's hearts. If people are to stumble, let it be over "Jesus Christ and him crucified" ... not our uptight, self-righteous, fear-based, religious and spiritually non-essential cultural preferences.

We must land on the things that made Jesus so winsome, compelling, appealing and attractive to ordinary folks, and seek to walk as he did in relating to them. May the Holy Spirit grant us a grand measure of Jesus' magnetic personality as we live in his light today and for all our days in this world.

78. The Renewal of Our Minds (12:2)

Don't let the value system of fallen humanity mold or dictate your life or lifestyle. Rather, cooperate with God's agenda to transform you through the spiritual renewal of your thinking, so that you may be able to discern the will of God, which is truly good, always acceptable and entirely perfect.

Comments ————————————————————————

Or as the NIV says: "Do not conform any longer to the pattern of this world, but be transformed by the renewing of your mind." As followers of Jesus, we all yearn to become perfected people ... to become like him. This longing for metamorphosis (the Greek root word for transformed) is a powerful motivation in our lives. (Sometimes religious teachers and movements that promise us powerful personal change exploit it, and this is something for which we must be on guard.)

Paul here is emphasizing that the renewal of our mind is an important key to our personal transformation into the image of Christ. A good place to begin the discussion about this vital subject is with a parallel passage in Ephesians that contrasts the old nature (self) and the condition of the mind with the new:

Now this I say and testify in the Lord, that you must no longer walk as the Gentiles do, in the futility of their minds. They are darkened in their understanding, alienated from the life of God because of the ignorance that is in them, due to their hardness of heart. They have become callous and have given themselves up to sensuality, greedy to practice every kind of impurity. But that is not the way you learned Christ!—assuming that you have heard about him and were taught in him, as the truth is in Jesus, to put off your old self, which belongs to your former manner of life and is corrupt through deceitful desires, and to be renewed in the spirit of your minds, and to put on the new self, created after the likeness of God in true righteousness and holiness. (Ephesians 4:17–24)

We can see in this passage how Paul viewed the mind's place in the context of the broader fabric of our lives that includes the heart, the self, the manner of life and the desires. There is a seamless connection between the components of the human life ... we are integrated beings. Additionally, in the approach to his challenge for us to put on the new self, which is already created (or re-created) within the believer by regeneration, Paul refers to Christ himself and implies his real presence in the process of our spiritual development. We have learned ... and must learn"... Christ himself. We aren't merely taught "about" Christ, we are taught "in" Christ ... Christ, who indwells us, teaches us.

A wonderful assumption lies beneath an effective transformation in our lives, lifestyles and relationships. Christ is in us ... really and truly! And because he is, we are explicitly empowered within to respond to the challenge to put off the old and put on the new. This reality and our awareness of it set the stage for us to cooperate with the renewing of the spirit of our minds—the essence of our thinking.

79. How to "Get Guided" (12:2)

Don't let the value system of fallen humanity mold or

dictate your life or lifestyle. Rather, cooperate with God's agenda to transform you through the spiritual renewal of your thinking, so that you may be able to discern the will of God, which is truly good, always acceptable and entirely perfect.

Comments

The most common question that comes my way as a spiritual director is: How can I know God's will? ... or sometimes ... How can I hear God's voice to guide me? This is a wonderful question for each of us to ponder long and hard. Deep within the renewed heart of a Christ-follower is a dominant desire to know God better, to please him and to fulfill God's plan for her/his life. The answer to such a question has many facets. Many dedicated believers also have a lot of misconceptions regarding their expectations about being guided into the Father's will. An implication of the above passage exposes one of these misconceptions.

First, it is important to note that being guided begins with a generalized consecration of our entire being and life under the lordship of Jesus ... before we know the specifics of what God's plans for us might be. Second, we are called to find the courage to think, live and choose outside the boxes that our earthly cultures have prepared to slowly squeeze us into ... to use us and keep us under their sway. Third, as this passage makes clear, we come to know the will of God most normally by an internal process, rather than by input from an over-powering external source ... like a robot that mechanically reacts to its user's inputs. Spiritual guidance in the disciple's life is more of an art than

a science ... living out an unfolding, colorful drama versus receiving a computerized printout of a
comprehensive blueprint ... a gracious, rhythmic
dance with our Guide in contrast to a goose-step to
orders barked out by a militant dictator. Spiritual
guidance most often integrates both divine inspi-
rations and human faculties within its processes.

A vital lesson in new covenant spirituality is
embedded in the story of Elijah's discovery that the
LORD was not in the whirlwind, the earthquake or
the fire. Instead he came to Elijah in the still, small
voice ... or within ... the sound of silence.

Because there is such a thing as a genuine experience of hearing the voice of God from beyond, many
believers imagine that, if they were really spiritually
mature and truly intimate with God, then this would
be the normal way that they would be guided by him
and land on his specific will for their lives. But this assumption has become the source for confusion, disil-
lusionment, frustration, self-condemnation and even
deception for too many disciples.

80. The Focus on Transformation into Christ's
Image (12: 2)

*Don't let the value system of fallen humanity mold or
dictate your life or lifestyle. Rather, cooperate with God's
agenda to transform you through the spiritual renewal
of your thinking, so that you may be able to discern the
will of God, which is truly good, always acceptable and
entirely perfect.*

Comments —————————————————————

Or, as the NKJV puts it, "Be transformed by the

renewing of your mind, that you may prove what is that good and acceptable and perfect will of God."

Before I move on and make one more point about the renewing of our mind, I think it's important to point out that landing on God's will for our lives directly relates to our progressive personal transformation into the image of Christ. If we focus on becoming more like him, we will find ourselves guided ... most often by a gentle, powerful, invisible hand upon us. Most believers can testify, on the other side of a particular chapter of their lives, that they didn't realize how closely the Lord was guiding them until that season ended. And they also speak of how they came to know Jesus better through that life experience. Our job is to be the responsive sheep. His job is to be the Shepherd, and he does it very well!

81. On Being Naturally Supernatural (12:2)

Don't let the value system of fallen humanity mold or dictate your life or lifestyle. Rather, cooperate with God's agenda to transform you through the spiritual renewal of your thinking, so that you may be able to discern the will of God, which is truly good, always acceptable and entirely perfect.

Comments —————————————————————————

For this reason I remind you to fan into flame the gift of God, which is in you through the laying on of my hands. For God did not give us a spirit of timidity, but a spirit [or Spirit] of power, of love and of a sound mind. (2 Timothy 1:6–7)

Whenever I get the chance to preach about the

Person of the Holy Spirit, I like to refer to this verse as a foundation. I believe that Paul is referring specifically here to the gift of the Holy Spirit, rather than one of the gifts of the Spirit. As we survey the Scriptures, we indeed discover that He is a Spirit of power. He is a Spirit of love. The Scriptures often refer to these two aspects of the Spirit's Person and Work. And this kind of language about him makes sense to us.

But then Paul says that the Holy Spirit is a Spirit of a sound mind, or discipline, or self-discipline ... depending on the particular translation. To me, this language is strange, and has inspired some further research and reflection on my part. It seems to be a neglected aspect of the Holy Spirit, yet it is as vital to a Spirit-filled human life as the first two.

It turns out that this passage is the only place in the whole Bible where this specific Greek word is used. Here is what Adam Clarke's commentary says about this word:

> "Of a sound mind", soophronismou (Gk 4995), of self–possession and government, according to some. But a sound mind implies much more; it means a clear understanding, a sound judgment, a rectified will, holy passions, heavenly tempers [thoughts and feelings]; in a word, the whole soul harmonized in all its powers and faculties; and completely regulated and influenced, so as to think, speak, and act aright in all things. The apostle says, God hath given the spirit of these things; they are not factitious [artificial, feigned, forced, engineered]; they are not assumed for times and circumstances; they are

radical powers and tempers [internal abiding realities]; each produced by its proper principle [i.e., it is expressed from the inside/out].

Related ideas: discipline, self-control, sobering, safe, self-restraint, to admonish[1]

My conviction is that only by the indwelling of the Holy Spirit can this kind of virtue be imputed and genuinely expressed through our lives. The pathway to self-government, self-discipline and a renewed mind begins with the presence of the Person of the Holy Spirit within us. He himself is the spirit—the animating secret—of the kind of sound mind and renewed thinking that living in Christ involves.

An astounding implication of this is that the Holy Spirit doesn't bypass and isn't superimposed upon our personality, but becomes deeply joined to us in a interactive partnership. He literally dwells within us and works through our human faculties. As a result of this reality, we become "supernaturally natural" ... maybe you've heard the term before? We are not the Holy Spirit (and we must never confuse this clear distinction between Creator and creature), but he enables us to become our truest selves as the faculties of our entire beings come under his divine influences. God wants us to be ourselves, and also wants us to allow him to be himself. I'm not him and he's not me ... but we make a great team! Does this bring as much peace and joy to your heart as it does to mine?

One of the most encouraging experiences we can have in life is to serve others in counsel, prayer, presence, acts of love and kindness ... along with

---

1 Adam Clarke, *Commentary on the Bible*, GodRules.net, http://www.godrules.net/library/clarke/clarke2tim1.htm

many other possible avenues ... only to later discover that the Holy Spirit was quietly inspiring what we assumed were our own ideas, words and choices. But the feedback we receive about how those encounters met the exact needs of folks that we didn't even know, convinces us that it was more than "merely us" who was working in and through us. This is what it essentially means to be "naturally supernatural" ... a style of living, relating and ministering that I heartily recommend.

82.   A Quiet Reformation (12:1–21)

I have camped out in Romans 12 for many years, and have become convinced that it holds a very relevant message and clear challenge for the expression of our faith in the modern Western world. I believe that it contains "seed thoughts" that can lead us into a needed rebranding of what it means and looks like for communities of people to genuinely follow Jesus Christ ... a new reformation, if you will. Romans 12 is the beginning of the practical and logical response to who Jesus is and what he has done for the cosmos and all humanity. That is our part of the deal ... which we can, in the end, only do well by the empowerment of the Holy Spirit. This kind of divine arrangement is what will save us from self-righteousness, yet allows us to progressively walk in authentic righteousness.

These are the four main reformational points of the chapter, which stand out to me as ideals we are called to passionately pursue:

- A more holistic spirituality (holistic simply means a well-rounded, fuller kind of spirituality).

- A more healthy community. God has called us to belong to a spiritual family that is wise in the matters of relationship building and community building. We need to learn the skills about what makes for healthy relationships and what makes for long-lasting friendships.

- A more humble ministry. It seems to me that God has been dealing with the Western church for years about pride in our lives and pride in our styles of leadership. We have allowed too much of the celebrity mentality and arrogant entrepreneurialism to dominate our church cultures.

- A more heartfelt set of values. Some vital biblical values in this great chapter have been generally overlooked in the personal and corporate expression of our faith in too many of our faith communities. May God help us to return with our whole hearts to the ancient, simple and pure devotion to Christ that the first apostles taught and lived out.

83. A More Holistic Spirituality (12:1–2)

So here's what I want you to do, God helping you: Take your everyday, ordinary life—your sleeping, eating, going-to-work, and walking-around life—and place it before God as an offering. Embracing what God does for you is the best thing you can do for him. Don't become so well adjusted to your culture that you fit into it without even thinking. Instead, fix your attention on God. You'll be changed from the inside out. Readily recognize what he wants from you, and quickly respond to it. Unlike the culture around you, always dragging you down to its level of immaturity, God brings the best out of you, develops well-formed maturity in you. (Romans 12:1–2, The Message)

Comments ————————————————————

In thinking about the first reformational point for the Western church in the 21st century—a more holistic spirituality—I don't think we could improve upon the way that Eugene Peterson translates these first two verses in The Message. The ordinariness of most of our hours and our lives is not an automatic hindrance to engaging and enjoying a genuine, interactive friendship with the holy Trinity in realtime, or to true biblical spirituality. The Father, Son and Spirit all promise to be with us and go with us in the full range of our being and activity. We are not called to strive to be extraordinary, when it is sufficient for us to live fully human lives (with all its joys, sorrows, blessings and trials) and "let" God be his extraordinary Self to us. This kind of approach, in the end, does indeed lift us up to live lives that are supernaturally natural.

84. A More Healthy Community (12:3–8)

By the spiritual authority that God has vested in me, I challenge every person among you not to think more highly of yourself than you should. We all need to receive reality checks. God has given to all of us a sphere of life and ministry in which to function, and for which we also have been given the corresponding necessary amount of faith. Our physical body is one, yet it has many members, each having a different function. So the body of Christ is one and each of us is one of its many members. But even though we have various roles to play, we are organically joined both to him and to one another. And since we have different gifts, let us excel in using what we specifically have been given: if prophecy, then prophesy within the boundaries of genuine faith; if service, then serve in a way that you can do it graciously; if teaching, then teach in the areas in which you have true authority; if exhortation, then exhort according to your spiritual passion; if giving, then give from your heart without second guessing; if leadership, then lead with excellence; if showing mercy, then do it with the joy of the Lord.

Comments

The second reformational point that I am positing from this chapter for us as believers and our groups is about moving toward a more healthy community. This involves creating a different kind of relational culture than what has been generally modeled to us in our histories, within our societies at large and, usually, within our families and churches as well. Unhealthy relational styles and patterns have been stamped deeply upon our souls to the point where it is often difficult and threatening for us to even be made aware of them. In the New Testament, the apostles of Jesus hold out some high ideals of what it looks like to glorify God in our inter-personal relationships—to genuinely walk in the love of God. Their basic model revolves around gracefully navigating the tensions of individuality and interdependence ... honoring diversity while maintaining an essential unity in the community of faith. In his epistles, Paul utilized the image of the human body to help us intuit and picture this dynamic.

Some years ago, I was privileged to become friends with Dr. Larry Crabb. Though separated by time and space, still we significantly touched hearts. His books had already been making a deep impact on my life when we met, and his writings have continued to help me greatly through the years. I believe the whole body of Christ is indebted to him for his wonderful contributions (forged in the fires of his own vulnerable journey and musings) toward understanding both the sanctification process and healthy relationships. He has helped to identify the radical middle between the traditional moralistic (You must try harder!) and therapeutic (You are a victim!) approaches to these two vital issues. He has done this by gleaning truths from each polar opposite and integrating them into a more biblical context, so that we can understand and engage in our personal life and our relationships with others. I will write more about some critical points from his book *Connecting: Healing Ourselves and Our Relationships* in the next readings.

85. Connecting (12:3–5)

God has given to all of us a sphere of life and ministry in which to function, for which we also have been given the corresponding necessary amount of faith. Our physical body is one, yet it has many members, each having a different function. So the body of Christ is one and each of us is one of its many members. But even though we have various roles to play, we are organically joined both to him and to one another.

Comments ———————————————————

In his book *Connecting: Healing Ourselves and*

Our Relationships,[2] Dr. Larry Crabb distills years of counseling experience, biblical research, intensive work of putting thoughts into words, and a whole lot of life lived to help us consider the essence of healthy interpersonal relationships. He steers us away from extreme but popularized views of how people are thought to overcome their personal and relational problems. Instead, he holds out to us a few simply profound and profoundly simple, yet to often overlooked, keys to this kind of health and holiness ... a pattern leading to maturity in Christ.

The two extreme views are what he refers to as (1) the moralistic model and (2) the therapy model. The first focuses on challenging people (often with hardly any empathy or compassion) that they simply need to begin to make better choices by trying harder to obey God and the Bible. The second focuses on trying, in various ways, to help people uncover the dynamic (subconscious) pains of injustice they have suffered and to which they are reacting. Larry acknowledges that we all certainly have made bad choices and that we have suffered injustices, but he posits the notion that most of us won't ultimately overcome either kinds of problems unless we connect with others in a healthy relational circle ... a community in Christ. We need to have our wills renewed by the Holy Spirit and our broken hearts healed by Christ, but do these kinds of things actually happen regularly without a vital connection to friends in Christ who can track with us through life's journey? Larry says no, through his astute observations and many years of helping people as a professional counselor.

2 Larry Crabb, *Connecting: Healing Ourselves and Our Relationships* (Nashville: Thomas Nelson, 1997).

Furthermore, he goes on to describe the three essential elements of the kind of Christ-centered interpersonal connections that we long to experience in our communities of faith. First of all, we need connection with some others (even a few connections make us extremely wealthy) who genuinely delight in who we are without reference to our failures or battles. Second, we need to realize that we all have something powerful (the Spirit's presence) in us, which enables us to speak profoundly to the good that is truly present (maybe hidden or buried) in a hurting or struggling friend in Christ and to call that good up and out. Third (and the order here is very important), we are called to gently, lovingly, and in a timely manner expose the sin or the pain in one another that we may be blind to or deny. All three elements are essential for well-rounded friendships.

These three elements of healthy relationships create a context for spiritual growth. I am convinced that unless we seek after and find this quality of connection, then we will be very limited in how to affect the kind of personal transformation in our communities we tend to admire, but often fail to achieve. The Spirit of God has always worked in this normal, mighty way in and through the friends of Jesus Christ.

86. The Longing for Belonging (12:3–5)

God has given to all of us a sphere of life and ministry in which to function, for which we also have been given the corresponding necessary amount of faith. Our physical body is one, yet it has many members, each having a different function. So the body of Christ is one and each of us is one of its many members. But even though we have various roles to play, we are organically joined both to him and to one another.

Comments ———————————————————————————

The second reformation point of the four that I derive from of Romans 12—a more healthy community—has to do with this vital issue of forming and living in a healthy network of relationships in our faith communities. The longing for belonging and interpersonal connection are basic to the way that we, as humans, have been created in the image of God. Because that image has been marred, though not eradicated, by sin, all our human relations are presently imperfect. God actually, and ironically, seeks to use this pain and ache to keep us from relational idolatry; therefore, we will long in a healthy way for the new heavens and earth in which we won't be tempted to worship anyone or anything but him. This will provide a perfect balance and harmony in all our other relationships, as the love of God will perfectly govern all things.

Still, we are called to experience a substantial foretaste of and prophetically model this relational fullness yet to come. We do this through the realism of the love and unity of the body of Christ that witnesses to the world the inauguration of God's new creation in Jesus. Walking out God's love in a practical way in our relationships with fellow believers should be a main priority for us, as it is fundamental to the release of so much good into this world. How often did the apostles of Jesus instruct us to love one another? This high calling and great challenge should be no wonder to us. May

God empower us to learn well what this kind of love looks like.

87. More Humble Ministry (12:3–8)

By the spiritual authority that God has vested in me, I challenge every person among you not to think more highly of yourself than you should. We all need to receive reality checks. God has given to all of us a sphere of life and ministry in which to function, for which we also have been given the corresponding necessary amount of faith. Our physical body is one, yet it has many members, each having a different function. So the body of Christ is one and each of us is one of its many members. But even though we have various roles to play, we are organically joined both to him and to one ... Since we have different gifts, let us excel in using what we specifically have been given: if prophecy, then prophesy within the boundaries of genuine faith; if service, then serve in a way that you can do it graciously; if teaching, then teach in the areas in which you have true authority; if exhortation, then exhort according to your spiritual passion; if giving, then give from your heart without second guessing; if leadership, then lead with excellence; if showing mercy, then do it with the joy of the Lord.

Comments ————————————————————————

The third reformational point that I see standing out in this chapter is what I would call a more humble ministry. An interesting way of studying Paul's epistles is to dig into the background of the cultures of the cities and regions to whom he wrote. Notice that the errors he sought to correct in the churches were a result of the cultures "baptizing" the church communities with their embedded evils. He labored to empower the followers of Jesus to stand against the sinful elements of these cultural tides.

Our culture at large has become deeply affected and oriented around celebrity. We are bombarded with both head-on and subliminal messages that if we are to achieve real meaning, significance and value, then we must strive to become noticed by many. All kinds of powerful tools are available to us to assist us in puffing up, projecting and managing our image. Still, most of us fail to garner this kind of attention and therefore kowtow to the satanic lie that we are living insignificant lives. This makes us vulnerable to finding some possible way to associate with someone or some group that is significant ... or, we simply resign ourselves to the fate that we must embrace our boring existence. That's when we become vulnerable to the plethora of the cultural "medications" that are available to dull our aching hearts.

The apostle would challenge us to embrace a radically different view of our lives—of how we are to be and what we are to do in this world. We can live truly significant lives without seeking or achieving celebrity. We begin by firmly rejecting the demonic lose-lose paradigm of life described above. On one hand, we must come to a point where we don't give a rip about how many people notice us or hear our voice. We must become oriented around living for the audience of One, and leave the degree of our impact on others in his capable hands.

Simultaneously, we must not submit to a false modesty about what God has called and gifted us to offer to others. Neither should we absolutely avoid using the tools available to us to offer our gifts to the people and world about us.

Humility is not about looking down on ourselves or pretending that we are less gifted, capable, experienced, intelligent or discerning than we are. Humility is realism ... not posing. C. S. Lewis said that humility is grounded simply in standing next to something infinitely larger and higher than we are and noticing the difference!

88. Heartfelt Values (12:9–21)

Love others without any pretense. Hate what is evil and embrace what is good. Really care about your fellow believers, and don't compete with one another, except in the "holy competition" of honoring and promoting others instead of yourself. Don't be lazy and irresponsible, but fervently serve the Lord in every arena of life. Let the expectation of your glorious future in the presence of God be the source of joy that strengthens you to endure the pressures of this life. Fill your daily life with prayers, generously share your resources to meet the needs of fellow believers and eagerly show hospitality to others.

Don't curse those who persecute you, but bless them instead. Celebrate with those who are rejoicing and sympathize with those who are weeping. Be thoughtful toward one another. Don't value the high and lofty things of life that feed people's egos, but deliberately identify with lowly things and people. Don't consider yourself as being above or too good for such mundane, ordinary things. Save your energies—if you value lowliness, then no one can put you down! Don't return an injustice for an injustice—two wrongs don't make a right. Walk in integrity of heart before all people. As much as it is possible and within your control, live at peace with others.

Don't take personal vengeance into your own hands, my dear friends. (You're not holy enough or smart enough to do it right anyway!) Leave room for God to act on your behalf according to his perfect wisdom and timetable. The Scripture says, "Vengeance is mine to dispense; I will repay, says the Lord." Rather, disarm and convict your enemy by shocking them with kindness. Again, the Scripture says, "If your enemy is hungry, give him some food. If he is thirsty, give him a drink." Doing this is the best way of helping them get in touch with and turn away from the wrongness of what they are doing. Don't be overwhelmed by evil, but overcome evil with good. Don't curse the darkness; turn on a light!

Comments ————————————————————

The fourth point of reformation that I see in this chapter is what I would call a set of heartfelt values. Since I was a new believer, I have always been struck by the comprehensive nature of Romans 12 when it comes to practical or pastoral theology. Internalizing the spirit of the simply profound, Christ-like way of life recommended here is a way of learning to navigate as spiritual people in a world (and a church world) that is dear to God, but never perfect.

Every sentence in this section of Romans 12 is loaded with meaning and exhortation for the gritty situations of our daily lives. Paul's first point is that we love others without any pretense. You can view the rest of what's on the list as teasing out what that life of love looks like ... how the love of Christ that genuinely courses through our beings leads us to respond to people of all kinds. It is a great passage to read over slowly, internalize and then rejoice over as the personal applications present themselves to our hearts and minds under the inspiration of the Holy Spirit.

89. God and Civil Authorities (13:1–5)

Every person must live in submission to the civil authorities. For civil government has been ordained by God, and he has overseen the installment of rulers into their offices. Therefore, whoever rebels against their authority is rebelling against something that God has established, and they will suffer very severe consequences for doing so. Such authority isn't intended to intimidate good citizens, only bad ones. So if you want to live free from this fear, obey the civil authorities, and they will reward your good citizenship. They are servants of God, given for the good of society. But if you are a lawbreaker, you need to be afraid, for these God-ordained authorities have been called to use force—even deadly force when necessary—in bringing criminals to justice. We need to obey the civil laws for both the sake of avoiding punishment and keeping our consciences clear before God.

Comments ————————————————————

The apostle Paul here addresses another very practical area of daily life ... the disciple's relationship to civil authority and law. It's important to

remember that he wrote these injunctions to believers who were living under the rule of imperial
Rome! This was a human government that could
be absolutely ruthless and violent. It was the government under which Jesus had been condemned
to a cruel and unjust crucifixion. When, in fact, Jesus was being judged by Pilate, he essentially said
to this ruler, who was flaunting his power, "You
have no authority except what my Father has given
to you." Jesus understood how the sovereignty of
his (and our) heavenly Father works in this fallen
world, and he modeled a belief and a pattern for all
who would follow him across the many cultures of
the world in every generation.

Though a number of thorny issues emerge in a
theological consideration of how followers of the
Christ relate to and navigate within the frameworks
of civil authorities of various kinds, an essential
simplicity underlies the appropriate discussion:
God is sovereign over all human governments, and
he will work within them and through them, despite their many flaws.

90. The Place of Civil Disobedience (13:6–10)

*Because civil authority is an instrument of God for
our good, we must give to it what we owe it. Pay all
your taxes and tariffs, show proper respect to officers and
officials, and honor all those in authority. Don't accrue
any debt to society by breaking your contracts and
commitments, but stay free to focus on giving to others
what you truly "owe" them—love. If you learn to love,
you will fulfill the essence and intent of God's moral
law. Whatever specific commandment of God's you can
name—"You shall not commit adultery," "You shall not*

murder," "You shall not steal," "You shall not give false testimony," "You shall not covet," or any of the others; they all are rooted in the concept of "You shall love your neighbor as yourself." It is impossible for genuine love to perpetrate an injustice toward others. That's why it fulfills God's moral law.

Comments

Paul sets forth a basic conviction that God is sovereign over the civil governments and works through them to bring order and justice to a society. In most cases, civil laws can be obeyed as disciples of Jesus navigate within our cultures by simply allowing what the love of Christ looks like to inform our attitudes and actions. This will lead to the conversion of some, or even many, and will also introduce a necessary spiritual tension into the cultures in which we live.

Of course, the matter of civil disobedience always come into view when we take seriously Paul's teaching in Romans 13 and Peter's in 1 Peter 2:13–17:

> *Submit yourselves for the Lord's sake to every authority instituted among men: whether to the king, as the supreme authority, or to governors, who are sent by him to punish those who do wrong and to commend those who do right. For it is God's will that by doing good you should silence the ignorant talk of foolish men. Live as free men, but do not use your freedom as a cover-up for evil; live as servants of God. Show proper respect to everyone: Love the brotherhood of believers, fear God, honor the king.*

What, if any, are the biblical limits to the biblical submission to civil authorities? Following is a link to an excellent article for further reading and some assorted quotes from some highly regarded teachers that will help set some parameters for civil disobedience from Scripture.

The Bible gives us numerous examples of civil disobedience in which God's people sought to do what is right in obedience to God, in spite of violating a civil law or decree. The Hebrew midwives defy an order by Pharaoh to kill all Hebrew males at birth, covering their action with a half-truth to Pharaoh (Exodus 1:1 5ff). Rahab hides the Israelite spies and refuses to surrender them to the messenger from the king of Jericho (Josh. 2:1ff.) During several years of David's life, he and his band of followers are fugitives from Saul, the civil authority of Israel (e.g., 1 Samuel 22). Daniel and his companions seek and gain permission from an official under King Nebuchadnezzar to set aside an assignment of the king to eat his delicacies; they test their health with a simpler diet (Daniel 1). Later, Shadrach, Meschach, and Abednego refuse to bow and worship King Nebuchadnezzar's image of gold (Daniel 3). Then under King Darius, Daniel refuses to obey the decree, which prohibits prayer for thirty days to anyone except the king (Daniel 6). Likewise, in the book of Esther, Mordecai refuses to kneel and pay honor to Haman, disobeying the command of King Xerxes (Esther 3). In all of these instances, a supreme loyalty to God, which includes his plan for his people, prompts them to set aside obedience to a civil law in order to be obedient to the will of God.[1]

So we believe that civil disobedience is justified only when government compels us to sin, or when there is no legal recourse for fighting injustice. The reason we draw the line there is simply because all the scriptural examples of civil disobedience fall squarely into those two situations. Any other kind of activism has no precedent in the Word of God and violates the spirit of Romans 13 and 1 Peter 2.[2]

[Civil disobedience] can be for two main sorts of reasons: when the state commands us to do that which the Bible forbids; or when the state prohibits us from doing that which the Bible commands.[3]

Here is "laid down the principle of civil and ecclesiastical disobedience". He continues, if the "authority concerned misuses its God-given power to command what he forbids or forbid what he commands, then the Christian's duty is to disobey the human authority in order to obey God's."[4]

---

1 Evangelical Presbyterian Church, "Pastoral Letter on Civil Disobedience," http://www.epc.org/about-the-epc/pastoral-letters/civil-disobedience. (This paper goes on to recount some examples from the New Testament and puts forth some practical applications for followers of Christ.)

2 John MacArthur, "Can Christians Participte in Civil Disobedience," Grace To You, http://www.gty.org/Resources/Articles/A120_Can-Christians-Participate-in-Civil-Disobedience.

3 D. A. Carson, quoted in "Christians and Civil Disobedience," Bill Muehlenberg's CultureWatch, http://www.billmuehlenberg.com/2008/11/02/christians-and-civil-disobedience.

4 John Stott, quoted in "Christians and Civil Disobedience," Bill Muehlenberg's CultureWatch, http://www.billmuehlenberg.

It is rarely good for a Christian to disobey even a bad law. That is why the Scripture so frequently urges Christians to obey even evil governments and laws that create trouble for them. Still, there are times when a Christian becomes thoroughly convinced that the total welfare of others would be significantly better if he disobeyed rather than obeyed a particular law. When that moment arrives he must obey God rather than man. God has commanded him to be concerned for the well being of all human beings, and the well being of human beings demands disobedience to that particular law at that particular time. The Christian in such a case must humbly, yet boldly, and with a prayer to God for forgiveness if he has judged wrongly, disobey the law and be willing to suffer the consequences of his disobedience.[5]

91. Thou Shall (13:8–10)

If you learn to love, you will fulfill the essence and intent of God's moral law. Whatever specific commandment of God's you can name—"You shall not commit adultery," "You shall not murder," "You shall not steal," "You shall not give false testimony," "You shall not covet," or any of the others; they all are rooted in the concept of "You shall love your neighbor as yourself." It is impossible for genuine love to perpetrate an injustice toward others. That's why it fulfills God's moral law.

com/2008/11/02/christians-and-civil-disobedience.

5   Kenneth Kantzer, quoted in "Pastoral Letter on Civil Disobedience," Evangelical Presbyterian Church, www.epc.org/mediafiles/epc-pastoral-letter-on-civil-disobediance.pdf.

Comments —————————————————————

Maybe a good way of summarizing the difference that Jesus has made in the world is to notice the above contrast. The Law of Moses often focused on "shall not" and the new covenant focuses on "shall." And ... the "shall" becomes more than a commandment. It takes on the form and power of a promise. In Christ and by the power of the indwelling Holy Spirit, we "shall" love both God and people from our renewed hearts. This promise works its way out to very concrete and practical specifics that then, as a naturally supernatural byproduct, keep us from sinning. This is why life in Jesus takes us far beyond a life of sin management.

> *For the law was given through Moses; grace and truth came through Jesus Christ.* (John 1:17)

92. Prophetic Witnesses of Resurrection Reality (13:11–14)

Since we all know that precious time is ticking away, we need to rise up from our spiritual slumber—the end of the age has never been closer! The sun rose some time ago leaving the night far behind. So let us cast off our old sinful "night life"—outrageous behavior, drunkenness, lustfulness, infidelity, contentiousness and envying. Rather, let us put on the shining armor of the daylight— honesty, integrity, sincerity and transparency. Constantly welcome the Lord Jesus Christ to live in you and through you, and don't be on the lookout for any loopholes for the expression of your selfish desires.

Comments —————————————————————

Paul was the New Testament theologian of the

new creation. The reality of the historical, bodily resurrection of Jesus Christ changed the essential dynamics of the heavens, of the earth and of their relationship. The new creation was powerfully and forever inaugurated via the first coming of Jesus, even though its consummation awaits his return. In light of this, Paul and the other New Testament writers constantly call followers of the Christ to live conscious of the reality of God's kingdom, which is both mysteriously and practically unfolding all about us in the midst of earthly cultures in which, assuredly, not everything goes well and nothing goes perfectly.

The apostles teach us that responding to the Holy Spirit in the context of our daily lives, our vocations and our relationships provides a substantial prophetic witness to people all about us. We are witnesses to that coming time in which all things will be properly reintegrated (with all goodness vindicated and evil divinely judged/banished) through Jesus Christ. Our lives and loving communities of faith are to manifest that the process is significantly underway. The Dawn is already here, since Christ's resurrection and ascension ... and so High Noon (the resurrection of all others—living or dead) is sure to follow. The climactic moment of God's Big God-Story arrived ahead of anyone's expected schedule, changed the fabric of everything and added a shocking twist to the plot line, yet has hardly been noticed by the powers that be. (Yet again—and don't you find it odd that the whole world seems to pause at Christmas Eve and ponder its repressed hope: that God himself actually did come to earth in humility and vulnerability as a human baby so long ago in Bethlehem.)

The practical apostolic advice on how to live here and now is simple: believers are not called to live as sleazy denizens and dealers of the spiritually/morally bankrupt "night" of previous ages, but as powerfully-equipped citizens and agents of the spiritually/morally vibrant "day" of the new creation. Christ is risen, and he is expressing his resurrection life in and through those who have courageously chosen follow him.

ROMANS CHAPTER FOURTEEN

93. The Art of Gnat Swallowing (14:1–6)

Don't refuse to recognize or fellowship with believers who disagree with you over non-essential matters—even if they're unenlightened about the truth. One believer has a clear conscience about eating anything. Another, who may be hypersensitive, is a vegetarian. The one who eats freely shouldn't get down on the one who doesn't, and the one who doesn't shouldn't get down on the one who does. God has accepted them both. Who are we to condemn another's servant? Before his own master he will stand or fall. And stand he will, for God himself is holding up his own!

Let's take another issue. One believer regards one day as more sacred than another. Another believer views each day as equally sacred. Things like this should be seen as a matter of personal conscience that allows for individual liberty. The one who celebrates a certain day as special does so as an expression of love for the Lord. The one who equally celebrates every day also does so as an expression of love for the Lord—just like the one who eats freely worships the Lord in his eating, and the one who abstains from meat worships the Lord by not eating. Can't you see that the truly important issues are

209

not the externals, but the motives of the heart—love and worship.

Comments

It has become common for Jesus-followers to claim that they are "spiritual" but not "religious." I personally like the distinction, and I think that the folks around us can relate to the statement too. Well ... Romans 14 is the chapter that can provide the theological basis for this important contrast. It has always been one of my favorites to ponder and teach. A well-known maxim attributed to Augustine captures the heart of Paul in Romans 14—*"In necessariis unitas, in non–necessariis (or, dubiis) libertas, in utrisque (or, omnibus) caritas."* In English we say: "In essentials, unity; in non-essentials, liberty; in all things, charity."

Of course, drawing the line between the theological essentials and non-essentials is a delicate, sweet science. Jesus chided the religious leaders of his day for straining out gnats, while swallowing camels (Mt. 23:24) ... surely one of his better jokes. You'd think that we'd normally be able to distinguish camel issues from gnat issues, but we do get easily-confused perspectives when our personal preferences and cultural/religious "golden calves" are potentially on the chopping block: our styles of dressing, eating, recreating, socializing; how we specifically "do church"; and our strong convictions regarding secondary doctrines and temporal politics ... just to name a few. It seems that Jesus is inferring that in order for us to avoid the discomforting act of consuming our mode of transportation (while mysteriously maintaining our dignity in the eyes of many people), we are going to have to get used to the bitter taste and brief choking sensation of ingesting some little bugs along our way in life with Jesus as our leader.

I think that Jesus also had in mind that gnats and camels tend to hang out around each other! So what's the spiritual moral of the story? If we're going to actually travel anywhere in our spiritual journey, we've got an unavoidable "dietary choice" to make. Is it going to be camels or gnats? Bad religion ironically snarfs camels while upholding its image of precision, yet getting us nowhere. Genuine spirituality chooses to choke down some bothersome gnats for the sake of riding, instead of eating, the camels that Christ provides us for his ongoing mission.

Lord Jesus, give me the grace to know the difference between these two animals and make the needed sacrifices of my preferences to actually make some progress in loving well—both our Father in heaven and other people.

94. Seeing Beyond Externals (14:5–6)

One believer regards one day as more sacred than another. Another believer views each day as equally sacred. Things like this should be seen as a matter of personal conscience, which allows for individual liberty. The one who celebrates a certain day as special does so as an expression of love for the Lord. The one who equally celebrates every day also does so as an expression of love for the Lord—just like the one who eats freely worships the Lord in his eating, and the one who abstains from meat worships the Lord by not eating. Can't you see that the truly important issues are not the externals, but the motives of the heart—love and worship.

Comments ——————————————————————

It is so natural for us to pick out external-oriented preferences in life and make them the measures by which we evaluate our own spirituality and the spirituality of others. (Consider things like preferences in clothing, fashion, food, beverages, hair styles, music, forms of praying, family traditions, spending money, entertainment, sports, language idioms, "secondary" doctrines, ways of "doing church" and the like.) This very human habit is rooted in our desire to look and be "right," and externals are easy targets for us to use to "prove" our rightness to ourselves and the people whose opinions matter to us. (I've heard that "being right" is the booby prize of life!) Yet, when we read through the gospels, we are confronted again and again with how Jesus lived, ministered and worked to undermine this kind of self-righteousness. We love him for it! He heroically sees beyond the externals of race, religious (or non-religious) background, cultural prejudices, social standings, religious titles, economic states and man-made traditions, and instead looks upon the heart of both matters and people.

Now there are obviously sinful external ways of living and relating that we can clearly identify and properly condemn. The New Testament has several contrasting lists of the kinds of attitudes and behaviors that are of the flesh or of the Spirit. (Galatians 5 comes to mind.) But the problem arises when we add to the list our own culturally/ personally derived taboos, do's and don'ts, and biases, and then place these matters into the "essential" category. We must make room in our church cultures, without being divisive, for fellow believers to have differing preferences and convictions regarding non-essentials. Beyond this, we must actually fight for their freedom to choose differently than we would. (When we apply this same principle to people who haven't yet come to faith in Christ, we often find ourselves tempted to write off people who have transgressed a true, ethical essential without offering them a chance at receiving God's mercy in Christ. Maybe they've blown it over and over again, but their hearts could truly be crying out for freedom; they could jump at the chance of receiving forgiveness and repent for their wicked ways.)

Romans 14 is an apostolic appeal to us to live in and proclaim the liberty that Christ has purchased for us with his blood. He has come to free us to live in God's love. We are called to yield to the love and personal leadership of the Holy Spirit to help us transcend fleshly hatred, prejudice and self-justification so that we can reach out to people who are either coming from a different place than we are on non-essential matters or to people who need to be touched by the good news of Jesus. May the Father help us to rise up from our insecurities and fear-based judgments to love others with his compelling, joy-filled and liberating love through Jesus Christ and the power of the Holy Spirit.

95. Pondering Our Approaching Death (14:7–9)

For we ourselves aren't the central focus of our lives or our deaths, loving and worshiping the Lord is. So if we're alive, Jesus is our reference point. And if we die, we'll be face to face with our reference point! We are owned and wanted by him, "dead or alive"! It was for this very goal that Christ died and rose again, that he might rightfully exercise his claim of lordship over both the dead and the living.

Comments ─────────────────────────

In the midst of his essay in chapter 14 on surmounting unrighteous judgmentalism in our lives, the apostle holds out a vital key for our success. If Jesus continues to wait to return, you and I are going to die! And our deaths aren't that far away. In the Sermon on the Mount, Jesus challenged us to judge with a righteous judgment and avoid the unrighteous sort. As many believers…and even non-Christians can tell you, "perspective is everything." Periodically contemplating our swiftly approaching death is one of the disciplines held out to us through the centuries by spiritual leaders in.

Our consciousness of how we will soon be face to face with Jesus is an excellent way to maintain the proper perspective on earthly life and relationships and to guard us from petty, unrighteous judgments. We seriously don't have time or energy to waste on self-justification, jealousy and envy, or on being cantankerous, cranky and contentious. Each one of us will give an account to God (and very soon at that!) regarding how much of his life and love we learned to allow into our hearts and to be expressed through our thoughts, words and deeds.

May Christ grant us great mercy and wisdom in this focused journey into his light and into his arms. Any and all deception we suffered or held

will peel off of us when he looks into our eyes. May
we seek to gaze into his eyes even now and shed as
many of those lies as we possibly can, by the grace
and power of the Holy Spirit, before that Day.

96. A Heart of Mission (14:10–17)

*So how can we condemn or disregard our fellow
believers? For we shall all have our individual turn before
the judgment seat of Christ. The Scripture says, "As
surely as I live, says the Lord, every knee will bow before
me, and every person will verbally acknowledge what is
true to God." Every one of us will give an account of
ourselves to God. So let's not get sidetracked by critically
evaluating each other, but zero in on evaluating what is
critical—how we can avoid causing another believer to
get tripped up by any insensitive attitudes or actions on
our part.*

*I know by personal revelation from the Lord Jesus
that no material thing is intrinsically evil, but to the
person who views it as unholy, it really is for him. If
your fellow believer's heart is grieved by observing your
liberty to eat anything, then you're not doing what love
would dictate. Don't crush another believer's spirit by
not sacrificing a petty liberty, when Christ sacrificed his
very life for him! Be concerned about even good things
you do that are easily misconstrued as being improper.*

*For the Kingdom of God cannot be reduced to
personal and cultural preferences like habits of eating and
drinking, but it is defined by the transcendent realities
of righteousness, peace and joy, which are inseparably
linked to the person and ministry of the Holy Spirit.*

Comments ————————————————————

Servants of God possess a missional heart. They cherish perspective, zeroing in on what is critical in any situation in which the Master has placed them. Helping to connect human beings with the Trinity and establishing as healthy (truly loving) of a relationship with them as possible are the two most important matters before them. Paul had been Jewish leader of a rigorous religious sub-group in the formative years of his life. But meeting the risen Christ on the Damascus road reformed his heart and liberated him. He gained a new perspective about the essence of true righteousness and the kind of robust spiritual bond between people and people groups that God has provided for the whole earth through Jesus.

When we are ushered into the real presence of God's kingdom through the Holy Spirit's ministry, the cultural preferences by which we naturally measure our (and others') degree of "rightness" pale in significance to witnessing to (and participating in) the radical transformation of human beings (whatever their cultural background) by the power of the gospel of Jesus. The presence of Christ's in their lives will enlighten them, causing them to turn away from the intrinsically evil aspects of their culture (various local expressions of pride, greed, hatred, envy, deceit and lust, which we are also called to lovingly point out in a timely manner). However, this renewed perspective of what is genuinely critical in God's eyes will give us tolerance for people and their different ways of living and relating.

Beyond this, when we touch and are touched by a different human culture than our own, we will inevitably learn many important new things that God himself has providentially placed in that culture, and that will draw us even closer to him. When we find the courage to cross over the cultural barriers for Christ's sake (and truly there are cultural barriers right in our own neighborhoods), we will joyfully discover that he has gone into that culture ahead of us and that he has been waiting to meet and partner with us there on that ground. Our eyes will be reopened to spiritual blind spots we've suffered from, and new levels of our self-righteousness will be exposed, sprinkled afresh in and washed away by the shed blood of Jesus Christ. This perspective on life gives new guts and meaning to "following Christ"!

97. Freedom in Christ (14:14–18)

I know by personal revelation from the Lord Jesus that no material thing is intrinsically evil, but to the person who views it as unholy, it really is for him. If your fellow believer's heart is grieved by observing your liberty to eat anything, then you're not doing what love would dictate. Don't crush another believer's spirit by not sacrificing a petty liberty when Christ sacrificed his very life for him! Be concerned about even good things you do that are easily misconstrued as being improper.

For the Kingdom of God cannot be reduced to personal and cultural preferences like habits of eating and drinking, but it is defined by the transcendent realities of righteousness, peace and joy, which are inseparably linked to the person and ministry of the Holy Spirit.

If you will embrace these values in your service for Christ, you will have favor with and affirmation from both God and others.

Comments ———————————————————

Romans 14 is the apostolic manifesto on liberty and freedom in Christ. In order for us to enjoy the liberty Christ has purchased for us, we need to have our minds renewed and our consciences strengthened regarding the nature of true spirituality.

This necessarily begins with an exposure of dualism. Dualism is the philosophy of life based in fear-driven and man-made religion that presumes that the visible/material world is intrinsically evil, while the invisible/immaterial world is intrinsically holy. Out of this philosophical goop come all sorts of weird religious practices, rituals, sacrifices, forms of worship and, ironically, both extreme abstinences and indulgences. The goal of dualism is to find ways to either escape or ignore the visible realm in order to connect with the invisible realm and be "spiritual." Thank God, there is no hint of dualism or the superstitions that spin off from it in the minds of Christ and his apostles.

The spiritual disciplines of Scripture encourage the reasonable, temporary, healthy, rhythmic and graceful denial of earthly pleasures in order to make more room for the pursuit of transcendent pleasures in Christ. Those disciplines are trampled upon by a conscious or repressed, yet guilt-driven and toxic, religious extremism. Dualism is found in many religions of the world, but it has also assaulted the church from her earliest days. Both Paul and John fought against the insidious encroachments of dualism (specifically Gnosticism) upon the believing communities in their epistles.

True spirituality in Christ gratefully acknowledges that all that God has made is good and that the proper use of the material world—which is to further the goal of loving both God and neighbor in concrete ways—is holy by nature. It acknowledges that both the visible and invisible realms have been infected by sin. It acknowledges that Jesus Christ came to purge both realms of evil through his birth, life, ministry, death on the cross, resurrection, ascension and gift of the Holy Spirit. It acknowledges that Jesus Christ has inaugurated a new creation: a new heavens wedded to a new earth, which is mysteriously already present, though not yet fully realized.

The blessings and pleasures that flow from the proper use and cultivation of God's creation are to be sources of inspiration for thanksgiving to and joy before our Creator. We need not fall into idolization of the creation. Such priestly human lives become both a living witness and a sure prophecy to the entire cosmos of the reality of the renewed creation, which will ultimately swallow up sin and death in all its forms. We are called to worship the Giver and enjoy his good gifts. This honors God, our souls, our bodies and our human relations.

> *For everything created by God is good, and nothing is to be rejected if it is received with thanksgiving.* (1 Timothy 4:4)

> *If with Christ you died to the elemental spirits [i.e. superstitions] of the world, why, as if you were still alive in the world, do you submit to regulations—"Do not handle, do not taste, do not touch" referring to things that all perish as they are used)—according to human precepts and teachings? These have indeed an appearance of wisdom in promoting self-made religion and*

asceticism and severity to the body, but they are of no value in stopping the indulgence of the flesh. (Colossians 2:20–23)

Every good and perfect gift is from above, coming down from the Father of the heavenly lights, who does not change like shifting shadows. (James 1:17)

[God brought his Son into the world] ... *to rescue us from the hand of our enemies, and to enable us to serve him without fear in holiness and righteousness before him all our days.* (Luke 1:74–75)

98. Keeping the Main Things the Main Things (14:14–18)

I know by personal revelation from the Lord Jesus that no material thing is intrinsically evil, but to the person who views it as unholy, it really is for him. If your fellow believer's heart is grieved by observing your liberty to eat anything, then you're not doing what love would dictate. Don't crush another believer's spirit by not sacrificing a petty liberty when Christ sacrificed his very life for him! Be concerned about even good things you do that are easily misconstrued as being improper.

For the Kingdom of God cannot be reduced to personal and cultural preferences like habits of eating and drinking, but it is defined by the transcendent realities of righteousness, peace and joy, which are inseparably linked to the person and ministry of the Holy Spirit.

If you will embrace these values in your service for Christ, you will have favor with and affirmation from both God and others.

Comments ———————————————————

The passage above paints a picture of the true freedom enjoyed by the children of God. We are liberated in our hearts to receive and embrace all the good gifts that our heavenly Father has provided for us through his creation. In fact, we are so free and our perspective is so keen that we are able to actually see the crowning touch of the original creation: other human beings that are made in his image. We are so free that we would quickly sacrifice a legitimate use of something God has made if another still views that use as illegitimate. Children of God are so free that we are behaviorally flexible in various relationships, cultures and life situations, all for the higher purpose of loving and connecting with others for Christ's honor.

Do you find it odd that the same behavior in two people can either be proper or improper in God's eyes, depending on the state of the consciences, or perspectives, of those two individuals? This principle, of course, does not apply to all behaviors, but to the "non-essentials" of life ... or cultural preferences, as I call them.

What kinds of behaviors do you think might be on such a list? I remember being a bit culturally challenged when our family was eating dinner with one of the most godly, humble men I have ever met. He had been imprisoned for his faith in China for over twenty years simply because he wouldn't say to the prison officials, "I don't believe in Jesus." In joyful celebration of the gift of food we were enjoying, he boldly belched several times during our meal with a big smile on his face! My grandmother would have been mortified. It wasn't quite as easy to tell my young children to behave themselves at dinner after that!

I actually find this Romans 14 way of God intriguing and joy-inspiring. It counters the temptation for me to know and control everything in my world. It challenges my fleshly desire to precisely know ahead of time what the right course will be for me and/or others to take. When it comes to these kinds of matters, the code for living in the genuine freedom of God's children is not written on stones or comprehensively recorded in a book of the Bible. Rather, it is written upon the renewed heart and mind of an individual child of God by the Holy Spirit himself, who indwells him or her. The child of God is encouraged to continually be alive and alert to the Spirit of God, who is also alive and moving within his or her being in realtime. We grow to learn to mind the Holy Spirit, as children mind their parents. We are not actually called to live by a code, but by "the law of the Spirit of life in Christ Jesus" (Rom. 8:2). By this we discover the mind of Christ.

This dynamic will inform us in every situation in which our Father places us what the love of Jesus looks like right here and right now. Knowing this and living it out is true freedom!

99. The Kingdom and the Spirit (14:17–18)

For the Kingdom of God cannot be reduced to personal and cultural preferences like habits of eating and drinking, but it is defined by the transcendent realities of righteousness, peace and joy, which are inseparably linked to the person and ministry of the Holy Spirit. If you will embrace these values in your service for Christ, you will have favor with and affirmation from both God and others.

For the kingdom of God is not a matter of eating and drinking but of righteousness and peace and joy in the Holy Spirit. Whoever thus serves Christ is acceptable to God and approved by men. (ESV)

Comments ————————————————————

"For the kingdom of God ... is in the Holy Spirit." One of the most profound theological truths in all the New Testament is embedded here in this very practical section of Romans. The Holy Spirit and the kingdom of God are inseparably linked. The kingdom of God is the natural habitat of the Holy Spirit. The Holy Spirit is the animating life force of Christ's kingdom. Where the Holy Spirit is working, the atmospheric conditions of kingdom of God are present and operative. Jesus said, "But if it is by the Spirit of God that I cast out demons, then the kingdom of God has come upon you" (Mt. 12:28).

It is often said that Christianity is not a religion, but a personal relationship with Jesus Christ. The same can be said about the kingdom of God. It is not about visible things like the many earthly kingdoms of this world, but it is centered in knowing— in having an interactive friendship and partnership with the Spirit of God. In the midst of this fallen creation, through Christ and the Holy Spirit, here and now, we have direct access to the powers and dynamics of the eternal, invisible kingdom of heaven. By relating to the Holy Spirit, we have access to genuine and fundamental righteousness, peace and joy. The children of this age grasp for these three qualities of life in various convoluted ways, but never truly find them... until they turn to Jesus.

From the fountainhead of experiencing this divine kind of righteousness, peace and joy, many other streams of spiritual life and power naturally flow... love, hope, faith, prayer, healing, reconciliation, justice, deliverance from evil, spiritual gifts, creative work and arts, purpose, mission and destiny, to name just a few. We should pray to be filled with the Holy Spirit each night and day, and then simply live in an attitude of open trust and shameless reliance, knowing that the Father and the Son will delight in answering such a bold request.

100. Beyond Rules (14:19–23)

Place working for and preserving unity with fellow believers, as well as building up one another, at the top of your list of life's values. Let the freedom to express your liberty in Christ in non-essentials come somewhere down the list! Don't destroy the work of God for the sake of something as boring as meat eating. Truly, all things are pure, but not all truths are equally important. And besides, if someone believes that eating meat is wrong, it's wrong for him to eat it. It is honorable to forego any liberty, like eating meat or drinking wine, if it somehow pressures a fellow believer to violate her/his conscience. Do you have a strong faith that can handle such liberties? Great! Enjoy them before God. Just don't project onto others the same expectation. We will be happy if we aren't self-condemned for the liberties we allow ourselves. But if you have doubts about the legitimacy of any behavior, like eating meat, and you do it anyway, your joy will evaporate because you aren't living by faith. And whatever cannot be done in faith is, by definition, sinful.

Comments ———————————————————————

In these last two paragraphs of Romans 14, Paul summarizes the main point of the passage on the sometimes-delicate ethical balance between living in both liberty and brotherly love. The way of Christ is the way of the heart. God and his word always penetrate to the heart of matters, and are never content to view human life and its choices on the superficial plane. Love is to be our motive and goal. In that context, God makes a lot of room for individual liberty based in the guidance of personal conviction and conscience.

Our faith can never be boiled down to a static set of rules for living because of God's deeper commitment to bring us into a personal, dynamic, interactive relationship with the Father, Son and Holy Spirit in realtime. In one situation or time frame, love may look like one thing, and in the next situation or season, it may look like the opposite: taking action or being patient; speaking up or being silent; showing mercy or applying justice; confronting or forbearing; working hard or simply trusting God to work; remaining peaceful or expressing righteous anger; resisting a trial or accepting it; expecting a miracle or leaving the matter to providence ... often the way of Christ's love implies a wise blending of both.

No written code could cover all the possibilities of what love looks like, nor could we memorize it and apply it perfectly if we had such a thing. The Scriptures tell us stories of God's love, the failures of human wisdom and foolishness, and prescribe ethical boundaries. It is vital for us to read and re-read the texts. However, the Trinity will work within us to bring these things to mind in timely ways and give us special wisdom in our hours of need.

101. Echoes of the Garden (15:1–4)

Those who have more personal strength must use it to lift up those who are weaker and not exploit it to their own advantage. Let each of us seek out ways to bless others and build them up. Even the most powerful man of all, Jesus Christ, didn't use his power to create for himself a pain-free and pleasure-filled earthly life. As Scripture says, "I have personally identified with and embraced the rejection they have shown you, O God." All the Scriptures have been written to impart knowledge, patience and comfort to us so that we can live in hope—a confident expectation of a glorious future.

Comments ———————————————————

I can't think of another value of the spiritual life that runs more contrary to fallen human flesh than what Paul states above. "Survival of the fittest" is one of the primary mantras of secular humanism. We witness the exploitation of the weak by the strong in our cultures every day. It long ago became the way of the world. On the other hand, when we consider the natural affection that parents often ex-hibit toward their children, we do get a glimpse into the kind of sacrificial love that the apostle holds out to us: it is a way of Christ that is meant to apply to the heart of all our relations with others. Parents often heroically offer their strengths to their children without thinking of getting anything out of it.

Along the way in my studies about the kingdom of God, I have come to believe that the kingdom is actually more native to human life than I once thought. Sin is actually a foreign invasion into human existence. There is something more original than sin in God's beautiful creation.

When Jesus came on the scene to reveal the kingdom of God, he was making a way for us to get back to the Garden ... and then beyond it! The echoes of the goodness of our Father's original intentions for humanity resonate within our deepest heart. In the beginning, the Son was the voice of God who initiated these echoes and now today pours substance back into them. When we come to Christ, we are actually coming home.

In whatever way God has blessed us with strengths (abilities, opportunities, resources, experience, relationships, etc.), we are called to walk in them. We must be conscious that these strengths are a gift from him, that he has bestowed them upon us so we can love others better and that we will ultimately answer to him for how we have stewarded them.

Father, what do I have at my disposal today, and how can I use it to benefit another who might otherwise not have access to it? Continually keep me from the boastful pride of life that sees my strengths as mine alone, for Christ's sake. Amen.

102. Hope (15:3–4)

Even the most powerful man of all, Jesus Christ, didn't use his power to create for himself a pain-free and pleasure-filled earthly life. As Scripture says, "I have personally identified with and embraced the rejection they have shown you, O God." All the Scriptures have been written to impart knowledge, patience and comfort to us so that we can live in hope—a confident expectation of a glorious future.

Comments ───────────────────────────────

What stands out to me in this little paragraph of Romans 15 is how vital it is for us to continually possess hope in our lives. Paul says here that the aim of all the Scriptures, and our Father's primary intent on providing them for us, is that we might have hope. In Colossians 1–5a, the apostle states, "We give thanks to the God and Father of our Lord Jesus Christ, praying always for you, since we heard of your faith in Christ Jesus and of your love for all the saints; because of the hope which is laid up for you in heaven." The implication here is that hope is the fountainhead of both faith and love ... the three virtues of a life lived in the Spirit, which receive special attention throughout the New Testament writings. Paul seems to say that if we possess this hope, then both faith and love will naturally, obviously spring forth from it.

Hope is always about our expectations of the future. And our expectation of the future continually affects our convictions, perspectives, attitudes, decisions, emotions, actions and reactions in the present. Can you personally identify with this connection? Having a Christ-centered hope is about having a genuine, undergirding, confident optimism about our lives in the future ... a kind of life that is truly, inexpressibly *full* of love, beauty, peace, harmony, understanding, purpose, satisfaction, joy and well-being. No more tears (as in ripping); no more tears (as in what flows from our eyes). This life will be lived in the very presence and fully displayed power of God. His entire eternal family will live in a renewed heavens and earth, in which the tension between the invisible and visible aspects of God's magnificent creation will be forever relaxed.

The circumstances of our lives in the future very often stand in stark contrast to the circumstances of our lives in this fallen age. The circumstances of Jesus' earthly life are an example for us regarding what we will encounter as we follow him in our earthly life. He experienced rejection and injustice in this world—though, paradoxically, he also walked in the joy of his Father's approval—and we also will have our share of the same. Yet the Holy Spirit and the Scriptures will supply for us the knowledge, patience and comfort we will need to not give up on this life, the people in our world and, especially, our unshakable belief in God's goodness. Hope informs us that all of our sufferings and sorrows have redemptive divine purpose and profound meaning. We foresee by the power of hope that patiently enduring the trials of life will be worth it all.

103. The Gift of Scripture (15:3–4)

Even the most powerful man of all, Jesus Christ,

didn't use his power to create for himself a pain-free and
pleasure-filled earthly life. As Scripture says, "I have
personally identified with and embraced the rejection
they have shown you O God." All the Scriptures have
been written to impart knowledge, patience and comfort
to us so that we can live in hope—a confident expectation
of a glorious future.

Comments ————————————————————————

As I stated earlier in the book, I have been very
blessed through many years to learn from Dr. Larry
Crabb—both through his groundbreaking books
and in person. (I have had the unusual and joyful
opportunity to get to know most of the authors of
our generation whose books have impacted me the
most.) For decades now, Larry has studied, pondered, wrestled with, prayed through, reconsid-
ered and written about the doctrines, instructions,
poetry and narratives of Scripture, and he has applied them specifically to the conditions of our individual lives and relationships with God and people. I have great admiration for this dear friend in
Christ and will say more about his teaching in the
next few readings.

I think of Larry's body of work when I reread
the final sentence of this paragraph from my devotional paraphrase of Romans 15: "All the Scriptures
have been written to impart knowledge, patience
and comfort to us so that we can live in hope—a
confident expectation of a glorious future." Wow,
what a lineup.

Let's ponder briefly the quote above.

First, God has given us the amazing gift of the

holy Scriptures. We are meant to meditate upon and apply them throughout our whole lives. They are an inexhaustible supply of reliable truths that are divinely inspired, or God-breathed. Are we doing this kind of study in both our personal and communal lives? So much more could be said about the power of the written and spoken word of God in this world and in our lives!

Second (and I'll start at the end point), to live in an atmosphere of hope is an experience whose power lies in a certainty about a marvelous future, because something absolutely revolutionary happened in the past: the resurrection of Jesus Christ from the dead. Followers of Jesus Christ are empowered by the Holy Spirit to live as prophetic witnesses to the kingdom of God that is truly here now, but not fully revealed or demonstrated, as it will surely be. Jesus is risen from the dead; therefore, all the other effects of the rebellion of both angels and humanity against God and its countless negative consequences will surely be undone.

Third, the Scriptures are filled with the knowledge we need to live lives of integrity (i.e. wholeness) and true success. At one point God laments through the prophet Hosea, "My people are destroyed from lack of knowledge. Because you have rejected knowledge, I also reject you as my priests" (Hos. 4:6). Followers of Jesus are called to live as royal priests in our fallen world, those who embody and radiate the wisdom, beauty and knowledge of the living God to all the earth. "But you are a chosen people, a royal priesthood, a holy nation, a people belonging to God, that you may declare the praises of him who called you out of darkness into his wonderful light" (1 Pet. 2:9).

Fourth, Paul refers to how the Scriptures inspire the cultivation of the virtue of patience in our lives. Without holding before us the perpetual example of the biblical heroes of faith, who loved and served God and people (and who also recovered from failing to do so!), we can easily lose heart in our struggles with injustice, rejection, abandonment, illness, material need, tragedy, seemingly unanswered prayer and personal failure ... to name just a few trials of life. But again and again, the Bible provides divine perspectives that equip us with the kind of "shock absorbers" for our life's "vehicle" so that our hope does not bounce out of the car. One of these primary perspectives is how patience (like the kind that God possesses) can only be worked into our souls through enduring and surmounting trials. Another is that we will receive a more than commensurate, eternal reward for the temporary sufferings we experience, if we do not give up.

Finally, God gives us comfort through our engagement with holy Scripture. I think that comfort is the most mysterious of the elements here in view. (Why do scrapes feel better when kissed by our amazing mothers?) We all long for comfort in our lives, and we too often settle for false comforts that do not go deep enough or last long enough to satisfy our aching hearts. So much could be said here, but it is sufficient to say that the most exquisite comfort possible comes to us by experiencing the genuine presence of the Trinity in the midst of an imperfect life. This, most often and most promisingly, happens for us as God interacts with us through his written word. The Holy Spirit who is called the Comforter, originally inspired the writings and has watched over their accurate transmission through the centuries. As we read, the very same Spirit draws near to us, rises within us, kisses our hearts and whispers the truth we need to hear into our spirits. There is no comfort in this hurting world greater than this.

104. Sullivant on Crabb (15:3–4)

Even the most powerful man of all, Jesus Christ, didn't use his power to create for himself a pain-free and pleasure-filled earthly life. As Scripture says, "I have personally identified with and embraced the rejection they have shown you O God." All the Scriptures have been written to impart knowledge, patience and comfort to us so that we can live in hope—a confident expectation of a glorious future.

Comments ———————————————

Years ago I did a series of pastoral sermons called "Sullivant on Crabb." The points of those messages have provided a very helpful framework, which became deeply integrated into my heart and mind as a follower of Jesus and a spiritual director to others. In the following readings, I will unfold the essence of this framework. It deals with our basic condition as human beings, how and why our problems develop, and how God works to help us face and surmount those problems as we who follow Jesus are progressively conformed to his image.

The framework begins with a biblical definition of the human being. We are the crowning touch of God's original creation, and were made according to his likeness and image. We are therefore image bearers. Yet, because of our first parents' tragic fall into independence from God (the essence of spiritual rebellion), the corruption of human nature, and the many-faceted death that resulted, we have inherited a terrible fallenness and brokenness that affects every aspect of our beings (the essence of depravity). So a paradox defines our condition—we are fallen image bearers. If we don't discern and navigate this paradox, we will be confused about our lives, our goals, this age, our relationships, our true enemies and God himself.

The second main point of the framework follows the first. On one hand, because we are image bearers, every human being possesses dignity that must be affirmed and respected. On the other hand, because we are fallen, we simultaneously possess depravity that must be exposed and overcome if we are to be restored to the unmarred image of Christ. Whole movements, institutions and both religious and secular worldviews have, throughout the centuries, emphasized one side of the paradox of the human condition to the neglect of the other, thereby offering a distorted view of humanity and insufficient solutions to our problems.

The challenge before us is to discover and expound upon the radical middle of this paradox, which holds these opposing truths in necessary tension. This results in the relaxation of a boatload of unnecessary tension.

Psalm 8:3–6 (Our Dignity)

When I consider your heavens, the work of your fingers, the moon and the stars, which you have set in place, what is man that you are mindful of him, the son of man that you care for him? You made him a little lower than the heavenly beings and crowned him with glory and honor. You made him ruler over the works of your hands; you put everything under his feet.

Romans 5:12,19 (Our Depravity ... and Our Destiny)

Sin entered the world through one man, and death through sin, and in this way death came to all men, because all sinned—for just as through the disobedience of the one man the many were made sinners, so also through the obedience of the one man the many will be made righteous.

105. Legitimate Longings (15:3–4)

Even the most powerful man of all, Jesus Christ, didn't use his power to create for himself a pain-free and pleasure-filled earthly life. As Scripture says, "I have personally identified with and embraced the rejection they have shown you O God." All the Scriptures have been written to impart knowledge, patience and comfort to us so that we can live in hope—a confident expectation of a glorious future.

Comments ─────────────────────────────

Moving more deeply into the heart of understanding how we, as fallen image bearers (who possess both dignity and depravity) develop and surmount problems, we see that human beings and relations are like icebergs. What you see on the surface of the water is much smaller than the mass of what lies below. This can complicate our lives a bit! Furthermore, we do not become easily conscious (self-aware) of what moves us at the core of our beings. We must turn to the wisdom of Scripture to help us pinpoint what goes on in the depths of the human soul. (How many of the Bible's narratives and its instructions are recorded to achieve this very end!) Then we must also rely on the Holy Spirit and the feedback of wise and loving friends to make it more personal.

Larry Crabb summarizes the essence of our nobility as the longing for intimacy and the longing for impact. From the very beginning of life we yearn to connect with and be loved by another, and to not be rejected. We also have a core desire to use our abilities to make an impact for good on the people and world around us. Dr. Crabb emphasizes that these desires, in their essence, should be affirmed, because they are aspects of the Imago Dei (the image of God) in the human being. We cannot actually repent of them, and the attempt to do so wastes our energies and damages our humanity.

The Imago Dei in a human being, according to the good doctor, consists of being, as God is, relational, rational, volitional and emotional. I imagine there are other classic aspects of the Imago Dei, but these certainly will do for a start. These things about us are also to be acknowledged, affirmed, accepted and celebrated. To do less is an insult to our Creator.

So ... our genuine problems do not lie with these two embedded longings. Rather, they develop from our profound reactions to how these longings become stymied as we live and relate in this broken world. Instead of experiencing the kind of intimacy we have been designed for, we experience insufficient love and even outright rejection from people. No one loves us the way we long to be loved. Instead of freely making the impact we long for, we experience injustices that hinder our freedom to use our talents. Some people, whom we expect will help pave the way for us to make our contribution, become envious of or threatened by our strengths, and intentionally undermine our efforts and/or discredit our motivations.

When left to our own resources to cope with the reality of this situation, extended over the course of some years, we feel a terrible, tragic pain at the center of our souls. Our very human reactions to this kind of pain deep in our hearts activates our own depravity. We have been victimized by others' sins of rejection and injustice and, out of our effort to survive, we become agents of sin ourselves. This age is weighed down by a vicious cycle of human depravity ... and the evil of it runs right through our own souls.

Yet still, there is hope for transformation.

106. Creatures of Reaction (15:3–4)

Even the most powerful man of all, Jesus Christ, didn't use his power to create for himself a pain-free and pleasure-filled earthly life. As Scripture says, "I have personally identified with and embraced the rejection they have shown you O God." All the Scriptures have been written to impart knowledge, patience and comfort to us so that we can live in hope—a confident expectation of a glorious future.

Comments ————————————————————

The terrible pain of rejections and injustices combine and add shame to our situation. We even feel ashamed of the very longings for intimacy and impact that are at the core of our being. Again, left to ourselves, we are driven to find a way to cope. Our strategies are erected upon a reactionary, firm commitment at our center to self-protect. We aren't speaking here of a kind of reasonable self-defense from physical harm, but a putting up of walls that generally shut out and shut down our relational vulnerability. This kind of self-protection becomes the subterranean, usually subtle, primary goal of our broken hearts. The Scripture states in Proverbs, "There is a way that seems right to a man, But its end is the way of death" (14:12, NKJV). To me, such self-protection seems to fit squarely into this warning.

On a surface level, we creatively make multiple choices, normally over the course of many years, that fit neatly with our now-embedded goal of self-protection. We learn to make such decisions so swiftly and deftly that we lose touch with the hidden agenda that is moving us through life and relationships. We also lose touch with the very fact that we are making choices at all. We imagine that we are just "being ourselves" ... though the joy of living ebbs out from us. (I am convinced that at this stage of the process, the ancient enemies of God and the human soul—Satan and his demonic host—are operating overtime and incognito to offer us false images of God, other people, our circumstances and ourselves. If we buy into these falsehoods, then the evil one's most basic work is accomplished, for he has received our personal support for his lies.)

In reaction to our profound pain (and our felt need for comfort of any kind), we form false images, we believe lies, we make unwise inner vows, we overuse our strengths, we transfer blame to undeserving people, we develop addictions, we mimic others and we employ any number of similar coping mechanisms. All of these things have a weird way of offering us a temporary comfort. This is why they are tempting to us. A particular way of being emerges and a style of relating ensues that is far from the genuine, whole person whom God intends for us to be and become. Some would call this, and I believe there is merit to this term, a false self.

Of course, many people realize along the way that they need God to forgive them for their depravity—their sins of pride, lust, greed, hatred, selfishness and the like. And God faithfully provides this forgiveness when we turn to Jesus Christ and believe in who he is and what he has done for us in his death and resurrection. Additionally, when the Holy Spirit enters our lives, he takes up residence in our innermost being and imparts to us a new nature ... a new heart ... a new creation. This reality provides the new baseline for us so that God and we can partner, through both crisis and process, to dislodge the sinful, hidden goal of self-protection. We can therefore successfully put off the old nature, or the false self—both its way of being and its style of relating.

A huge battle is inaugurated in order for this to be realized! But, we are no longer alone in the fight, and One who has already conquered all sin and death is our Bodyguard.

107. Negative Strongholds (15: 3–4)

Even the most powerful man of all, Jesus Christ, didn't use his power to create for himself a pain-free and pleasure-filled earthly life. As Scripture says, "I have personally identified with and embraced the rejection they have shown you O God." All the Scriptures have been written to impart knowledge, patience and comfort to us so that we can live in hope—a confident expectation of a glorious future.

Comments ───────────────────────

I like to refer to the sinfully self–protective strategies that we choose and then repress as "strongholds". In 2 Corinthians 10:3–5, the apostle Paul makes reference to this challenge and battle we all face: "For though we walk in the flesh, we do not war according to the flesh. For the weapons of our warfare are not carnal but mighty in God for pulling down strongholds, casting down arguments and every high thing that exalts itself against the knowledge of God, bringing every thought into captivity to the obedience of Christ."

The locus of the fight to tear down the strongholds of human depravity begins with our own thoughts—our images of reality, beliefs, attitudes, perspectives and mindsets. In the language of Romans 12, displacing strongholds has to do with the renewing of the mind: the practical way that we put off the old self (or false self) and put on the new self (or new creation).

Strongholds are things that block us from the knowledge of God—a kind of knowledge that is rooted in an experiential intimacy with the Father,

Son and Holy Spirit ... relational knowledge, if you will. Strongholds hinder healthy interpersonal relationships with others and our self-awareness as well. I truly mean no disrespect, but, without substantial divine intervention, we all tend to slowly and progressively get "jerked into being jerks" by the evil one and our willful reactions to the pains of living in a fallen world in which our deepest longings are profoundly thwarted.

We may become religious jerks or irreligious jerks. Either kind serves the enemy's broader schemes in our world. As Dr. Crabb would say in the many lectures I attended, we are victims of sin, but we are also agents of sin. Our sinful strategies need to be graciously disrupted and displaced by God's love through the power of the Holy Spirit in the context of Christ's community. It can and does happen, and has happened throughout the centuries in the lives of ordinary folks like us. Strongholds are stubborn and deeply embedded, but also recall from the Scripture above that the spiritual weapons at our disposal are mighty through God. When we rightly apply them, we demolish strongholds.

I will yet come to the good news of how a more radical transformation into the image of Jesus Christ happens in us by bringing every errant thought captive to him, but I believe we need to ponder the anatomy and scope of our brokenness in order to be prepped to take in, cooperate with and forever appreciate the remedy!

108. The Golden Goal of Life (15:3–4)

Even the most powerful man of all, Jesus Christ,

didn't use his power to create for himself a pain-free and pleasure-filled earthly life. As Scripture says, "I have personally identified with and embraced the rejection they have shown you O God." All the Scriptures have been written to impart knowledge, patience and comfort to us so that we can live in hope—a confident expectation of a glorious future.

Comments

We buy into various false beliefs about reality because they offer us some kind of temporary comfort, distraction or protection from the pain and shame of past rejections and injustices that we have not found a way to resolve. The embedded goal of self-protection is what fuels the fires of our negative strongholds. Scripture refers to a positive kind of stronghold as well. Psalm 27:1 is just one example of many: "The LORD is my light and my salvation—whom shall I fear? The LORD is the stronghold of my life—of whom shall I be afraid?"

The Lord himself desires to become the one legitimate stronghold of our life. Crabb would tell us that in order for this to happen, the illegitimate, hidden/denied goal of self-protection must be displaced by vulnerable trust in God. I believe that a deliberate, conscious exchange of a primary goal at the core of our being is the key to our freedom. This recommended, new, supreme life goal is thoroughly biblical. There are many ways to state this goal, but I believe it is the one golden goal that we all are designed to share.

Beyond this goal are many legitimate desires we may have in life and many prayers we are encouraged to pray, so that those desires might be satisfied;

however, none of these noble desires should ever be elevated to the place in our hearts of a supreme goal. It is vital that we do not confuse our desires with our goal, because human beings can thwart our desires, but no one can keep us from our goal if it is the proper one. Is there any rejection or injustice that can automatically keep us from getting to know God better or from vulnerably trusting in God? Such negative experiences should be thought of as sufferings. When we give them to the Lord as an offering from a broken heart, they become sanctified as legitimate sufferings, or even sufferings for the sake of Christ. Is not the Scripture full of promises of how God can use sufferings to deepen our relationship with him? In fact, there are aspects of knowing God and identifying with him that can only be learned through pain.

Paul says it this way in Philippians 3:10–11: "I want to know Christ and the power of his resurrection and the fellowship of sharing in his sufferings, becoming like him in his death, and so, somehow, to attain to the resurrection from the dead."

109. Only God Can Meet Our Deepest Longings (15:3–4)

Even the most powerful man of all, Jesus Christ, didn't use his power to create for himself a pain-free and pleasure-filled earthly life. As Scripture says, "I have personally identified with and embraced the rejection they have shown you O God." All the Scriptures have been written to impart knowledge, patience and comfort to us so that we can live in hope—a confident expectation of a glorious future.

Comments ——————————————————————

So, continuing to diagnose the pattern of how we form deeper, subterranean problems and a false self that is beset with negative strongholds ... Why is it so difficult to displace the clenched fist of self-protection in our gut with the golden goal of vulnerably trusting God or getting to know God better? Is it not simply because God is the One who gave us the longings for intimacy and impact, and then placed us in the environment of a broken world? A world in which he knew that these longings would be significantly undermined and remain unsatisfied (though not fully so)? We have a subtle, profound controversy with God that is challenging to settle on a deep heart level. It's hard for many of us to admit, because it seems so irreligious. Yet how can we realistically trust him on a gut level when we have doubts about his goodness? We instinctively don't trust anyone we don't believe is good. This was the original temptation offered by the serpent to Eve and Adam in the garden: "God is not good ... he cannot be trusted ... take your destiny into your own hands."

So we are in a bind that we desperately need to address. We must somehow become reconciled to the pain of the sufferings that God has, at least, allowed to come our way in the course of life. We must make peace with the reality that no human being on earth will meet our deepest need for intimacy ... not the best parent, the closest friend or the most faithful mate. We must face the fact that we live in a world in which not everything is going well and nothing is going perfectly, and that it never will until we are face to face with Christ. We must learn to navigate in cultures in which obstacles will always hinder us from freely making the impact we long to make and achieving the purposes we long to fulfill.

Yes, only God himself can possibly meet our deepest yearnings for intimacy and impact. He will, but even then he requires us to wait for another age for full satisfaction. (Though surely, he does provide tokens and a down payment on the reality of our yearnings by being with us here and now by his Spirit. Moreover, he uses blessed people in this world as instruments of his love in our lives. He also showers us with many simple joys and blessings of life.) Self-protection seems reasonable, but tragically, it blocks us from receiving the generous love that God has to give us (and that he desires to flow through us to others) even in this fallen world. Experiencing and passing on his love is the very reason for our existence on the planet! It is the essence of the only thing that really matters in our lives. And ... unfortunately or not ... a life of love is simply incompatible with the goal of self-protection!

Somehow we must discover that the inevitable pains and sufferings of living in this age have a redemptive purpose. This is what Jesus and the apostles say to us over and over again in the gospels and epistles in so many ways. Yes, yes, yes ... God is good. Do you believe it? Do I? Do I ... really?

> *Therefore we do not lose heart. Though outwardly we are wasting away, yet inwardly we are being renewed day by day. For our light and momentary troubles are achieving for us an eternal glory that far outweighs them all.* (2 Corinthians 4:16–17)

Consider it pure joy, my brothers, whenever you face trials of many kinds, because you know that the testing of your faith develops perseverance. Perseverance must finish its work so that you may be mature and complete, not lacking anything. (James 1:2–4)

Life in this world can be extremely hard, but God is still good. (Thankfully, there is also much of God's beauty still to behold as it is reflected in this world, so we should drink it in whenever we can and wherever we discover it!) Our pain is not the end of the story; the Scriptures have been written to impart to us knowledge, patience and comfort by the power of the Holy Spirit so that we can live in hope. This is what all those Bible stories point to and what all the letters instruct us about.

Overzealous revivalists often lead us to think that an unprecedented move of God across the globe will negate and transcend our need for "low-level" virtues like patience, comfort and hope. But they are badly mistaken, and they always leave many well-intentioned believers disillusioned along the roadways of life after human zeal subsides. But God is full of his own zeal, and his intentions for our lives—both now and in the age to come—will not be deterred as we grow to put our trust in him.

110. The Irony of Our Pain (15:3–4)

Even the most powerful man of all, Jesus Christ, didn't use his power to create for himself a pain-free and pleasure-filled earthly life. As Scripture says, "I have personally identified with and embraced the rejection they have shown you O God." All the Scriptures have been written to impart knowledge, patience and comfort

*to us so that we can live in hope—a confident expectation
of a glorious future.*

Comments

Our friend, Steve Morrison of Healing for the
Nations, opened one of his teaching sessions at
a conference we sponsored last year by asking,
"How many of you would like to have your sense
of physical pain taken away?"[1] Of course, after a
bit of thought, everyone realized that our ability to
feel pain is needed to keep us from greater harm
or alert us to a condition that could be fatal. C. S.
Lewis wrote, "God whispers to us in our pleasures,
speaks to us in our conscience, but shouts in our
pains: It is His megaphone to rouse a deaf world."[2]

We are not easily reconciled to the fact that we
will experience pain in this world—even profound
pain—and that everyone does, though we imagine that the "beautiful people" do not. It isn't true,
despite the images that the media and advertising
industry throw our way. God's truth in Scripture
teaches us over and over that we will have our
share of pain, but that he still is good and that he
loves us more than we can imagine. He teaches us
that there is meaning and purpose for the pains we
experience as we live in a fallen world. Pain is pro-
ductive, though it doesn't feel like it to us when we
are going through it.

Somehow we need to grasp and internalize the
reality of 2 Corinthians 4:17–18: "For momentary,

---

1   Steve Morrison, Hillcrest Covenant Church Life Conference,
    March 2010.
2   C.S. Lewis, "C.S. Lewis quotes," ThinkExist.com, http://thinkex-
    ist.com/quotation/god_whispers_to_us_in_our_pleasures-
    speaks_to_us/180233.html.

light affliction is producing for us an eternal weight of glory far beyond all comparison, while we look not at the things which are seen, but at the things which are not seen; for the things which are seen are temporal, but the things which are not seen are eternal" (NASB).

Notice the juxtapositions here: *momentary* and *eternal*; *light* and *weight*; *affliction* and *glory*. Then notice the word *produce*. Finally, notice that we become conscious of these very real connections of opposites only when we look at our situation from a particular perspective ... looking with a set of eyes that sees into the invisible realm. This kind of sight is essential if we are going to move beyond being victims of life to being victors in life—without becoming obnoxiously triumphal! Pain is real. Pain is hard. Don't go looking for pain ... it will find you on its own. But pain itself is not our enemy.

I am convinced that the inferior goal of self-protection lodged in our souls must be displaced by the Holy Spirit's power for us to be and become our truest selves ... the genuine persons that Jesus came to save and display to creation. This is a practical way to think of and apply our need for co-crucifixion and resurrection with Jesus. If we cooperate with the heavenly Father's agenda for our lives, then we will be able to slough off the childish and sinful strongholds that we have accustomed ourselves to hide behind. We will be able to forgive as we have been forgiven because we realize that another human being cannot thwart our life goal, no matter what they have done or not done. (Larry Crabb expounds on this as it relates to marriage problems in his classic book, *The Marriage Builder*.) We will cast off our energy-draining false selves—all the lies and foolish inner vows; the overuse of our strengths; and the silly ways we try to mimic others instead of being comfortable in our own skin.

As the Holy Spirit brings his timely and compassionate exposure of our childish ways of coping—especially through the Word of God and the people of God—the invisible walls we've activated since our youth will gradually, and sometimes dramatically, dissolve. We will settle the controversy with our great, good Father in heaven regarding why he has given us such longings, allowed them to be thwarted, and reinforced to us that only he can fully satisfy our desperate thirst, but made us wait for their full satisfaction until a future time (though he strategically provides substantial tokens of the reality of this promise, which make living in sin a boring and unsatisfactory proposition). New dimensions of our hearts will come alive to receive the Father's love, return this love back to him and then receive more of it again so that it can flow freely though us to other people of all kinds.

We will begin to walk in love, and the guidance and faith we so often fret over getting from God will catch us up in its current. If we love, we know God and we do his highest will ... it becomes naturally supernatural.

> *For through the Spirit, by faith, we ourselves eagerly wait for the hope of righteousness. For in Christ Jesus neither circumcision nor uncircumcision counts for anything, but only faith working through love. You were running well. Who hindered you from obeying the truth?* (Galatians 5:5–7)

111. Resistance Builds Muscles (15:3–4)

Even the most powerful man of all, Jesus Christ, didn't use his power to create for himself a pain-free and pleasure-filled earthly life. As Scripture says, "I have personally identified with and embraced the rejection they have shown you O God." All the Scriptures have been written to impart knowledge, patience and comfort to us so that we can live in hope—a confident expectation of a glorious future.

Comments ──────────────────────────────

So to conclude these "Sullivant on Crabb" series of readings from this little paragraph in Romans 15, God has permitted for us to be born into and live within a context of conflict ... or spiritual warfare, if you will. The "good fight of faith" (1 Tim. 6:12) revolves around securing and maintaining a confidence in the depths of our being regarding his goodness, despite the adversity we continually face. This requires embracing a perspective that perceives that resistance has a divine purpose and a noble end: to build spiritual and relational muscles that equip us both for this life and the age to come.

From our earliest days we have learned to rely on our own distorted, sinful strategies of coping with the pain of rejections and injustices. We have developed ingrained styles of relating that (1) rob us of the freedom to be the truest selves that God wants us to become in Christ and (2) blind us to our negative strongholds, which empower our reactions to people and events that pose a threat to our self-made, fragile comfort zones. All the while, the evil one subtly entices us to buy into lies that are camouflaged as the best ways to navigate the dangers of living in a fallen world.

Genuinely becoming more like Christ, then, involves (1) welcoming the Holy Spirit's work to graciously expose these lies (normally done through Scripture and wise friends over the years), (2) learning the art of not overreacting to perceived threats, but rather trusting God for the help to discern what his love and liberty look like for us like in any given situation and 3) boldly choosing to live in this love and freedom and to leave the consequences in God's mighty hands.

This crisis/process journey results in our discovering an authentically spiritual way of being— one which informs a way of relating and of doing that glorifies God, honors Jesus Christ and invites the power of the Holy Spirit to trump the inferior powers of human culture, our own foolish ways and spiritual darkness.

Romans 15 states that all the Scriptures have been written so that we might receive:

(1) The knowledge we need to see what is really going on in our great Father's mind, our fallen world, the war room of our enemy, our broken and longing hearts, our ingrained overreaction to life's pains and the way that Christ's love can win out;

(2) The patience that will be required for us to continue to trust God and his goodness over the long haul of many years, despite the adversity and the adversaries;

(3) The legitimate, blessed comfort coming from God's good hand that helps to regularly

compensate and reinvigorate our hearts when they get so battle-weary.

We are liberated and empowered from within to radiate the transcendent life of Jesus Christ and become the person he has planned for us to be. Then we will naturally/supernaturally do what he has created us to do.

112. Negative Strongholds—Redux

The New Testament doesn't go into a lot of explicit details about the nature of strongholds as they have come to be understood among many believers in our generation ... the kind of embedded problems (even subconscious ones) like I have been describing. The passage from John's first epistle below may be the best New Testament passage in which to see how the apostles thought about nature of these stubborn strongholds of darkness, which commonly become lodged deep in the hearts of human beings ... even though John doesn't call them strongholds. I think this is one of the most profound passages in all of Scripture regarding personal transformation into the image of Jesus Christ.

16 By this we know love, that he laid down his life for us, and we ought to lay down our lives for the brothers. 17 But if anyone has the world's goods and sees his brother in need, yet closes his heart against him, how does God's love abide in him? 18 Little children, let us not love in word or talk but in deed and in truth. 19 By this we shall know that we are of the truth and reassure our heart before him; 20 for whenever our heart condemns us, God is greater than our heart, and he knows everything. 21 Beloved, if our heart does not condemn us, we have confidence before God; 22 and whatever we ask we receive from him, because we keep his commandments and do

*what pleases him. 23 And this is his commandment, that
we believe in the name of his Son Jesus Christ and love
one another, just as he has commanded us. 24 Whoever
keeps his commandments abides in God, and God in him.
And by this we know that he abides in us, by the Spirit
whom he has given us.* (1 Jn. 3:16–24, ESV)

I will simply point out some of my observations
on this passage as it relates to the framework about
human problems and divine solutions I have previously written about. See if you agree.

V. 19: God's intention is to "reassure" our heart
in the light of his grace and truth. This Greek word
can also be translated "persuade." Our hearts need
some persuasion to become free and whole.

V. 21: Our hearts tend to "condemn" us and this
robs us of our "confidence before God." Our hearts
are the focus of the needed persuasion ... from condemnation to confidence.

V. 22: In turn, this lack of confidence before God
in our heart hinders our intimate communion, or
our conversational relationship, with the Trinity.

V. 23: If, however, we gain confidence before
God, our friendship with him achieves new heights,
depths and breadth. We will discover a naturally
supernatural flow of prayer, obedience, discernment, faith, love for others, and ...

V. 24: ... the grace and ability to remain present
with God—and he with us—at all times (a good
definition for "abide"). Finally, we realize how close
the Holy Spirit is to us, how involved he is with us
in this process and how accessible his presence and
power is to us.

V. 16: The genesis of this transformation of heart

is based in "know[ing] love"—first, knowing the sacrificial love of Jesus for us personally; secondly, as a direct outcome, knowing our sacrificial love for others.

V. 18: This love is authentic, genuine, divine, true, beyond rhetoric ... practical and concrete.

V. 17: We can choose to "close [our] heart" to self-protect in the face of others' needs (as one example among many), which effectively walls us off from the love of God. The result of the profound closing of the heart, which can be sudden or gradual—today we call it "shutting down"—is the formation of a stronghold like the kind I have been describing.

V. 20: When we discover a stronghold, which John describes here as a area of our life in which our heart "condemns" us, we need not panic—strongholds are common to us all. The self-awareness, or the exposure, is a gift from God. The reality is that we do not even know the depths of our own heart. Fortunately, the self-talk of our own hearts is not the final judge of our lives, for "God is greater than our heart" and he knows everything! Nothing true about us can shock him, scandalize him or deter his pursuit of cleansing and healing our hearts through Jesus the Son. We need his light to even see the precise nature of our heart's conflicts. We can fall back safely into his strong, waiting arms when we are bowled over by the blows of life and our own compromises.

V. 19: By this, our hearts go on this journey of discovery and transformation. By what? By our ongoing experience of living in a culture in which the love in human relations goes beyond rhetoric to a more genuine, practical expression. It involves dwelling in a sweet society—the true church of Jesus Christ, which understands the nature of the needs, longings, tendencies, temptations and strongholds of our hearts ... and that helps create a practical pathway out of condemnation into confidence for spiritual pilgrims. I call such a culture a human life refuge for the wild at heart.

However large it becomes in terms of numbers of people, the believing community must be structured in such a way that it will continue to include: the centrality of God himself, Scripture and devotion; knowing others and being known by others on a heart level; taking genuine delight in knowing and supporting one another; the freedom to be transparent without rejection; the welcoming of accountability for sins (confession, restoration and restitution); generosity and compassion for the needy; family-friendliness; affirming of vocation; a sense of mission to those who have yet come to faith and a reliance on the Holy Spirit's gifts and graces.

113. Substantial, Yet Imperfect, Love (15:5–7)

Now may the God of patience and comfort help you to live in deep harmony of spirit with one another, so that with unified hearts and voices you may glorify God, the Father of our Lord Jesus Christ. Therefore, accept one another just as Christ, to honor his Father, has accepted each of us.

Comments ⎯⎯⎯⎯⎯⎯⎯⎯⎯⎯⎯⎯⎯⎯⎯⎯

The remaining paragraphs of Romans 15–16 are inspired endings to this great epistle. The above section could have been put at the very end as a benediction, but there are a few other things that Paul just has to say before the real end comes.

A part of dwelling in the sweet society of the community of Christ, to which I referred in my last post, revolves around a basic core value of receiving and accepting one another as spiritual kinfolk, if we name the name of Christ as our Lord. The body of Christ on earth is not yet a perfect community (nor or its many individual members), and we will certainly need the patience and comfort that our Father in heaven provides if we are to experience the kind of harmony for which the apostle prays. (I once heard a preacher state, "The Church is like Noah's ark…if it weren't for the flood outside, you couldn't stand the smell inside"! Maybe he was a bit too jaded, but there is some realism to the joke.) In my early years of ministry I believe that I fell prey to over-idealizing the visible church. Somehow we must find ongoing grace from God to seek to live out our ideals in our communities of faith without succumbing to either relational cynicism or relational idolatry.

In John's gospel, Jesus also prayed for this kind of glorious relational unity among those who chose and those who would, in the future, choose to follow him. He stated that the world would both know that we are his disciples and that the Father had truly sent him because of the quality of unity and love that characterizes our relationships as fellow believers.

The love and unity among the followers of Jesus Christ is to be a wonderful, mysterious magnetic force that pricks the consciences of those who have yet to believe in Jesus. It should stir them to seek out how they also might experience the kind of basic acceptance and noble purpose they long for but fail to find in the Christ-less institutions of this age.

One of the greatest helps to the personal faith of my children was when they witnessed the innate love and unity we all experienced with believers from other cultures, whom we visited in our travels and who often visited with us in our home. When their faith was tested in young adulthood by their exposure to the secularized higher education of our culture, they remembered and compared the quality of love they witnessed and experienced in our family—and even cross-culturally—with the lack of love they witnessed in the lives and relationships of many "educated" and "successful" unbelievers. In remembering, they realized that they were deeply marked by the love of God, and they never found it necessary to walk away from the faith in Jesus they had confessed as little kids. Rather, they committed themselves to their Savior afresh, in a fully adult way ... and each one, along with his/her spouse (four of our five are now married), walk closely with him today.

I must confess that my papa's heart bursts like the apostle John's: "I have no greater joy than ... that my children walk in truth" (3 John 1:4).

114. Bursting Our Bigotry (15:8–12)

Allow me to summarize the mystery I have unveiled to you in this letter. Jesus the Messiah was sent to the Jews to confirm the truth of the prophetic promises God gave to the Jewish patriarchs. He was also sent to make a way for the Gentiles to glorify God for the extension

*of his mercies to them. For Scripture says, "To this end
I will declare your truth to the Gentiles and sing to
them about your great name." And again he says, "You
Gentiles, rejoice together with the Jews." And again,
"Praise the Lord, all you Gentiles and exalt him all you
nations." Isaiah also prophesied, "The root of Jesse will
rise to reign over all the Gentiles, and they will put their
trust in him."*

Comments ——————————————————————

I believe that this is the main biblical thematic
context for all that Paul has to say in the book of
Romans—his inspired understanding of the big
God-Story that arches from Genesis to Revelation.
The mystery is something that was previously
hidden from the understanding of God's people
(even the Hebrew prophets themselves didn't always understand what the Holy Spirit was indicat-
ing through their inspired proclamations), but that
has now been explained by Jesus Christ's advent,
teaching and the spiritually-authoritative revelation that he imparted to his apostolic scribes.

God gave the magnificent promises of the universal, eternal good news of the Messiah to all the
ethnic groups of the earth and to the whole of creation in "seed form"—given to and through the
Abrahamic patriarchs and Jewish prophets of long
ago. These prophetic promises converged and co-
alesced in the Person of Christ Jesus. The result is
that the chosen people of God now includes both
believing Jews and Gentiles, who have had the ancient wall of separation between them demolished
... they have come together in Jesus to make up "one
new man" through their faith in him.

Paul states this clearly in Galatians 3:28–29 (as well as in many other passages in his epistles):

"There is neither Jew nor Greek, there is neither slave nor free, there is no male and female; for you are all one in Christ Jesus. And if you are Christ's, then you are Abraham's offspring, and heirs according to promise."

Those who insist on continuing to make distinctions of personal spiritual status between Jews and Gentiles based on their ethnicity are, often unwittingly, minimizing the work that Jesus Christ finished on the cross (and in his resurrection and ascension). This is a terrible, tragic mistake that does theological violence to the gospel.

Challenging the racism that lurked in the hearts of people in the first century was a significant part of what led to the executions of both Jesus and Paul. This same kind of racism still lurks in the hearts of the people of our time, and it is the source of much ongoing conflict, tragedy and anguish to this day, all across the world. The resurrection of Jesus represents, among many other wonderful things, the defeat of all hateful bigotry and a faithful witness to the ultimate triumph of God's love in the human drama.

115. The God of Hope (15:13–14)

I pray that the God of hope will fill you with abundant joy and peace through your belief in him, and that you will also overflow with this strong hope by the power of the Holy Spirit. I am confident that you, dear friends, are also full of goodness and knowledge and are therefore able to effectively counsel and teach one another.

Comments ──────────────────────────────

As Paul continues his many-phased benediction of Romans, he refers here to a fabulous title for our heavenly Father: "the God of hope." He is the One who definitively holds the future of all things in his heart and in his hands ... and it is a marvelous future that Jesus Christ came to inaugurate and secure for the entire creation. It is a perfect future ... one filled with love, justice, beauty and ongoing adventure. God is with us now through Jesus, and He offers himself to be the source of the renewed hope that we so desperately need as we endure and grow through the adversities of life in this world. The apostle prays for us, his readers, to be filled with abundant joy and peace (those characteristics of being that spring up, by the Spirit's power, from God's hope over us and in us) as we hold fast to our trust in Christ Jesus. To live in hope within this realm requires the power of the Holy Spirit, a power with a source beyond this realm,. Followers of Jesus are a prophetic sign on display to the entire creation of God's ultimate victory over all that is evil and broken.

As we are filled with these heavenly graces, we are empowered to offer this overflowing strength to one another in the community of faith and to those who are on their way into it. We not only need what God supplies directly to our hearts and minds, but we also will need brothers and sisters in Christ all along the journey—vessels of God's goodness and truth, who will be used by the same Spirit to convey God's loving messages and support into our lives as needed. The church is meant to be a network of Christ-centered friends who band together through all seasons of life and help inspire one another to keep moving forward to our personal finish lines.

May you be filled afresh this day with abundant joy and peace. May you abound in hope through a power beyond your own as God allows you to see what he sees and shares his very thoughts with you. May he bless you with true, wise friends now and all throughout your life, until that great day comes when the old creation is seen to be swallowed up by, fully digested by and entirely assimilated into the new. Amen.

116. Gutsy Friendship (15:13–14)

I pray that the God of hope will fill you with abundant joy and peace through your belief in him, and that you will also overflow with this strong hope by the power of the Holy Spirit. I am confident that you, dear friends, are also full of goodness and knowledge and are therefore able to effectively counsel and teach one another.

Comments ─────────────────────────────

There are over thirty *one anothers* in the New Testament that, when combined, give us a fairly great list of how to practically walk in love within a community of faith. We all need a network of believing friends in Christ in which our fellowship experience is face to face, and with whom we have ongoing interdependent relationships. One of these relational responsibilities is to instruct, or admonish, one another, which the meaning of the one Greek word used here (*nouthesis*) that I paraphrase in the second sentence above: "effectively counsel and teach."

Admonish is a word that, in our culture, has come to have negative overtones. This seems sad to me, because it refers to a very needed element in healthy friendships; admonition brings some risk to the table and adds vital texture to a great friendship. Unless I am sometimes challenged by my friends, loved ones and co-workers when they point out something I am missing, neglecting, overdoing, falling short in, etc., I tend to settle down into a self-satisfied comfort zone and not put my whole heart into something I have said I am committed to. Of course, I need to know that such friends are for me and that they are compelled by their love for me as they present their challenge. The love motive is actually embedded in the original meaning of this Greek word. Additionally, in the context of this passage, Paul outlines the qualifications for the people who can effectively admonish another. They are to be filled with goodness and knowledge. And even more than this, the context indicates that those who are equipped to teach others well are those who are filled with joyful hope by the Spirit's power. In other words: Don't mess with my personal business if you haven't done your homework, don't have a track record of having substantial goodness and kindness rooted in your soul, don't have the joy and peace of Christ humming within you, or if you've lost all hope for me. But, if you've got all that ... bring it on, because I want to keep growing. And please do it with a song in your heart!

> *Let the word of Christ richly dwell within you, with all wisdom teaching and admonishing one another with psalms and hymns and spiritual songs, singing with thankfulness in your hearts to God.* (Colossians 3:16)

117. New Testament Priesthood (15:15–16)

But in light of the special calling God has placed upon me, I have had the boldness to write to you this rather heavy letter. He has called me to be a servant of Jesus Christ by serving his good news. I'm like a priest offering up an acceptable sacrifice that has been consecrated by the Holy Spirit. It's not animals that I offer, but rather the whole Gentile world!

Comments ——————————————————————

Priesthood is a concept to which the evangelical wing of the church does not generally have an emotional connection. We have lost a major living truth that is all throughout the writings of the apostles of Christ. The main point of the book of Hebrews is that we have, in Jesus, a high priest who is interceding for us in the Father's presence in the highest heavens (cf. Heb. 8:1f.) All believers are qualified, through the regeneration of the Spirit, to function as a part of a royal priesthood in this world. I believe that being conscious of our priesthood is a primary identity issue for us, because it is meant to inform all of our worship and work.

In the garden, Adam and Eve were not just stewards over the earth that God gave them to share in with him, but were sacred stewards—priests of the original creation—and the garden in Eden was the holy of holies within the cosmos. Temple language surrounds their callings and duties to God and creation in the Genesis account. This sacred stewardship was restored through the life and ministry of Jesus to humanity—to those who would identify with him through simple faith. Only now, it is taken to unprecedented heights in God's economy because we are royal priests of both creation and the new creation, which was inaugurated by Jesus' resurrection and ascension to the Father's right hand.

In this passage, Paul views himself as a priest who, through the agency of embodying and spreading the great news of Jesus, is envisaging gathering up the whole Gentile world in his apostolic arms. He will offer their lives, "redeemed by Christ through grace and faith," to the Father as a sweet-smelling sacrifice, for they are the reward of the sufferings of Jesus his Son. The Father promised to give the nations to Jesus the firstborn (of both "creation" and "from the dead"; see Colossians 1:15, 18) as his inheritance in Psalm 2.

We also are called to view our entire lives and labors in this world as a sacred offering to the glorious Trinity—both our occupation of handling the created order and our preoccupation of sharing the news of Christ with our fellow human beings, whom he so dearly loves and died to save. The duty of royal priests can be summarized by saying this: we gratefully receive what God has put into our charge; we add our love, labor and human creativity to those divine gifts; we offer back to God what we have cultivated for his honor; and then we trust him to sanctify and crown—with salvific power—what he, in response, gives back again into our hands for the good of all creation and its creatures. As one wise Eastern Orthodox priest noted, "In the Lord's supper, we don't offer to God wheat and grapes, but bread and wine."[3] It is these elements

---

3   Vassilios Papavassiliou, "Creation in Genesis," Archdiocese of

that he graces with new life and healing power.

118. Two Sides of God's Power (15:17–24)

I am not making an empty or presumptuous boast concerning my service for God. I would not dare to talk about things the Lord has not done through me to help the Gentiles passionately obey God in word and deed. But I will testify concerning what he has done through me. I have fully preached the good news of Jesus from Jerusalem all the way around to Illyricum in the power of the Holy Spirit, with signs and wonders confirming its reality. I have sought to be a pioneer and preach the good news in areas where Christ has never been proclaimed so that I wouldn't build the churches on another divine ambassador's foundation. I have taken this Scripture personally: "Those shall see to whom he was not spoken of, and those who have not heard will understand." This very mission is what has thus far kept me from coming to you in Rome. But now the season has changed for me, and since I have wanted to come and see you for many years, I will visit when I am on my way to Spain. I hope the Lord will permit me to do this and enjoy your company for a while.

Comments ————————————————————

God is, at all times and in perfect balance, above and beyond all things, yet passionately involved with the smallest of the things he has created. These two apparently opposing attributes are what theologians have respectively called transcendence and immanence. The major religions' conceptions of God have tended to think of God as "either/or,"

Thyatira and Great Britain, http://www.thyateira.org.uk/index.php?option=com_content&task=view&id=294&Itemid=122

while holy Scripture presents him as "both/and."

Flowing out from these two aspects of God's nature are two similar, related descriptors of his astounding and mysterious power: providence and miracles. Both equally display his personal creative energy, but Scripture points out a definable difference between them in many places. This distinction boils down to something quite simple. Providence is the "usual" acts of God's power (i.e., he causes the sun to set and rise each night and day), and miracles are the "unusual" acts of God's power (i.e., he once caused the sun to stand still and lengthened the daylight when Joshua prayed during a critical battle [see Josh. 10]).

Furthermore, flowing down from these two aspects of divine power are two divine ways of being with his creation: omnipresence and manifest presence. God is always present everywhere, yet retains the ability to localize his presence to make his creation keenly aware of how nearby he is. The God who is everywhere is well able to show up! Both Scripture and history teach us that when he draws near, great and mighty things tend to happen. Various movements within church history have emphasized one aspect of his power to the neglect of the other. Still, both must be held together in grateful tension (we feel the tension, God does not!) in order to understand God's nature and ways. The God who heals the sick and raises the dead also exercises his power to cause the deer in his fields to give birth and the flowers all about them to bloom and grow. His power is what keeps your heart and mine beating without our effort.

We should regularly pray for the power of God

to come near to us, touch people's souls and bodies and meet their needs in miraculous ways. This activity is to be normal to faithful, missional believers and the rich spiritual culture believers together invoke. Still, miracles are the unusual acts of God, and we must beware of presuming that the Holy Spirit of God is under our control ... though he is generous toward and responsive to us. May we live daily under his dominion, be his servants and celebrate both aspects of the great presence and power of God all about us.

119. Signs, Wonders and Miracles (15:17–24)

I am not making an empty or presumptuous boast concerning my service for God. I would not dare to talk about things the Lord has not done through me to help the Gentiles passionately obey God in word and deed. But I will testify concerning what he has done through me. I have fully preached the good news of Jesus from Jerusalem all the way around to Illyricum in the power of the Holy Spirit, with signs and wonders confirming its reality. I have sought to be a pioneer and preach the good news in areas where Christ has never been proclaimed so that I wouldn't build the churches on another divine ambassador's foundation. I have taken this Scripture personally: "Those shall see to whom he was not spoken of, and those who have not heard will understand." This very mission is what has thus far kept me from coming to you in Rome. But now the season has changed for me, and since I have wanted to come and see you for many years, I will visit when I am on my way to Spain. I hope the Lord will permit me to do this and enjoy your company for a while.

Comments ————————————————————————

Paul was a wonderful, rare combination of a theorist and a practitioner when it came to the worship of and service to God. His life experiences and his sacrificial lifestyle gave him the kind of intrinsic authority needed to speak and write to others with a challenging, vigorous, life-altering theological message. Additionally, Paul had witnessed many miracles as a divine endorsement that confirmed the graceful, penetrating truths he was commissioned to proclaim. Of course, the greatest miracle he witnessed was how the simple news of Jesus combined with a childlike response of trust in the human heart. That combination radically overturned ingrained sin patterns and unleashed the love of God and neighbor like a torrent into the souls of the once-unbelieving outsiders of his day. The power of God is embedded in the gospel of Christ, and when it is delivered with spiritual authority, it transforms people's lives for good.

I too have seen some miracles of healing, guidance, answered prayers and permanently transformed lives throughout my years of ministry, beginning in 1973. I have been blessed to know many others who can say the same and more. God still endorses the simple gospel of Jesus with signs and wonders ... especially on the front lines of sharing Christ's love with those who have no clue who he is or what he's done. I am always thrilled with the accounts of God's miraculous activity in our day. I recount some of the miraculous testimonies from my experience in my book, *Prophetic Etiquette.*

Sadly, as in Jesus' day, people can become pre-occupied with a desire to see the spectacular and miss the heart of why divine miracles happen. This eccentricity has led many people into fanaticism and into being deceived by the counterfeit works of religious charlatans. In all of our longing prayers for God's genuine power to be displayed, it is so vital to remember that signs point to something beyond themselves and wonders occur to inspire us to wonder, "Who is like God?" Miracles (unusual acts of God's power) happen to remind us that Providence (the usual acts of God's power) sustains all things. I see this truth reflected in Paul's words to the Greek philosophers in Athens in Acts 17:24–31:

> *The God who made the world and everything in it is the Lord of heaven and earth and does not live in temples built by hands. And he is not served by human hands, as if he needed anything, because he himself gives all men life and breath and everything else. From one man he made every nation of men, that they should inhabit the whole earth; and he determined the times set for them and the exact places where they should live. God did this so that men would seek him and perhaps reach out for him and find him, though he is not far from each one of us. "For in him we live and move and have our being." As some of your own poets have said, "We are his offspring." Therefore since we are God's offspring, we should not think that the divine being is like gold or silver or stone—an image made by man's design and skill. In the past God overlooked such ignorance, but now he commands all people everywhere to repent. For he has set a day when he will judge the world with justice by the man he has appointed. He has given proof of this to all men by raising him from the dead.*

May we be in that number who have repented (changed our minds) and are prepared for a day of justice (which will not be deterred or escaped), because we have personally agreed with and truly accepted God's message of great grace to the entire world through Jesus Christ the Lord.

120. Remembering the Poor (15:25–29)

But first I have to go to Jerusalem to bring a gift to the believers there. God moved upon the hearts of the believers in Macedonia and Achaia to take a collection for the poor believers there. They were very pleased to do this, because they realized that they are indebted to the Jewish believers for the spiritual heritage that they have shared with the Gentiles, and they feel an obligation to serve them in a material way as a token of their gratitude. After I deliver this "spiritual fruit basket" to them, I will come by to see you on my way to Spain. And I am confident that I will come to you overflowing with the fullness of the blessing contained in the good news of Christ.

Comments ———————————————————

When Paul was first converted to Christ, the apostles in Jerusalem were suspicious of him and his motivations. Along the way, he had his tensions with those leaders from Jerusalem as they were all seeking to understand what God actually required of the Gentiles who were turning to faith in Jesus. They were very unlike the Jewish believers in their cultural backgrounds, and there was some religious pressure on them to conform to various cultural preferences of the Jewish believers—preferences that were not essential to obeying the gospel and to pleasing God via genuine spirituality in Christ.

However, it is very interesting to note that as they hammered out their different strategic thrusts in ministry, they heartily agreed on one thing from the very start:

> *And from those who seemed to be influential (what they were makes no difference to me; God shows no partiality)—those, I say, who seemed influential added nothing to me. On the contrary, when they saw that I had been entrusted with the gospel to the uncircumcised, just as Peter had been entrusted with the gospel to the circumcised (for he who worked through Peter for his apostolic ministry to the circumcised worked also through me for mine to the Gentiles), and when James and Cephas and John, who seemed to be pillars, perceived the grace that was given to me, they gave the right hand of fellowship to Barnabas and me, that we should go to the Gentiles and they to the circumcised. Only, they asked us to remember the poor, the very thing I was eager to do.* (Galatians 2:6–10)

Paul remembered his commitment to his friends in Jerusalem. When the believers in Jerusalem found themselves many years later suffering from a poverty primarily due to a drought, Paul inspired the Gentile believers across his mission fields to give generously in a material way to these very people.

May we also open our hearts to Christ—to be eager, in light of the many things we are eager for, to help those in need ... so help us God.

121. The Mystery of Prayer (15:30–33)

Finally, I appeal to you dear friends, for Christ's sake

and because of the love we share in the Spirit, that you partner with me and one another in prayer to God on my behalf. Ask God to deliver me from the unbelievers in Judea and that the believers there will be pleased with the offering I am bringing to them. And that he will send me to you with joy so that you may be refreshed. So may the God of peace be with you. Yes, Lord, let it be!

Comments ————————————————————

Prayer ... it's a strange and mysterious thing from a certain angle. An all-knowing, all-powerful and everywhere-present Creator-God commands us to tell him things that he already knows and has will to shape. Yet he draws our attention in Scripture to examples of human beings just like us who have influenced him to do or not do specific things throughout history. They evoked a response from God that he would not have initiated if they had not offered heartfelt words to him. Though he dwells in a high, holy, eternal realm, he seems to desire a genuine, interactive relationship with us in realtime. To me this communicates to us an amazing message about some aspects of God's nature—that, in spite of his penultimate self-sufficiency, he is also humble and welcomes our influence upon him. This is hard for us to imagine and believe, and probably is one of the main subconscious reasons most of us don't find it easy or natural to pray. After all, we think, "There are so many things to do, and God will do what he will do without my assistance." Right? Apparently, this is not the real picture.

From another angle, prayer makes complete sense, because every genuine relationship is sustained by a mutual exchange of communication of heart and word. The Scriptures teach us that God desires to have a friendship with us human beings. Despite our weaknesses, he wants us. Moreover, he wants to be wanted by us. God has the longing passionate heart of a father and of a lover. The heartfelt words we sing and pray to him from our innermost guts move him. They move his heart, and his heart moves him to act in response to our longings, needs and wants. He longs to hear, like any lover does, the oft-repeated "I love you" that comes from the beloved. He wants us to tell him the things about him that we have come to understand, about how awesome he is—things about him that have stunned and overwhelmed us ... his beauty, justice, mercy, compassion, forgiveness, miracle power, infinitude, holiness and the like.

In addition, God has always looked for willing human partners to work with and through him as visible agents of his grace and truth, ministering to others who are estranged from him and who are striving to survive in a sin-burdened creation. We live in the battle zone of a noble war against evil. Our conversation with him relates not only to our worship of him, but to the co-mission we are on with him in this fallen world. It is absolutely essential to have an open line whereby we may exchange many words in the midst of this dramatic, sometimes dangerous adventure. For our own sanity, safety and success, we need to continually tell him what is on our hearts and what we need. He will regularly draw near to us on the mission and carry both us and our hearts, if we will honor him by remembering that we are neither self-sufficient nor self-reliant. Prayer is a natural, essential outcome of such consciousness.

If we will repent from wrongly taking our lives, relationships and destinies into our own hands and make worship and mission our preoccupations, then we will see marvelous provisions appear from our conversations with the Trinity:

> *You desire and do not have, so you murder. You covet and cannot obtain, so you fight and quarrel. You do not have, because you do not ask. You ask and do not receive, because you ask wrongly, to spend it on your passions ... Submit yourselves therefore to God. Resist the devil, and he will flee from you. Draw near to God, and he will draw near to you.* (James 4:2–3, 7–8)

ROMANS CHAPTER SIXTEEN

122. Heroic Women of God (16:1–7)

I highly recommend Phoebe to you. She is a servant of the church in Cenchrea. Receive her freely as a servant of the Lord and show her your hospitality. Assist her in her mission to you, whatever it may be, for she has helped many, including me. Give my love to Priscilla and Aquila, who have assisted me in Christ Jesus. They have laid their lives on the line for me, and not only am I grateful, so are all the churches of the Gentiles. Also greet the church that gathers in their home. Say hello to my dear Epaenetus, who was the first believer in Christ in Achaia. Greet Mary, who worked hard for our sakes. Honor Andronicus and Junia, my relatives and one-time fellow prisoners. They were in Christ before me, and they have a great reputation among all the divinely appointed ambassadors of the Church at large.

Comments ───────────────────────────────

It seems that a lot of folks have an image of Paul being caustic and impersonal in his style of relating to others. This is probably because he didn't live in the fear of man, and his letters often reflect his boldness to confront erroneous teachings and the people behind them. However, if we dig a bit deeper into the narratives and letters, we discover that the apostle was very warm and deeply connected to other people. This chapter in particular reveals how he took the time to encourage, affirm, remember and express gratitude to other people who had touched his heart.

Moreover, because Paul highlights some wise, basic differences in divine design between females and males in some of his writings, many folks throughout the centuries have concluded that Paul is down on women—specifically, down on women assuming leadership roles within the church of Jesus Christ. Much ongoing debate surrounds this issue among Scripture-believing teachers and movements, and all of the points that need to be considered are far beyond the scope of my purposes here.

However, I think it is sufficient to say that to examine the narrative sections of the gospels and epistles is vital. It helps provide a context for interpreting and applying the didactic portions of the epistles when it comes to such a vital issue as (and the serious danger of) potentially putting artificial, inconsistent, hypocritical and misguided limits on so many believers ... a criticism I am indeed leveling against many in the fundamentalist traditions. (I would guess that more women in the earth truly follow Jesus than men.) Here is my challenge: Those who would put limits on women filling leadership functions in the body of Christ need to make room in their practical theology for heroic leading women like Phoebe, Priscilla and Junia, not to mention other biblical characters and the hundreds of ladies like them—those who have risked all and sacrificed so much throughout church history and in our own generation in order to promote and live out the message of Jesus Christ in this world.

123. Koininia (16:8–16)

Give my love to all of these people: Amplias, my dear friend in the Lord; Urbane, who has helped us in Christ; Stachys, my beloved friend; Apelles, whose loyalty to Christ has been proved; the whole household of Aristobulus; Herodion, my relative; the household of Narcissus, who are all believers; Tryphena and Tryphosa, who are Christ's workers; Persis, who has worked hard for the Lord; Rufus, who is chosen by God, and his mother, who is like a mother to me also; Asyncritus, Phlegon, Hermas, Patrobas, Hermes, and all the believers with them; Philologus and Julia, Nereus and his sister, Olympas and all the believers with them. Greet each other with a holy embrace. The churches of Christ send their greetings to you.

Comments ────────────────────────────

The affection we feel for and express to our fellow believers can be infectious ... a holy virus. I refer to fellowship, or *koininia* (Gk.) as an ordinary miracle of the Christian experience—a literal exchange of Christ's very life between one person and another. The loving, healthy relation between the followers of Jesus may be the most powerful witness of genuine faith to folks who have yet to come to worship Jesus.

I can't count the times that I have experienced a keen awareness of how Christ has been present as

I and other believers have shared with each other
our dreams, hopes, fears, failures, food, adventures,
victories, songs, love, sufferings, joys and prayers,
as well as the word of God, the Lord's supper and
many other things of life. As we relate to and work
with each other in the networks of our faith communities, what a wonderful challenge it is for us to
ensure that we put our whole hearts into maintaining this quality of shared life in Jesus. We must not
allow the weeds of dissension, unresolved conflict,
jealousy, resentment, offense, competition and the
like to grow up and pollute our relational gardens.

124. Reality Check (16:17–20)

*I urge you to take note of and avoid those people
who cause divisions and offenses by embracing or
promoting doctrines that are contrary to the ones you
have learned. These kinds of people are not concerned
with serving the Lord Jesus Christ, but with filling their
unsatisfied desires. They employ good-sounding words
and manipulative monologues that deceive the hearts
of the undiscerning. The testimony of your faithfulness
to God has been reported throughout the whole world,
and I am glad that you've been honored like this. Just
make sure that you preserve your spirit of innocence—be
"streetwise" in good, but not in evil! Soon, the God of
peace will crush Satan under your feet. May the grace of
our Lord Jesus be with you. Yes, Lord, let it be!*

Comments ───────────────────────────

We are nearing the end of this extensive,
intensive world-changing letter. It seems to me as if
Paul keeps thinking of final words to say and blessings to offer and, as a result, we end up with several

benedictory closings in this final chapter. He is like a proud father who boasts in the well-being and well-doing of his children, though he had never had the opportunity to visit the believers in Rome in person. It was a great victory for the believers throughout the world to have a faithful, vibrant congregation of Christ-followers in the capital city. It would be so wonderful if church communities never had to deal with negative influences or deceptive, destructive people in their midst. Sadly, it has never been and will never be so in this age.

The church is planted in the earth in the midst of a spiritual battle zone. God's ancient enemy, who cannot overthrow God himself, is always at work to assault and tear down the people of God—and God's beloved creation—on every possible front. Satan does this primarily on the visible level by using both witting and unwitting people as ambassadors of error, disruption and deception.

Still, though it is tempting to use unholy means of dealing with these kinds of people and their influences, believers must rise above evil and overcome it with good. The church has been compared to a mighty rescue ship in the ocean in which shipwrecked people are drowning. Many are saved by the efforts of the ship's crew. The ship is in the sea by design ... but if the sea gets in the ship, then the ship will tragically lose its purpose for being and fail in its mission. The church is called to navigate within the broken, sinful cultures of the world, but it must be on guard to not allow sinful cultures to invade it. How can we do this without becoming overly defensive, unloving, self-righteous, negative, controlling and fearful?

The New Testament offers us a godly polity—
a way of governing the community of faith—that
equips us to deal effectively with troublesome people and influences and to live out the challenge of
Micah 6:8, which is to do justly, to love mercy and
to walk humbly with our God. Believers need to be
forearmed to deal with these inevitable situations
and people so that we are not left to our own de-
vices when such events crop up.

125. Bringing Correction by the Spirit of Christ (16:17–20)

*I urge you to take note of and avoid those people
who cause divisions and offenses by embracing or
promoting doctrines that are contrary to the ones you
have learned. These kinds of people are not concerned
with serving the Lord Jesus Christ, but with filling their
unsatisfied desires. They employ good-sounding words
and manipulative monologues that deceive the hearts
of the undiscerning. The testimony of your faithfulness
to God has been reported throughout the whole world,
and I am glad that you've been honored like this. Just
make sure that you preserve your spirit of innocence—be
"streetwise" in good, but not in evil! Soon, the God of
peace will crush Satan under your feet. May the grace of
our Lord Jesus be with you. Yes, Lord, let it be!*

Comments ————————————————————

Romans is such a positive, powerful letter, and
it would be nice to not have to address the issue of
difficult people or the devil. But that wouldn't really do justice to the reality of living out the gospel
in the community of faith. The truth is that when
believers put our hearts together and commit to

function as the body of Christ in our cultures, hellish forces are pitted against our progress and fruitfulness. Believers and the leaders of their communities must be equipped to deal well with both the evil spirits and the deceived people who will seek to disrupt our communities. We must bring needed correction while being Christ-like—in a way that embodies his compassion and respect for people and his great heart of hope and redemption.

Sadly, the seminaries have rarely taught their ministers-in-training the art of dealing with deceived people and the demonic realm. Most church leaders have a very rude awakening—one of the main areas of their jobs ends up being the need to address the hardships, setbacks and sufferings associated with spiritual warfare and interpersonal conflicts in the lives of their members.

Early on in my pastoral ministry, I internalized an important passage that helped me to navigate the waters of spiritual warfare and relational conflict:

> *Have nothing to do with foolish, ignorant controversies; you know that they breed quarrels. And the Lord's servant must not be quarrelsome but kind to everyone, able to teach, patiently enduring evil, correcting his opponents with gentleness. God may perhaps grant them repentance leading to a knowledge of the truth, and they may come to their senses and escape from the snare of the devil, after being captured by him to do his will.*
> (2 Timothy 2:23–25, ESV)

Through many years, this passage helped to brace me for the challenges that I would face in pastoring God's people and in creating a Christ-centered culture around my own soul (and, by extension, the whole community). The inspiration from this passage empowered me to gracefully handle the presence of unstable people, their false beliefs and destructive actions, and the manipulative enemy working beyond and through them. The key to honoring Christ and accessing the Holy Spirit's power in these difficult, often tragic situations is to find a way of being that helps us remain poised under the pressures they create. If we can invoke and remain in the Holy Spirit's presence, then the best practical steps to take will present themselves.

In my early years of ministry, I found myself tightening up in ways that were counterproductive to solving, or at least containing, these kinds of problems. My own zeal and personal power became dominant and interfered with the display of the Lord's wisdom in the matter. Over time, I learned how to reign in my fleshly reactions and follow the Spirit's leadings. When we do this, the outcome is not always positive (as we can see from the above passage, via the word *perhaps*), but we do provide people with the best opportunity possible for a deliverance from evil and a sweet resolution.

126. The Importance of Good Doctrine (16:17–18)

I urge you to take note of and avoid those people who cause divisions and offenses by embracing or promoting doctrines that are contrary to the ones you have learned. These kinds of people are not concerned with serving the Lord Jesus Christ, but with filling their unsatisfied desires. They employ good-sounding words and manipulative monologues that deceive the hearts of the undiscerning.

Comments —————————————————————————

Errors, schisms, sects, divisions and cults have plagued the church of Jesus since her earliest days ... and what a downer this is. Dealing with these matters is a challenge and a suffering that believers, especially church leaders, have to endure. Just to read church history takes a lot of guts; to make history in one's own generation takes even more. Our wise, great, powerful Father in heaven does not over-control the choices, beliefs, behaviors and practices of human beings. For this we should be grateful. He doesn't immediately sort out truth from error in this world, but one day his inscrutable judgments will forever establish absolute truth and righteousness (justice) in the new heavens and earth.

One important point to note is that holding to sound doctrine is of vital importance to every Christ-follower and fellowship. Like it or not—acknowledge it or not—what we believe ultimately affects how we live. It's an immutable reality of human psychology. Believing well is essential to living well. (Too often people claim they believe well but not actually live well. But we will never truly live well without believing well.)

However, it is overly idealistic to think that all true Christ-followers will agree on every point of doctrine. All truth is true, but not all truths are equally important. So we are left with the sensitive task of identifying the scriptural truths essential to saving faith, witnessing to them and distinguishing them from secondary doctrinal matters that can be righteously debated among those who belong to Christ.

I must add that Jesus does have the power to save an untaught person who has yet to be exposed to or who is confused about essential doctrines. In our important quest to land on essential truths, we must be very cautious not to limit what the Father, Son and Holy Spirit can do for and in a human being, apart from their ability to clearly reason! My conviction is that one who has been saved by the power of Jesus Christ will deeply resonate with essential doctrine when she/he has the opportunity to hear it taught. Her/his entire being will thrill to have words put to what she/he has encountered. Words do matter ... they always have and always will.

Fortunately, much great work has already been done throughout the history of the church to identify the essential truths of holding genuine faith in Christ. They are few and clear in the New Testament.

An example of such follows:

For I delivered to you as of first importance what I also received: that Christ died for our sins in accordance with the Scriptures, that he was buried, that he was raised on the third day in accordance with the Scriptures, and that he appeared to Cephas, then to the twelve. Then he appeared to more than five hundred brothers at one time, most of whom are still alive, though some have fallen asleep. Then he appeared to James, then to all the apostles. (1 Corinthians 15:3–7)

It is also my conviction that the many groups of Christ-followers in the earth—large or small, old or new—must grant themselves, their leaders and teachers the liberty to state with conviction their personal and corporate positions on secondary doctrines. Making these statements helps to create the spiritual culture of their spiritual families, which is their divinely assigned realm of responsibility. This kind of freedom of expression among the various groups of believers in this earth is probably a beautiful thing in the end. We will all laugh together in the age to come about how limited our views actually were.

Still, we must not automatically think of doctrines that are nonessential to salvation as unimportant for the health and growth of a body of Christ-followers, though some are certainly unwise to over-emphasize or require adherence to. Choosing wisely on how to distinguish essential truths (our primary responsibility) and also how to steward the teaching and incorporation of nonessential, yet still important, truths is a spiritual art—one that teachers, preachers, prophets and leaders must seek and master. May Christ grant his great and beautiful church wisdom and discernment in this regard.

127. True Peacemaking (16:17–18)

I urge you to take note of and avoid those people who cause divisions and offenses by embracing or promoting doctrines that are contrary to the ones you have learned. These kinds of people are not concerned with serving the Lord Jesus Christ, but with filling their unsatisfied desires. They employ good-sounding words and manipulative monologues that deceive the hearts of the undiscerning.

Comments ————————————————————————

Dealing with divisive, offensive people and/or groups is always difficult and can tend to distract us from a positive, forward movement in life and ministry. It can also be confusing and oppressive. A number of questions rise as I ponder this subject.

Do we forbear or confront? How can we measure if a matter is worthy of a confrontation? Do we go to someone who has offended us in private or bring a few others into the mix for counsel, prayer support and/or as witnesses? Do we warn others of spiritual danger? Do we speak out publicly on a matter and expose falsehood? Does God call some to such tasks, but not others? Do we leave a matter in the hands of God alone to deal with? Do we simply avoid a matter—even a person or a group? Now that the globe is connected via mass communications, which errors do we pick to confront and/or expose, since we can research them all? Presuming to be the cops for the earth's spiritual landscape could swallow up our entire lives. I know this last option is not for any of us!

Over the years of leading communities of faith, practical and workable actions have presented themselves. Some of my convictions follow below.

I am convinced that these kinds of situations and our proper responses can always be located a spectrum of severity, usually without dividing lines between the phases. We need more than raw principles or laws to go by in these situations. We need God's realtime, direct spiritual wisdom to settle upon us for the proper timing and application of scriptural principles. We are called to be peacemakers as children of God, but this is not the same thing as being a peacekeeper. Peacemaking involves putting things in their proper places, and this can often involve confrontation, righteous judgment and sanctions. Sometimes a confrontation, rebuke or fight becomes a necessary evil. However, peace-making is always about praying and looking for minimal fallout and for the redemptive purposes of God to win the day.

Another thing is that the closer our relationship is to people or a matter, the more we have a right and responsibility to face them/it. Often, our designated function within a community can also inform us of our right and responsibility to deal with a difficult person or matter. Another principle is that it is good to confirm, confine, contain and rectify an error to as small a circle of people as possible. However, when a scandalous sin or a crime has been committed, it is better for the guilty to suffer than for the innocent, and confession should cover the same social scope as the knowledge and damage of the offense.

One final thought on this complex issue (and so much more needs to be said): When others go public with their erroneous, sometimes dangerous beliefs and teachings, public challenge and criticism are warranted. We must be careful to not misrepresent what another is actually teaching. A personal, behind-the-scenes inquiry and/or challenge might be called for, but ultimately, if a person has the moxie to take his/her teachings to the public square, it is only fair to expect those who may disagree to openly say so. If you can't take the heat, get out of the kitchen!

128. Satan (16:19–20)

The testimony of your faithfulness to God has been reported throughout the whole world, and I am glad that you've been honored like this. Just make sure that you preserve your spirit of innocence—be "streetwise" in good, but not in evil! Soon, the God of peace will crush Satan under your feet. May the grace of our Lord Jesus be with you. Yes, Lord, let it be!

Comments

I think it's interesting that, given the broad scope of the book of Romans for living a truly spiritual life, Paul only mentions Satan by name this one time at the end of his letter. I don't believe that this is because we should deny the reality of, ignore or underestimate the kingdom of darkness and its many hosts. Rather, I think that it is because the reality of evil and the entities behind it all, who manipulate humanity and so many cultural systems of this age, are a given in the worldview of his readers. And the apostles' focus seemed to be overcoming evil with good, first on a personal level and then corporately as the body of Christ, versus hastily and angrily lashing out against all the evil about us in the name of serving God. (Notice the very practical nature of the whole armor of God that Paul exhorts us to put on in Ephesians 6:12ff that enables us to stand in an evil day.) Their instruction to us is not to panic or be overly-conscious of evil spirits and their craft, but to proclaim and live out the truth of the gospel of Jesus Christ. We are to call all people to believe in and follow him; to leave sin in the dirt behind us where it belongs; to live in healthy, interdependent, relational networks called local churches; and to lovingly reach out to the needy, broken people all about us with Christ's love and compassion.

When evil spirits confront us, which will

happen in the normal course of living out our mission, we simply exercise the spiritual authority freely entrusted to us in Christ and express the power of the Holy Spirit through our prayers, words and deeds. We often see God's power working through us, his servants, in ways that trump the powers of darkness. Yet having access to this power doesn't imply that everything will be fine here and now. This war has casualties. We triumph through Christ, but not in a manner that smacks of the bloated triumphalism of so many modern (and ancient!) movements and sects. We have both many victories and many sufferings in our mission, and God will use them all to make us more like his glorious Son.

Though Satan and his kingdom have been legally defeated and overthrown through all that Jesus accomplished in his first coming (his death and subsequent resurrection and ascension), the power of his deceptive lies still holds significant sway over many people and nations of this fallen world. Satan received a mortal blow at the cross, but he is a wounded, dying beast who is enraged at God, and he is determined to destroy as many human lives as he can before his final judgment is leveled. Yes, we are to be well aware of the ancient enemy of all that is good and just, and of his classic schemes that keep so many people captive to do his will. We are aware of and buffeted by his constant attempts to hinder what God wills to do through Christ-followers and our new covenant communities.

Finally, we are joyfully aware that though we will experience painful and disappointing losses in this battle, we minister, persevere, labor and fight with an indomitable declaration and promise of

hope—one that resonates throughout our entire being and throughout the entire cosmos. It is a hope
based on an inarguable eschatological certainty,
made so by Jesus Christ's resurrection and ascension to the place of highest honor and supremacy:
soon, the God who brings true peace will crush Satan under our feet.

129. The Problem of Evil (16:19–20)

*The testimony of your faithfulness to God has been
reported throughout the whole world, and I am glad that
you've been honored like this. Just make sure that you
preserve your spirit of innocence—be "streetwise" in
good, but not in evil! Soon, the God of peace will crush
Satan under your feet. May the grace of our Lord Jesus
be with you. Yes, Lord, let it be!*

Comments ————————————————————————

The problem of evil in this world has been pondered and debated with great angst and energy by
many throughout human history. And it has been
maybe the major stumbling block for people accepting a belief in the all-powerful, good God that
the Scriptures clearly declare him to be. We may not
be able to fully comprehend the why of evil, but we
all must face the fact that evil exists. Moreover, we
must face the fact that we ourselves are more than
capable of choosing an evil course of being and/or
doing ... and indeed, that we have done so at times.

Why would an all-powerful and good Creator allow an enemy to even exist, much less mess up his
creation? Apparently he has. However, the two basic
philosophical alternatives to this difficult scenario

are even more troubling in my estimation: (1) There is an all-powerful God, but he is not good. (2) There is no creator and we are the products of the impersonal forces of time plus chance. I won't take the time to elaborate, but embracing these two alternative philosophical viewpoints creates very troubling ramifications, which pose more difficulties than simply accepting the biblical premise that our all-powerful, holy, loving Creator has allowed evil to affect his good creation.

Here is a brief overview of what the Scripture teaches about the problem of evil:

(1) Long ago, a holy archangel rebelled against God in the highest heavens. He was powerful and seductive enough to lure a third of the holy angels into his ill-fated attempt to displace God. This rebellion was the genesis of sin, of Satan (the accuser) and of the demonic forces that are present in and around our world.

(2) Rather than immediately eradicating his fallen angelic enemies, God banished them from dwelling in his highest heaven. However, he allowed the devil and his hosts to continue to exist and operate within a limited realm.

(3) In addition—and this is where the high drama of it all takes on new dimensions— he wisely chose to incorporate Satan's presence and plots into a greater master plan. This plan would mysteriously reveal his love, power, mercy and glory to the crowning touch of his creation— human beings, whom he made to reflect his own image and likeness back to him, and from there to the

whole of his creation.

(4) In order to prepare human beings for our eternal destiny (to rule and reign with him over all other things in the ages to come), he has used the presence of evil and our exposure to evil spirits as a testing ground that challenges us to surmount sin, Satan, demonic powers and death. This has all been a part of his loving master plan. It can even be said that love is not full and mature if it is not tested, tried and entered into with freedom of choice.

(5) Our first parents succumbed to the wiles of Satan in a garden paradise, which they were divinely called to rule, cultivate and, apparently, export to the rest of the planet. However, as a result of cooperating with the devil, sin, and its consequences, death—spiritual, social and physical—entered the human nature. In the aftermath, both sin and death spread throughout the nations of the earth and throughout all human history. We live in a fallen world that is agonizing under the burdens that evil and its ripple effects have created for us all.

(6) But God has not been distant or silent throughout the centuries, though a spiritual war has been raging and there have been many sobering casualties and tragedies. His heart of love and his powerful acts have been at work. He has been passionately involved with humanity and patiently working out his master plan—what I have called "God's Big God-Story"—to rescue and redeem his

beloved creation from the grip of evil.

(7) God carefully prepared the earth for this intervention through many centuries by making amazing promises to his chosen human vessels (Abraham, Isaac and Jacob, and others of their progeny), sending prophets to foretell the future and tell forth his will, raising up and removing regimes, performing astounding signs and wonders, and providentially sustaining human life with his good gifts of food and water, in addition to many other such kindnesses. Then, at a strategic moment in human history, he visited the earth. He sent his Son, who co-created all things and who dwelt with the Father and the Holy Spirit in fully divine union from eternity past, as a fully human being. He came in love to show the face, or the nature, of God. He also came to deal radically with the problem of evil in both the invisible and visible realms by the reality and ramifications of his incarnation, life, ministry, death, resurrection and ascension back to highest heaven.

(8) The kingdom of darkness and its principalities and powers were dealt a mortal blow through all that ensued with the first coming of Christ. Those who put their personal trust in Jesus Christ receive into their souls his eternal life here and now, and they enter into his victory of love over all evil (sin, demons and death). This regeneration and the empowering of the Holy Spirit in their lives equip them with the divine grace needed

to progressively overcome evil, just as their Lord and King overcame evil. They are living witnesses to the fact that the new creation, which will assuredly swallow up the old, has already been inaugurated. They execute the judgment that has been written (Ps. 149:9) against evil as ambassadors of Jesus the Christ and of his mercy, truth and justice. The conflicts continue throughout this age— temptations, hassles, persecutions, trials, disappointments, human failures, tragedies, wars, afflictions, false accusations, imperfections and physical death. But God does not just provide many experiences that help Christ-followers to counteract and surmount these evil assaults. He also uses the spiritual warfare that they endure to both conform them more fully to the image of his Son Jesus and to prepare them to receive their full inheritance and walk in their destiny in the age to come.

(9) On a personal level, the powers of darkness still have the oppressive ability to whisper accusations, lies, temptations and horrendous thoughts of evil into the souls and minds of people ... even the followers of Jesus. Satan's main weapon is deception that leads to the committing of sins, which destroy the joys of human existence. This is a suffering that we encounter and must endure during our pilgrimage in this life. However, a Christ-follower is called to be awake to these subtle schemes of the devil, expose their source and firmly resist his attempt to lodge deception or compromise within them. The Holy Spirit

will warn them about and grant them the power to rebuke and overcome these crafty camouflaged demonic affronts and assaults. As they grow in their spiritual life they can also train others to do the same. This is the joy of partnering with the living Christ in ministry.

(10) Ultimately, when Jesus Christ returns and the visible and invisible realms are fully integrated into a new heavens and new earth, God will banish Satan and his hordes to a divinely constructed hell. They will never be able to escape and again spread their evil influence amidst God's redeemed, renewed creation. They will suffer an unimaginable, actually indescribable, eternal punishment away from all that is good. More tragically, many humans who sided with God's ancient enemy and who rejected his Son will be forever banished from God's presence as well. This alone should break our hearts for the salvation of other people through Jesus, even our greatest enemy. On that day, no fallen angel and no human being will be able to point a finger at God and accuse him of being unjust or lacking in love or wisdom (as they do now).

Everything will be righted; all our doubts and troubling questions will be resolved; all our tears will be wiped away; all our temptations will disappear; all weariness and heaviness will flee away; and our true identity and calling will be known, seen and affirmed by all. Our innate longing for true justice, which can become so confused and twisted in this life, will actually be fulfilled. We will be perfected people living fully in a perfect place ... forever and ever in the love of God.

130. Final Words of Glory (16:21–27)

My co-worker, Timothy, Lucius, Jason and Sosipater, my relative, send their greetings as well.) My host, Gaius, and the whole church here say hello. Erastus, the chamberlain of the city, also sends his greetings, along with a brother in the Lord named Quartus. The grace of our Lord Jesus Christ be with all of you. Let it be so, Lord!

Now we honor him who has the power to firmly establish you in this good news and in an intimate relationship with the Person of Jesus Christ. This is the revelation of the mystery which was hidden from the beginning of the world, but is now manifested, and which is a fulfillment of many prophecies in Scripture. And now, by the express commandment of the everlasting God, it is to be made known to all the nations of the earth, and will lead them into the passionate pursuit of God that flows from genuine faith.

Comments ———————————————————

Some final personal greetings and a summary of what Paul has written in his letter to the Romans, penned as a thanksgiving prayer, brings us to the end. The doxology (Gk.; it means "glorious words") is highly reminiscent of his opening purpose statement in the first five verses of chapter 1:

This is a letter from Paul, a servant of Jesus Christ, called to be a divine ambassador. I was apprehended for the express purpose of spreading the good

*news of God that was spoken of in times past by
the prophets in the holy Scriptures. This message
centers on his Son, Jesus Christ our Lord, who, in
his humanity, was the Son of David. He was also
proven to be the Son of God when he was raised
from the dead through the power of the Holy Spirit. Through the same Spirit, I have received this
ambassadorial commission to introduce many
people from many nations, for the honor of Christ,
into the passionate pursuit of God that flows from
genuine faith.*

At long last, God revealed God's Big God-Story
for all to see and understand—the penultimate focus
of the Old Testament prophets and their messages
to Israel and the nations; the longings and sighings
of the prayerful Hebrew fathers and mothers, that
which the angels long to fully comprehend (see 1
Peter 1:12); and the mysterious, divine construct
that would provide the previously-missing code
for integrating into a whole all that God had done
with his ancient people. The Person of Jesus Christ
and his gospel exploded onto the scene of human
history. God is able and willing to firmly establish
Christ-followers in understanding the points of this
now-revealed secret, which had been prophesied
throughout the previous generations and had been
preserved in Old Testament scriptures.

Paul is boldly declaring that his letter to the Romans captures the essential points of this divine
revelation, which had been hidden from all people
throughout all human history. The Jews and their
rabbis, scholars and scribes; the Gentiles and their
philosophers and religious mystics; and even the
Hebrew prophets themselves who were used by

God to utter his very words ... none of them had received a divine understanding of what has now come to light in Jesus the Messiah. The Son of God's incarnation and the cosmos-shifting events that followed in those thirty-three years were required to bring an unveiling of what had previously been hidden. This new revelation was based on Jesus' own authoritative commentaries on the Old Testament Scriptures, which he passed on directly to his apostles both before and after his resurrection ... and which provided the hindsight needed to unlock the mysteries of God's Big God-Story.

A major paradigm-shifting part of this great news, upon which Paul expounds in chapters 9–11, was that the Gentiles could now—if they would receive and follow Jesus as Lord and Messiah—be freely grafted in to the ancient "olive tree" of Israel that God planted in the earth when he cut his original covenant with Abraham. For the "natural branches," the Jews, their long-awaited Messiah had arrived, and they must personally receive him to remain in the covenant. Otherwise, they would be pruned from the family tree for their blatant rejection of Jesus as Messiah. (And though many first-century Jews—a believing remnant—accepted Jesus, the vast majority did not. Even so, an outstanding prophecy declares that God has not forgotten them as a people group, but that many Jews will yet come to faith in Jesus as Messiah.) They would not be saved and at one with God on the basis of their natural Jewish heritage, their knowledge of Scripture and/or their performance of Jewish cultural and religious rites and traditions.

Moreover, God had not lied or broken his word

to the Jews in the revelation of the gospel of Jesus, or the gospel of the Kingdom of God. But over time many of them had forgotten, twisted and misinterpreted the natural and spiritual roots of the salvation he had promised to them (and ultimately the Gentiles) from the very beginning. The "Substance" of all that was foreshadowed had arrived, and by his coming introduced a fateful, personal life or death moment of decision ... his intervention. It was a watershed moment in human history, and nothing would, or possibly could, ever be the same again.

> *Therefore remember that you, once Gentiles in the flesh—who are called Uncircumcision by what is called the Circumcision made in the flesh by hands—that at that time you were without Christ, being aliens from the commonwealth of Israel and strangers from the covenants of promise, having no hope and without God in the world. But now in Christ Jesus you who once were far off have been brought near by the blood of Christ. For he himself is our peace, who has made both one, and has broken down the middle wall of separation, having abolished in his flesh the enmity, that is, the law of commandments contained in ordinances, so as to create in himself one new man from the two, thus making peace, and that he might reconcile them both to God in one body through the cross, thereby putting to death the enmity. And he came and preached peace to you who were afar off and to those who were near. For through him we both have access by one Spirit to the Father.* (Ephesians 2:11–18)

Jesus was and is the integrating element for the

Story that is now fully declared in the light of the Day of the new creation, which dawned with his personal arrival to the earth. Those who put their faith in him, whether Jew or Gentile, would become "one new man" (Eph. 2:15)—a new kind of humanity that possesses the very uncreated life of God in their souls ... in Messiah Jesus. A new temple of God has been erected in the earth, one made "without hands" (Mk. 14:58) that consists of Holy Spirit-indwelt human lives scattered throughout the whole earth and gathered in local networks. Race and religious (or irreligious and/or falsely religious) backgrounds are irrelevant in light of the coming of the Christ. The gospel of Jesus eclipses all that human beings use to pridefully distinguish themselves from other people. God put an exclamation point on the inauguration and dedication of his new temple in Christ, fulfilling the tragic prophecies of Jesus recorded in the gospels concerning the utter destruction of Jerusalem and its Jewish temple in A.D. 70 by the Romans.

Through the gospel of Jesus, God himself is holding out a final, authoritative divine revelation to humanity that is intergenerational, international, inter-gender and inter-aeon in scope. Ever since the resurrection and ascension of Jesus Christ, God has been holding out that same moment of decision to individuals, tribes and nations. Who do we say Jesus of Nazareth is? Who do you say Jesus of Nazareth is? Who do I say Jesus of Nazareth is? Will I attempt to ignore him? Will I reject him for who he says he is? Or will I agree with who God says he is and pledge my allegiance to believe in and follow him? This urgent question requires a response from every person who hears of Jesus and his message.

This message must also be urgently shared with all the peoples on the face of the earth.

Indeed it is worth our while to drink deeply of this inspired letter, which is brimming with words of grace and truth written by this brilliant apostle. I pray that God will use this devotional paraphrase and my musings on the meaning and application of Paul's exquisite letter to bring greater spiritual life, encouragement and empowerment to my readers. May our hearts continually burn within us as we eagerly wait for his second advent.

BIBLIOGRAPHY

"Praxis." DIE.net. http://dictionary.die.net/praxis.

C.S. Lewis. "C.S. Lewis quotes." ThinkExist.com. http:/thinkexist.com/quotation/ god_whispers_to_ us_in_our_pleasures-speaks_to_us/180233.html.

Carson, D.A. Quoted in "Christians and Civil Disobedience." Bill Muehlenberg's CultureWatch. http://www.billmuehlenberg.com/2008/11/02/ christians-and-civil-disobedience.

Clarke, Adam. *Commentary on the Bible.* GodRules. net. http://www.godrules.net/library/clarke/clar-ke2tim1.htm

Crabb, Larry. *Connecting: Healing Ourselves and Our Relationships.* Nashville: Thomas Nelson, 1997.

De Chardin, Pierre Teilhard. "Pierre Teilhard de Chardin: The Phenomenon of Man." Wikiquote. http:// en.wikiquote.org/wiki/Pierre_Teilhard_de_Chardin.

Deasley, A.R.G. "Flesh." In Baker's Evangelical Dictionary of Biblical Theology. Edited by Walter Ewell. Grand Rapids, MI: Baker Books, 1996. http://www. biblestudytools.com/dictionaries/bakers-evangeli-cal-dictionary/flesh.html.

Evangelical Presbyterian Church. "Pastoral Letter on Civil Disobedience." http://www.epc.org/about-the-epc/pastoral-letters/civil-disobedience.

Flowers, Michael. Email message to author. July 16, 2009.

Foreman, Jon and Tim Foreman. *The Beautiful Letdown*. Switchfoot. Columbia Records.

Kantzer, Kenneth. Quoted in "Pastoral Letter on Civil Disobedience." Evangelical Presbyterian Church.   www.epc.org/mediafiles/epc-pastoral-letter-on-civil-disobediance.pdf.

Morrison, Steve. Hillcrest Covenant Church Life Conference. March 2010.

Peterson, Eugene. *A Long Obedience in the Same Direction: Discipleship in an Instant Society*. Downers Grove, IL: InterVarsity Press, 2000.

Preston, Eby. "The Ashes of a Red Heifer." Kingdom Bible Studies. http://www.kingdombiblestudies.org/ashes/ashes1.htm.

Stott, John. Quoted in "Christians and Civil Disobedience." Bill Muehlenberg's CultureWatch. http://www.billmuehlenberg.com/2008/11/02/christians-and-civil-disobedience.

The Arbinger Institute. *The Anatomy of Peace: Resolving the Heart of Conflict*, 104-106. San Francisco: Berrett-Koehler Publishers, 2008).

Vassilios Papavassiliou. "Creation in Genesis." Archdiocese of Thyatira and Great Britain. http://www.thyateira.org.uk/index.php?option=com_content&task=view&id=294&Itemid=122

Wright, N.T. *Simply Christian: Why Christianity Makes Sense.* New York: HarperOne, 2006.

If you have benefited from *The Romance of Romans: God's Big God Story*, please consider recommending it to your network of friends and acquaintances.

If you would like to inquire about having Michael or Terri come and speak to your group, please write and let them know.

Michael Sullivant
mwsullivant@gmail.com
Blogsite: *www.michael-radius.blogspot.com*
Websites: *www.radius-group.org; www.fullyalive5.com*